Joseph is Dead

THE UNTOLD STORY OF JESUS' FAMILY

By D. Paul Schulz

Jesus' Family Ministries
MILWAUKIE, OR

Copyright © 2016 by D. Paul Schulz

All rights reserved. No part of this publication may be reproduced, distributed or transmitted in any form or by any means, including photocopying, recording, or other electronic or mechanical methods, without the prior written permission of the publisher, except in the case of brief quotations embodied in critical reviews and certain other noncommercial uses permitted by copyright law.

Jesus' Family Ministries
4141 SE Jackson St
Milwaukie, OR 97222

Book Layout © 2015 BookDesignTemplates.com

Joseph is Dead/ D. Paul Schulz. —1st ed.
ISBN 978-0-692-81851-0

Contents

Preface		1
CHAPTER 1	Homage to the King in Nazareth	5
CHAPTER 2	Interpreting the Gospels	10
CHAPTER 3	Mary	20
CHAPTER 4	Joseph	30
CHAPTER 5	Before the Wise Men Visit	33
CHAPTER 6	When Was Jesus Born?	40
CHAPTER 7	Fleeing into Egypt	55
CHAPTER 8	Growing Up in Nazareth	65
CHAPTER 9	Joseph is Dead	76
CHAPTER 10	John the Baptist	86
CHAPTER 11	Jesus Moves Out	98
CHAPTER 12	Calling of the Disciples	112
CHAPTER 13	A Divided Family	129
CHAPTER 14	Judas' Father	144
CHAPTER 15	The Blessing of Simon Peter	154
CHAPTER 16	There is Something about Mary	163
CHAPTER 17	The Preordained Resurrection	169
CHAPTER 18	Called Out of Egypt	178
CHAPTER 19	Jesus Appears to Simon Peter	187
CHAPTER 20	Ye of Little Faith	194
CHAPTER 21	Encore	201
EPILOGUE	This World of Zeros	213
Appendix: Mary and the Apostle Family Genealogy		219
Notes		221

Dedication

To the mothers who teach their children to follow Jesus.

*Two mothers stood by Mary, the mother of Jesus, at His cross.
Their names were Salome and Mary, mother of James and Jose.
Both parents raised their children to follow Jesus and
hence they both had multiple sons who became His apostles.
They are therefore great in Scripture
and yet not known by many Christians.*

*While Bible expositors have virtually ignored them,
they play an integral part in the gospel, standing through
thick and thin with the greatest mother of them all.
Many men have given long speeches, but the mother of Jesus
gives the greatest sermon ever with just a few words:*

Whatsoever he saith unto you, do it (John 2:5 [KJV]).

Preface

Ironically the teachings of Christianity haven't noticed the fact Jesus was a family man, as a consequence, most believers don't know what Jesus did before He was thirty. The Gospels have made it apparent that Joseph, Mary's husband was dead when Jesus was on the cross. Jesus gave His disciple John charge over His mother, and he took her home straight away. This should highlight the fact to believers Jesus took care of His widowed mother and His siblings in Nazareth before He began His ministry. Many Christians have been taught that when Jesus was thirty, He walks past strangers and says "follow me" further adding to their unfamiliarity of His family connections. There is so much more to His story, and this book is about connecting dots the original writers assumed future followers would naturally make by understanding that family is important to God. Such as the fact Joseph was dead, and Jesus last actions at the cross were to care for His beloved mother.

Our families are the most influential people in our lives. Jesus had a family, too, and (besides Him) they were the most prominent members in the Gospels. Even though the Gospel of Luke introduces Mary's relatives at the beginning of his Gospel story, they are mostly ignored by Bible expositors. It seems no one has noticed that one side of Jesus' family embraced Him, while the other branch completely rejected Him. Jesus had twelve apostles, including three sets of brothers, yet His own brothers were not among them or at the foot of the cross. Consequently, Jesus asked another family member to care for His mother. Many believers are unaware that John was Jesus first cousin who was standing by his own mother who was Mary's sister. Bible expositors have neglected this and many other significant family associations that have major implications in the Gospels. For example, Jesus was a cousin to John the Baptist, and they contributed to each other's ministries, but this has been ignored. The same is true with many other relatives—including numerous cousins—of Jesus and the Baptist. Some were disciples of the Baptist who later became Jesus' disciples. Jesus' first apostles were family members from the region around Capernaum, where Mary, His mother, had a sister. That's why Jesus made Capernaum His headquarters.

Many believers are unaware of Jesus family associations which demonstrate there is a great deal missing in our teachings of Him today. Jesus appeared to his family in the resurrection appearances, and their witness gives us the Gospels we have today.

Of thirty-six miracles (before His resurrection) documented in the Gospels, Jesus performed eleven in Capernaum because the people there believed in Him. They knew Him as a boy because they were acquainted with the miraculous family stories of both John's and Jesus' birth. Seminaries have not comprehended the scene of the cross, where some members of Jesus' family didn't abandon Jesus or His mother in their darkest hour. God created families and would want us to know the importance of their bonds, and to stand in their strength against the ungodliness of this world.

Most believers are unaware of the break in Jesus family and don't notice the heartwarming story of a divided family finding healing in Christ in the book of Acts. A great teaching is missed by not observing how Jesus handled his own broken family. This story is empowering and can give believers who have experienced broken families hope during the dark times.

The Easter story of Jesus is paramount to the Christian faith; many believers haven't heard of Cleopas, one of two men first to witness the resurrection. Neither have they been taught who Mary Magdalene was probably related to, nor why Jesus chose to appear to her first. Instead of a cohesive, beautiful story of encouragement, believers have been taught that the Gospels are contradictory. Some of the resurrection accounts perplex Bible expositors to this day because they get hung up on semantics, instead of focusing on context, which connects to the storyline the writers are conveying to us. Many believers who have been taught that these distortions contradict each other, not knowing the difference, have accepted these beliefs without question.

Consequently, millions of Christians today have never understood the full implications of the greatest story that has ever been told. Jesus' purpose was to reconcile the world's lost children to His heavenly Father's family. Hence, before Jesus' ascension into Heaven, He reconciled His own earthly family to His heavenly Father's family.

God wants believers to know their story, which is why He repeatedly gave particular names in the four Gospels, to encourage us.

CHAPTER 1

Homage to the King in Nazareth

Joseph, the husband of Mary, Jesus' mother, prepares to go to the synagogue. It is the Sabbath Day. He walks past some neighbors and hears the usual snickers. "Mary is pregnant again. And she had a baby girl just six months ago." He has heard the jokes before. "Who is the father this time?"

At the synagogue, the Torah is read. Today's Scripture is from Psalms:

> Yea, all kings shall fall down before him:
> all nations shall serve him.
> For he shall deliver the needy when he crieth;
> the poor also, and him that hath no helper.
> He shall spare the poor and needy,
> and shall save the souls of the needy.
> He shall redeem their soul from deceit and violence:
> and precious shall their blood be in his sight.
>
> And he shall live,
> and to him shall be given of the gold of Sheba:
> Prayer also shall be made for him continually;
> and daily shall he be praised.
> There shall be an handful of corn in the earth
> upon the top of the mountains;
> The fruit thereof shall shake like Lebanon:
> and they of the city shall flourish like grass of the earth.
> His name shall endure for ever:
> his name shall be continued as long as the sun:

And men shall be blessed in him:
all nations shall call him blessed.

Blessed be the LORD God, the God of Israel,
who only doeth wondrous things.
And blessed be his glorious name for ever:
and let the whole earth be filled with his glory;
Amen, and Amen.

The prayers of David the son of Jesse are ended.

—Psalm 72:11-20 [KJV]

The last words linger. The scribe is about to open his mouth to teach when a shout interrupts: *"It's the Romans!"*

Men jump up and run outside. *"They are coming in great number!"* Women emerge from their houses. Someone screams in the distance. *"They know it's the Sabbath. They are coming to slaughter us while we are defenseless and gathered together."*

Then one man says, *"They're not Romans."*

Who are they, then? Now, even greater panic breaks out. Men scramble for weapons—not swords, but staffs and pitchforks. They wonder if this could be a band of raiders from one of Israel's old enemies, like Syria.

"Who are they?" Another man exclaims.

"A band of men whom I do not know."

"They're riding camels, wearing coats of many colors."

As the company approaches, men send their wives into hiding with the children. Silence settles over the town as the band approaches the village elders.

"What do you want?" asks the chief elder.

No reply. The riders are mostly young, but one older man dismounts his camel. He is dressed like a wealthy king. *"He's a wise man. From the East,"* whispers a village merchant, who has traveled abroad.

The wise man faces the elder. *"We have come to worship and pay homage to the King of the Jews."*

The elder replies, *"What King? We know not of any King in Nazareth."* Now, many in the village are even more frightened. The visitors are well provisioned, well armed, and trained to fight. Women and children peek through the windows.

The elder asks, *"What is your name, and where do you come from?"*

"My name doesn't matter. Nor is where we came from. Only the King is important, and we've come far to pay homage to Him. Now, where is the son of David, the son of Jesse, who was born in Bethlehem?"

The village residents gasp. Then Joseph steps forward. *"Sir, I am Joseph. My wife gave birth as a virgin to a child in Bethlehem. Come with me, and I will show you where He is, in my home."*

From the crowd, Joseph hears the mocking words: *"Virgin! Joseph is a fool!"*

The wise man spins to face the villagers. *"You all are fools! For one of your own has been born King, and yet you know Him not. We have seen His star from far away, and it led us to your village. You speak evil of your King, and of him who cares for Him. If the King so willed, I would remove all your heads at His whisper."*

The story you just read did not actually happen this way, but it's more accurate than the Christmas story that has been passed down through the ages. The Scriptures tell us that Jesus was born in Bethlehem and that angels appeared to shepherds, who then visited Him in a stable, where He lay in a manger. But the common folklore of Christianity has the three wise men visiting Jesus in the stable. This never happened. The wise men visited Jesus in Nazareth because that's where He was after His parents presented Him to Jerusalem. Then they took Him home. **And when they had performed all things according to the law of the Lord, they returned into Galilee, to their own city Nazareth** *(Luke 2:39 [KJV])*.

Our nativity scenes celebrate a stable with three wise men in it. Yet, they will come to a house with a number that was much greater than three; for their company was so great, it alarmed Jerusalem at their visitation. **When Herod the king had heard these things, he was troubled, and all Jerusalem with him** *(Matthew 2:3 [KJV])*.

As with many issues, this should reveal that we commemorate, or give attention to, things that most likely didn't happen. Our celebration of Christmas is not even close to the date on which Jesus was born. I believe this is significant. If we can't get critical events correct at the beginning of the Gospels, we are going to end up with inaccurate perceptions later in the Gospels.

The Gospels communicate that the Pharisees had knowledge of Scriptures, but lacked understanding of the visitation of Christ. Ironically, this same preoccupation with knowledge precepts has been passed down through seminaries to believers even until this day. There is a huge contrast between knowledge and understanding. For example, did Joseph and Mary go to Bethlehem to have the baby? The knowledge answer is "yes", but the understanding answer is "no". Joseph and Mary went to Bethlehem to fulfill Caesar's law, and when they did so, Mary happened to go into labor and delivered Jesus. They did fulfill God's will and prophecy.

Luke tells us at the beginning of his Gospel that Mary had family close by Bethlehem. Luke did this so we'd understand that God protected Mary's family from Herod's future wrath by having her deliver the baby away from them. Luke would assume readers would naturally know a woman would not choose to have a baby in a stable when she had family close by. The Gospels' writers did not write them so that believers could have historical knowledge of certain events in Jesus' life. They were written so we would understand the human relationships and how The God used them to bring us the Gospel.

Christmas is the second most significant day of the calendar, for believers. In a sense, we celebrate what did not happen, and we miss the human story of what did happen. Some Bible expositors had minimized Jesus' humanity; consequently believers don't know what Jesus did before He started His ministry in His thirties. Yet, the Scriptures give us clues, and when we connect the dots, we come to some great understandings about His "silent years."

Families are important to God because He created them, and yet, the story of Jesus' family has been underemphasized. For this very reason religion has no concept of His perfect humanity. Jesus was the most humble and meek person ever to walk this planet and His grace overcame the hatred poured out against Him in the "silent years."

At times in this book, I use my imagination to see through the eyes of Jesus' family, so the reader can consider different perspectives in the Gospels that have not been shared. Come with me on a journey and see how Jesus used not money, but the love of his family to spread the Gospels that we have today.

CHAPTER 2

Interpreting the Gospels

The purpose of this book is to highlight the Christian faith has neglected central teachings that are paramount to its edification. I suspect the primary culprit is the original translator's view of family life choices. At some point, Christianity became a religion that controlled access to the scriptures by compelling those who wished to study them to forgo a life that involved family. Consequently, a religious heresy was introduced and fully accepted even to the present day, that Jesus abandoned a life involving family to accomplish God's will. This belief is subtly ingrained into mainstream Christianity and yet is contrary to the oracles of God. In Genesis 18:19 the Lord states emphatically that revelation and blessing is given of God's word to Abraham because he is a father that leads his household to know the living God. Furthermore, God describes Himself as a Father and chooses Godly parents throughout the Old Testament because the Messiah will come from their loins.

The early translators looked through the lenses of indifference towards family relationships, which explain their disregard of the preponderance of Scriptures that underscores Jesus kindred interconnections throughout the Gospels. For example, John the Baptist is associated with sixty-two Scriptures in the New Testament. Clearly, God is designating that the Baptist relationship with Jesus is instrumental in the Gospels. Nevertheless, interpretations passed down to believers in all translations have the Baptist not recognizing his cousin whom he regularly saw at feasts—who grew up with Jesus—whom he preached was the Messiah because he comprehended Jesus immaculate birth even before he left the womb—all transpired before Jesus asked him to perform his baptism. Therefore an abstruse interpretation was introduced into the scriptures by translators who had no comprehension of family relationships in their own life let all alone the central role that relatives played in Jesus' life.

Jesus is the Good Shepherd to all believers, and as such, He was a shepherd to His household and earthly family. Subsequent chapters in this book will demonstrate religious prejudice introduced a European Christianity that disrespected Jewish traditions such as Jesus' actual birth observance further detaching from the centrality of Jesus' life. Jesus was not European but a Jew; as such He fulfilled Jewish law by attending feasts biannually with His household and extended family that celebrated God's incarnation to the Jewish people. Consequently, all His movements involved his family. Therefore it is my contention that the early translators were totally oblivious that Jesus loved his family and that many were devoted to him at his birth and throughout his life became instrumental in the Gospels. They were the first Christians, and God used them to give us the Gospels, and believer's ignorance of them has led to severe dysfunction throughout Christianity.

Jesus' relationships with His family are the foundation of the Gospel and yet translators utterly disregarded them, which resulted with Christianity being splintered into thousands of denominations without unity. Inexplicably, missing God's predominate purpose of the household has compounded the misinterpretations not even to acknowledge Jesus' family at His birth and Resurrection encounters.

The fact the Gospels were written almost two thousand years ago does increase the complexities in understanding them. While today, we may be perplexed by certain verses in the Gospels, we should be aware that this is contrary to the original writers' purpose. The authors were writing to an audience of simple folk who would have understood their communication. After we explore the possible reasons for today's misunderstandings of their words, we can have total confidence that God has preserved His Word that we might know and walk with Him.

Format

All four Gospels were passed down to us in Greek, yet what language Jesus spoke during His time here on Earth is disputed. He most likely spoke Aramaic, but some believe he utilized either Hebrew or both Hebrew and Aramaic. It is important to note that whatever language Jesus spoke, it was not Greek. The original Gospels are gone but were preserved by unknown scribes, who copied them. The process of copying began before 100 AD and is the reason we even have the Gospels today (this is disputed by many in religious studies). Errors and corrections were entered into the text over the centuries, but we now have so much manuscript evidence that we are virtually certain of what the original writers wrote. The original Gospels did not contain chapters or numbered verses. In fact, the words and sentences ran into each other without spaces or paragraph breaks. Centuries after the originals, scholars made the manuscripts more readable, using practices with which we are familiar today.

One example of formatting excellence is the movie *Pulp Fiction*, which received many acclamations in the nineties. One reason was due to its nonlinear storyline. The scenes were isolated stories within a story, and they didn't occur in chronological order but were tied together by common themes and characters. Each segment had its own title, alerting the audience that a new mini-story was commencing.

Unlike *Pulp Fiction*, however, the Gospels don't provide such clear visual clues to guide us. There are clues in some places, but even then, one must be familiar with the time and writing styles to recognize when the scenes have shifted and how they relate to the story line. Sometimes paragraphs and sentences run into each other, and the Medieval scholars didn't always get the verse and chapter divisions right. Or at least, there's room for debate. Sometimes we don't know if one sentence describes an event that occurred one day, one month, or even one year after the previous sentence. And sometimes the events are purposefully placed within the text out of chronological order possibly because God inspired the author to put them in a topical or thematic order, instead.

Our minds assume that each Gospel is a story with a chronological flow, yet it is not believed that the Synoptic Gospels (Matthew, Mark, and especially Luke) occur in strictly chronological order, and they don't correspond perfectly to each other with something that seems to us like a natural flow. Hence, we don't know with certainty the order of all events in the Gospels, and the Resurrection events have been particularly difficult to put into cohesive form. Unfortunately, this means that many movies, books, and teachings have missed key elements of the Resurrection.

Word Meanings

Mathematics is a universal language and, as such, has many fewer understandings than the world's spoken languages. The language that governs our society is full of misunderstandings; therefore, disagreements frequently occur. Unlike a whole number, which corresponds to just one integer, human words mean different things depending on how they're used in a sentence. **Let us go down, and there confound their language, that they may not understand one another's speech** *(Genesis 11:7 [KJV])*. And so it is today: Even though we may speak the same language, we often do not understand each other.

If we have misunderstandings when speaking a language, we have all shared from childhood, how many more misunderstandings might we encounter when interpreting the Gospels from a language that isn't utilized today? Adding to the confusion are words and phrases used in the New Testament, the meanings of which Bible expositors sometimes must take an educated guess.

Communication and understanding require one to correctly interpret the meanings of words and to do so in the correct context. Take, for instance, the word "appendix," which can be used to reference either an organ within human anatomy or a portion of a document or book that appears at the end of the paper or book. Two entirely different meanings of the same word and they are completely dependent on the context in which they are applied in communication.

The Greek (and a little Aramaic and Hebrew) employed in the Gospels does not always translate easily into similar words and phrases in English. That's one reason why skeptics mistakenly believe they've found contradictions in the Bible. Take, for example, Jesus' post-resurrection statement: **Behold my hands and my feet** *(Luke 24:39 [KJV])*. Modern movies show a nail hole in the palms of Jesus' hands, but Rome crucified criminals by placing the spike between the two bones of the forearm, so the body's weight would be held securely. The Greek word Luke used (translating the Aramaic that Jesus spoke among His friends) was understood in that day to include the wrist and forearm, not just what we call the hand, in today's English. We should understand some words are hard to convey briefly in an English translation accurately. Many translators do attempt to clarify the issue in a footnote, but readers sometimes come away with inaccurate perceptions.

Another example: The Gospels use a Greek word translated as "desert" or "wilderness." A standard concept of a desert is the Mojave Desert, with no water and only a few cacti, if even that. Some commentators suggest the Greek word was used to describe grassland that has been trodden down by livestock. In the past, many have pictured Jesus walking around in the Mojave Desert for forty days, but, in fact, Jesus did not wander far from water, because a human can't live without water. He didn't have to survive by supernatural means, and so he behaved consistently when he refused to perform miracles after each of Satan's suggestions.

One more area of confusion is the fact that the genealogies of Jesus in *Matthew 1:1* and *Luke 3:23* are quite different because Luke traces the lineage of Jesus' mother (his biological parent) and Matthew traces the lineage of Joseph (considered His legal "parent"). Some translators' word choices read as though both describe the lineage of Joseph. One commentator suggested that Luke couched his genealogy in Jewish patriarchal terms, while still implying Mary's lineage, to avoid unnecessary insult to the Jewish tradition of never posting a woman's genealogy.

Bible critics complain about what they believe are contradictions but which, in fact, are only *apparent* discrepancies caused, in part, by variations in Greek and English word usage, and by difficulties in the translation process. As such, there is some debate between believers regarding which translations are the most accurate. The problem is that teachers who come from seminaries are indoctrinated with the Greek translations, which I believe miss the context of the original writers' words.

Culture

When scholars attempt to precisely and accurately interpret the Bible, they encounter problems because people alive today generally cannot fully understand the correct meanings of some words used two to four thousand years ago. Of course, some words, such as *adultery* or *lying*, are distinct. But many believers have misperceptions about words they read outside of the original cultural and historical context. And a translation that might attempt to capture everything with complete accuracy would be so massive and expensive that no one could afford it. Reasonably-sized translations are limited in their ability to reproduce the full understanding of the original writers and readers, so we rely on commentaries and educated teachers.

As an example of the importance of cultural context, Bible skeptics point out that the apostles have different names in different Gospels. But they argue from a basis of cultural ignorance. They don't realize that people often had more than one name—like Simon Peter. Sometimes the Gospel authors give us some help, like pointing out that Judas Iscariot was so called to set him apart from the other Judas. There was James, the brother of the Lord, but also James, the brother of John. Places also had different names: The Sea of Galilee was interchangeable with the Sea of Tiberius.

The problem occurs in the translations where the authors described how people addressed one another or described a place, a number, or a sequence. For example, **He stood by the Lake of Gennesaret** *(Luke 5:1 [KJV])*. When I previously read this verse, I interpreted it to mean that Jesus was standing by a lake *called* Gennesaret. There are only two freshwater lakes in Israel, and I wondered if this was the small one instead of the Sea of Galilee. But Jesus called to Peter and John while they were fishing, and I know they lived off the Sea of Galilee. Footnotes in Bibles say that Lake Gennesaret was the Sea of Galilee. I've read different translations, but they haven't helped: **One day as Jesus was standing by the Lake of Gennesaret** *(Luke 5:1 [NIV])*. This doesn't make sense because there is no other Scripture about a lake called Gennesaret. Then I found a commentary stating that a certain plain of grass by the lake was called Gennesaret. That's where Jesus was speaking to the people. The people kept moving toward Jesus, so He asked the fisherman if He could get in the boat. Suddenly, the verse makes sense and is without contradictions, but it doesn't work the way it's written. This example highlights the fact the original translators had difficulty getting ever word perfect. It's my belief at times they made the wrong assumption, and some of those errors have hidden Jesus family's participation in the Gospel story.

Names

Names are critical for us to identify the players of the story and understand the simplicity of the Gospel. Different spellings identify some names for the same person. Why? Names were originally either Hebrew or Aramaic and had been translated into Greek names and then into English. A name such as Peter (English) is also referred to as Cephas in Aramaic. The name "Cleopas" is spelled differently in another Gospel as "Cleophas." Making our job even more challenging is the fact that in biblical times, people went by more than one name. Simon is a main character and is clearly identified by the Gospel writers to be also known as Peter, yet Cleopas, also known as Cleophas, wasn't; and there is some debate regarding if he is also referred to as Alphaeus.

Family

The Gospel of John gives us associations that are paramount, by stating them throughout his gospel, and ultimately with Judas. The one who betrayed Jesus and his family connections should be critically important to note, and yet apparently it's not. Bible expositors have apparently neglected the influence of Judas' father, and consequently, they have missed why Judas was induced to betray Jesus. Believers' connection to the story is then inhibited, such as, why Judas kissed Jesus. Knowing this climax is paramount to what God would want believers to understand about dysfunctional families. Ironically, God gave us genealogies throughout the Old Testament which many of us believers, including myself, skip over them. Perhaps the reason He did this, was so we understand family associations were paramount for us to understanding the scriptures.

There is a subtly distorted message in some interpretations of Jesus' teachings; one can abandon their family responsibilities and serve God. Cults minimize the family relationships and ultimately sabotage them to control their members. Yet, God would also have us understand we are not to betray our consciences but to detach from the dysfunction (not our family) that has been passed down to all our respective families.

Some Bible expositors miss the fact that when the Gospels were written by the players in the story, their contemporaries knew the back story that we don't know. It's easy to miss the simple humanity of Jesus, His personal relationships, and how He related to His immediate and extended family—especially before His thirties. God limited Himself by adding humanity to His deity, and while living as a human on Earth, He did great deeds so believers of all ages could be encouraged to face their limitations.

The Gospel of John was written by a blood relative and Jesus' first cousin, John, the son of Zebedee. Organized religion has largely ignored this connection. By understanding that a relative was writing to us, we can make sense of the Synoptic Gospels when we put them together with the Gospel of John. Many insights now open to us as we connect the dots of Jesus' family relationships. The family is vital to God; the marriage was His creation. They offer purpose, self-respect, protection, and dignity to humans. Jesus had no money, for a while it is useful, it does not equal love. Jesus used the love in families to spread the Gospel, as He does to this day.

Jesus was a family man, and ignorance of this fact opens the door to cults that have no respect for God's provision for the household. When we see through the lens of family, we understand why Jesus made Capernaum His capital. We see His travels with His family, and our perspective broadens. Knowing the love that Jesus had with His family shows us more of His humanity. It also opens our understanding of His deity and His personal love for us. We see Jesus overcome the same kinds of family dysfunction that torments Christians today, as well as conflicts that rise out of bitter resentment from family.

I am going to use Scripture to identify some facts that many have missed—highlights that all believers should know about Jesus' personal life and His relatives. Then I will attempt to show how these relate to the Gospel story using a much different storyline than what believers have been told. At times I will be presumptive of what I consider the motivations of the characters involved so that believers will feel the humanity and how that relates to the Gospel writers' accounts. I hope to portray a much more accurate story that movies should represent the influence of His family, culminating, with believers having a greater connection to how beautiful Jesus was when he walked this Earth.

King James Version

I will be using the King James Version (KJV) to identify most verses in this book. Where I don't, I will indicate which translation I am using. I do not use King James because I believe it's perfect; on the contrary, there are some who argue that the translators' agenda was for it to correspond to the interpretations of the Church of England. That is a red flag, if there ever was one, that agendas may have been introduced into the translations.

Why would I use it? In my opinion, it is the most consistent in that it corresponds to the Old or New Testament Scriptures. For example, I can compare Mark's to Luke's version of the resurrection and have the same words and not fall into further confusion.

Later in the book, I will demonstrate why the other translations have not led us to know the obvious: the relationships that Jesus had with His family.

Bible Expositors/ Seminaries/Teachers

My tone in this book may give off the impression I have little regard for the great men who have dedicated their lives to the study of Scriptures. On the contrary, I wouldn't have been able to write the book without their tireless and fervent dedication to God's word. Such as J. Vernon McGee, who blessed many with his *"Thru the Bible"* radio program whose books I find fundamental in sound doctrine of God's grace.

Most Christians understand there is nothing more important in this life than their family. That they are a gift from God and His will is that they love them. Yet centuries of interpretations have excluded Jesus family participations in our teachings of the Gospels. Consequently teachers do not present the beauty of Jesus loving His family or the fact that Mary's family loved Him. If they did, then the world would know what Jesus did before He was thirty. He took care of His widowed mother and younger siblings when Joseph died. As a family oriented person, I understand the huge lesson in that teaching instead of the detached Jesus that is presented in translations where He gets started doing God's work after he was thirty. This is a dark message that has been passed down to believers throughout the ages and has kept them in bewilderment of what Jesus did in His early life. Jesus did God's will loving His family and providing for them. We as Christians should recognize that God never wills us to be in the dark but in the light of God's love and see it in the Gospels.

CHAPTER 3

Mary

Bible expositors have largely neglected the family stories of John the Baptist and Jesus, so I wonder how many believers have contemplated the great faith which Mary demonstrated in accepting being pregnant without a husband. What should encourage us is her great faith in God by letting go of her own understanding. We can be sure that God took notice and honored her throughout her life.

And in the sixth month, the angel Gabriel was sent from God unto a city of Galilee, named Nazareth *(Luke 1:26 [KJV])*. It is assumed that Mary was from Nazareth, because of this verse. I hope to give you a different perspective on Jesus' life, in part by pointing out the importance of Mary's family in the Gospels. We read of events pertaining to Mary's family in Judea, Cana, and Capernaum. Jesus performed miracles in every one of these locations. We will see that Jesus used his mother's family to propagate the Gospel, but we never see Joseph's family contributing to Jesus' ministry.

The Gospels never record anyone from Nazareth believing in Jesus except Joseph, and he was born in Bethlehem. The Gospels do not describe any particular miracles being performed by Jesus in Nazareth. Nazareth is recorded as rejecting Jesus, and some there even tried to kill him. We should ponder why "he did not many mighty works there" *(Matthew 13:58 [KJV])*. I wonder if believers have pondered the difficult state Mary was put in. It's my belief she was intelligent and fully understood that it was unlikely that anyone would believe she was pregnant as a virgin. We will see later Nazareth rejected Jesus' virgin birth and the mother who claimed it. We should note that Jesus was not born in Nazareth, but in Bethlehem, fulfilling the prophecy.

One of the Bible's biggest miracles was Jesus' incarnation. His conception had nothing to do with Joseph of Nazareth. God makes it clear that Joseph was not Jesus' father and the address of His heavenly Father wasn't even close to Nazareth. Since God is not the author of confusion then doesn't it make sense that He wouldn't want Mary to be tarnished as a fornicator and the appearance that Joseph was the father? This rumor will be the story of Mary's life in Nazareth, and ironically our Bible interpretation has subtle innuendo confirming it. It's my belief that Jesus' conception was a big deal to God and He would highlight the location with miracles. It's not a stretch, then, to suspect that Jesus was not conceived in Nazareth, especially since Mary's hometown was likely where her relatives lived and where Jesus performed miracles. Therefore Jesus was conceived in Mary's hometown, and we will consider evidence as to its location as we go through the story.

Besides Jesus, Mary is a central character of the Gospel story, and Bible expositors' disregard of her importance has sabotaged understanding of the resurrection accounts to this day. Jesus' claim of incarnation would be without foundation if it were not for Mary's testimony, given to us in the Gospel of Luke. Some believed her then, and some did not, as it is to this day.

Mary was the only pure blooded relative Jesus had since He didn't have an earthly father and His siblings would be half-brothers and sisters. Joseph is nowhere to be found in the Gospels after Jesus started His ministry. Mary appeared at the beginning and the end of Jesus' life. The only parent at the cross was Mary, because by then, Joseph was already dead.

Nazareth was hostile to Jesus because it rejected Mary. The town never believed that Mary had conceived Jesus by the Spirit of God, and its people judged Mary to be a fornicator. Jesus' siblings were raised in the faithless environment of Nazareth, and they, too, did not believe in Him. The town is thought to have had a population of four hundred. If Mary had relatives in Nazareth, they would have supported Mary (as Luke tells us in the beginning and throughout the Gospels) and believed in Jesus. For this reason and from other clues, which we will see, it makes sense to suspect Mary was from Cana, just six miles away.

The Scripture that has been given to us reads that God sent the angel Gabriel to appear before Mary while she was at Nazareth. I believe her family had visited Joseph's family who were from Nazareth (parents commonly arranged marriages) and they had just made wedding plans. There was some connection between the families that we are not directly informed of. **And the angel came in unto her, and said, Hail, thou art highly favored, the Lord is with thee: blessed art thou among women** *(Luke 1:28 [KJV])*. While many religions esteem the superiority of man over woman, God offers a different viewpoint. In *Genesis 3:15* is the first Scripture reference to the promised Deliverer, where God said the Messiah would be born from the seed of the woman. Throughout the Old Testament, genealogies are given from Adam and Abraham's line. These genealogies did not, however, point toward a man, but, rather, to the woman God was going to choose to bring forth His Son.

Later, God gave prophecies relating to the son of David being the Messiah. Both Mary's and Joseph's fathers' lines came from the descendants of David. Mary was descended from David through his son Nathan, whereas Joseph descended in the royal line of Solomon, who succeeded David to the throne. However, in the book of Jeremiah, God rejects the royal line of Solomon as a precursor of the Messiah's birth.

Perhaps Mary was pondering her future with Joseph, and the wedding date could have been within a day, as far as we know, or a few years. What we should note is that the angel created a big wrinkle in the wedding plans. **And, behold, thou shalt conceive in thy womb, and bring forth a son, and shall call his name JESUS** *(Luke 1:31 [KJV])*. We should also observe that the angel neither mentioned Joseph nor explained how things were going to work out for the young couple. **Then said Mary unto the angel, How shall this be, seeing I know not a man?** *(Luke 1:34 [KJV])*. We will never know if Mary pondered if she was destined to be husbandless after agreeing to be pregnant. From her perspective, she was going to get married, and the angel interrupted those marriage plans.

And, behold, thy cousin Elisabeth, she hath also conceived a son in her old age *(Luke 1:36 [KJV])*. The angel Gabriel encouraged Mary to witness another miraculous birth in her family: that of Elisabeth's son, John, who would be known as John the Baptist (see *Luke 1:5-20*). Recognizing the magnitude of this miracle is critical to understanding the Gospels we have today. Elisabeth's pregnancy parallels that of Abraham's wife, Sarah (see *Genesis 18:12*), who was ninety years old, and who laughed at the Lord when she was told she would have a child. Elisabeth, too, was very old, and her husband, Zacharias, did not believe God could make his wife pregnant at her advanced age and was struck deaf and dumb for a period of time. **For with God nothing shall be impossible** *(Luke 1:37 [KJV])*. To build Mary's faith, God sends her immediately away before facing a society that would judge her unmercifully for being pregnant before marriage. It should be apparent that Luke is giving us Mary's testimony, and we should note that Mary's family was her only encouragement during this trial.

And Mary arose in those days, and went into the hill country with haste, into a city of Juda *(Luke 1:39 [KJV])*. She awoke the next day, pregnant, and immediately ("with haste") sought out her cousin, Elisabeth, as per the word of the angel. Who else could she talk to? Who would believe her? The angel had asked Mary whether she was willing to have the child, **And Mary said, Behold the handmaid of the Lord; be it unto me according to thy word...** *(Luke 1:38 [KJV]*. Mary could have been very young; perhaps only fourteen years old. From the Gospel of Matthew, we can infer that she didn't tell Joseph, but was likely in a state of shock and immediately traveled to see her elderly cousin. Elisabeth was probably a contemporary of Mary's grandmother or great-grandmother.

Mary's Possible Family Connection to Elisabeth

```
                    Mary's Maternal Great Grandmother — Mary's Maternal Great Grandfather
                                                    |
                    ┌───────────────────────────────┴───────────┐
Zacharias — Elisabeth                           Mary's Maternal Grandmother — Mary's Maternal Grandfather
            |                                                       |
      John the Baptist                                    Mary's Mother — Heli
                                                                |
                                                               Mary
```

Elisabeth's home today is called Ein Karem, a suburb four miles west of modern Jerusalem, where monuments have been erected to commemorate the event of John the Baptist's birth. Lost in the dogma of translations that believers have been taught is how close this location is to Bethlehem, which is just five miles' line of sight to the south. We should make a note of it, and then we might understand why God chose Bethlehem to be the birthplace of Jesus. Bible expositors believe Ein Karem was around seventy miles from Nazareth, not a few hours' walking distance; nor did Mary have a BMW to make the trip in a couple of hours. Family members likely accompanied her to see her cousin's miraculous pregnancy.

Blessed art thou among women *(Luke 1:42 [KJV])*. Women can be contentious when it comes to their kids. Elisabeth could have been riding a high horse, bearing a child that an angel pronounced would go before the Lord in the spirit and power of Elijah. Instead, she spoke of love and reverence towards her much younger cousin.

And whence is this to me, that the mother of my Lord should come to me? *(Luke 1:43 [KJV])*. Elisabeth knew that Mary was pregnant with God's Son. How? According to Luke, the angel told Zacharias that their son would "make ready a people prepared for the Lord." Mary's family had been informed that Mary was a virgin and was bearing God's child. It was not a secret to them.

From the very beginning, John the Baptist prepared the way of the Lord by preparing Mary's family for the Lord. No doubt the family was shocked at the possibility that an eighty-year-old, childless Elisabeth was pregnant. So, the family was prepared for another bombshell: A Virgin was pregnant. Without the miraculous birth of John, Mary's family would not have believed her. God, in His infinite wisdom, knew this and prepared Mary's family so they would support her through great difficulty throughout Jesus' life. The family stands ready to help John, and then Jesus. As we continue the story, we will find that some of them became disciples of them both.

Elisabeth wanted to be a blessing to her cousin and would have done all she could to encourage Mary through the hardships she would face. **For, lo, as soon as the voice of thy salutation sounded in mine ears, the babe leaped in my womb for joy** *(Luke 1:44 [KJV])*. An unborn child was filled with the Holy Spirit and leaped at the knowledge that the Son of God had entered the room. We should suspect the boys spent time together growing up. Imagine young John pestering his parents: *"When can we see Jesus?"* We will explore what their natural response would have been in some upcoming chapters. We should suspect John likely asked Jesus every question imaginable. They loved one another because they were the only two people on the planet known to be filled with the Holy Spirit before they were born!

Elisabeth was not present at Jesus' crucifixion more than three decades later because she had most likely died well before John started his ministry.

If Mary visited Elisabeth and stayed with her for three months before they both gave birth, then probably the two visited each other after that. A godly woman like Elisabeth would have been a great encouragement to her devout cousin through her tribulations.

The movies show John the Baptist meeting Jesus for the first time at Jesus' baptism. This is contradictory with what the Spirit has told us: that even when still in his mother's womb, the fetus John recognizes Mary's voice. Jesus and John the Baptist would grow up together. This intimate relationship has been ignored, for Jesus was baptized by a family member, not a stranger, as portrayed in movies.

And her neighbors and cousins heard how the Lord had showed great mercy upon her; and they rejoiced with her *(Luke 1:58 [KJV])*. Elisabeth was not the only cousin to support Mary during this time. Mary stayed with other relatives who supported both women. Luke points out the role of families from the very beginning of Jesus' story. We will see that family plays a huge part in Jesus' and John's ministries.

I've never heard Bible expositor mention the fact that Mary's relatives were from the tribe of Levi. The Levites were the only tribe permitted to serve as priests (see *Numbers 18:1-3*). Zacharias served as a priest, so he was a Levite. But we are also told: **His wife was of the daughters of Aaron; her name was Elisabeth** *(Luke 1:5 [KJV])*. We should ask ourselves why God found it necessary to include that bit of information. The answer, to me, seems that Mary's mom was related to Elisabeth and was then also from the tribe of Levi. For Mary's father was from the tribe of Judah; hence, Elisabeth is related to her mother.

In *2 Kings 15:5*, King Uzziah was struck with leprosy for acting as a priest when he was not a Levite but was from the tribe of Judah. God was harsh because Uzziah showed disrespect for God's Word and disrespected God's chosen High Priest. **Seeing then that we have a great high priest, that is passed into heavens, Jesus** *(Hebrews 4:14 [KJV])*. God's Word says that Jesus was a high priest, and since God ordained everything, then, of course, Jesus could be from the Levite tribe through His mother. The tribes intermarried; Mary's mother was Levite, and her father was from the tribe of Judah. Joseph's father was also from the tribe of Judah, which could explain their families' connections to each other. In *Matthew 21:12*, Jesus cleared the temple. The only way Jesus would have the authority under Jewish law to do what He did was as a priest.

Jesus performed the highest priestly function by dying on the cross, atoning for the sins of all who would believe in Him. **Thou art a priest for ever** *(Psalm 110:4 [KJV])*. Jesus was a King, yet He was rejected, but He performed the priestly action on the cross, which was accepted by God the Father. No one else could fill those shoes. If Mary's mother's mother was from the tribe of Levi, perhaps her grandmother was sister to Elisabeth.

Mary's Sister

Now there stood by the cross of Jesus his mother, and his mother's sister *(John 19:25 [KJV])*. Mary had one sister at her side at the crucifixion, and we can surmise that she believed Mary was a virgin who gave birth to a Savior. She very likely stood by Mary when others accused and slandered her.

And I will put enmity between thee and the woman, and between thy seed and her seed *(Genesis 3:16 [KJV])*. Mary had enemies, but God blessed her with a family who supported her through incredible hardships. God chose not only Mary but also her godly family. Mary's family helped and encouraged her as society sought to destroy her emotionally. This is God's plan for all of us: to be blessed with our families and to support one another through a godless society that damages its members psychologically.

When Jesus says to Peter "upon this rock," I like to think the rock is Christ and is interchangeable with love. The gates of Hell came after Mary, and her sister stood right by her side because love stands in union against this divided world. Love does not blink. It prevails, for love comes from its source: God. Mary's sister had faith that Jesus was God's Son, and she didn't back down. We will discover her name shortly. She, too, had children who played an integral part in the Gospel story.

My suspicion is that Mary's sister, along with other relatives (whom Luke is partially talking), traveled with Mary to see Elisabeth. Her closeness to Mary at the cross indicates she may have been close to Mary during her pregnancy. Let's find out her name.

The Gospels of Matthew, Mark, and John mention three women at the cross besides Mary. They were the same three women, but the Gospel writers identify them with different titles, except for Mary Magdalene. Since all three Gospel writers name Mary Magdalene, the other two were the same women in all three Gospels. If we cross-reference them, we understand the Gospels more clearly.

Now there stood by the cross of Jesus his mother, and his mother's sister, Mary the wife of Cleophas, and Mary Magdalene *(John 19:25 [KJV])*. Mary apparently didn't have one child comfort her at the crucifixion of Jesus, but this verse identifies her sister standing beside her. Let's try to determine who she was.

This illustration was taken with permission from website of La Vista Church of Christ

> *Matthew 27:56*: **Mary Magdalene + Mary the mother of James and Joses + the mother of Zebedee's children.**
>
> *Mark 15:40*: **Mary Magdalene + Mary the mother of James the less and of Joses + Salome**

Assuming that these are the same three women, we see that Salome is the wife of Zebedee, mother of James and John, two of Jesus' disciples.

> *John 19:25*: **His mother, and his mother's sister, Mary the wife of Cleophas, and Mary Magdalene.**
>
> (Flip *John 19:25*) **Mary Magdalene + Mary the wife of Cleophas + his mother's sister**
>
> (Compare Mark) **Mary Magdalene + Mary the mother of James and Joses +the mother of Zebedee's children**

The wife of Cleophas was Mary, mother of James and Joses. She cannot be the mother of Zebedee's children, too. Therefore, Jesus' mother's sister was also the mother of Zebedee's children.

The reason John gave her a title is the same reason he gave himself a title. John didn't use his first name in his Gospel. "The disciple whom Jesus loved" was how John referred to himself (see *John 21:20*). John referred to his mother as "the mother of Zebedee's children," using a third-person expression. John didn't even tell us he was the son of Zebedee; nor did he directly disclose Jesus' call to him in the first person. For this same reason, John didn't tell us he was Jesus' cousin. John humbly avoided abusing his familiarity with the Son of God. A great teaching is missed by not recognizing this with Jesus Himself. He was (is still) meek and speaks of Himself in third person and as such, didn't take things personally throughout His life.

Fortunately, Matthew told us that James and John were sons of Zebedee. **He saw two brethren, James the son of Zebedee, and John, his brother, in a ship with Zebedee their father** *(Matthew 4:21 [KJV])*. Perhaps the Spirit of God wants us to know that Zebedee was important, he is mentioned thirteen times in scripture.

Mark named Mary's sister as Salome. She had two sons, one of them (John) coincidentally named the same as John the Baptist. If she traveled with Mary and saw the miraculous birth of John the Baptist, this would likely have an impression on her. Her firstborn was named James, coincidently the same as Mary's firstborn, with Joseph. But her second could have been named after John the Baptist. The mother of James and John plays a prominent role in Scripture: She is recorded asking Jesus for places in His Kingdom (see *Matthew 20:20-23*). Through deduction, we can understand why she was so bold to ask, and why Jesus did not rebuke her: As His aunt, Salome was dear to Jesus, and this gives us more of an understanding of their relationship; to see that she held Him as an infant.

CHAPTER 4

Joseph

And there shall come forth a rod out of the stem of Jesse, and a Branch shall grow out of his roots *(Isaiah 11:1)*. Isaiah gave this prophecy around five hundred years before Jesus' birth, indicating the Messiah would be from David's line, yet born a peasant as Jesse (David's father). After David had died, his sons ruled Israel until it was divided and later scattered by Assyria and Babylonians. When the scribes looked at the line of Jesus, they saw the royal line through David to Joseph.

And Mary abode with her about three months, and returned to her house *(Luke 1:56 [KJV])*. Scripture already told us that Elisabeth is six months pregnant before Mary visits her. Upon returning to Nazareth, Mary was at least three months pregnant. No doubt Mary wanted to see the miraculous birth, as well as draw courage from Elisabeth before returning to face a horrible ordeal. The interesting question most believers have never contemplated is: did she tell Joseph she was pregnant before she left to visit Elisabeth?

She was found with child of the Holy Spirit *(Matthew 1:18 [KJV])*. Mary was publicly pregnant. We should understand this wasn't an everyday occurrence. Mary didn't know what to do but followed the angel's instructions for her own well-being. Luke told us she left the next day, and if she told Joseph, it's unlikely we have the next series of events. It is also more understandable when we see that Mary left

Cana immediately, obeying God without going to Nazareth to tell Joseph. **Then Joseph her husband, being a just man, and not willing to make her a public example, was minded to put her away privily** *(Matthew 1:19 [KJV])*. Who can blame Joseph for thinking the worst of Mary, after she leaves and comes back pregnant? Most believers have not considered the ordeal Mary went through. She had to ponder staying with Elisabeth and having the child under the shelter of her family's protection. After all the angel told Mary to spend time there in the first place. Mary's family (the first believers) no doubt offered prayers for her, and I suspect some accompanied her home to attest the miraculous birth of John the Baptist. We are not told by Luke, but apparently, Mary came to the knowledge of God's will and, by faith, returned to face Joseph.

We are told Joseph had no desire to shame Mary publically. The tradition would have been for him to go to the gates of the city where the elders were, and inform them about Mary. Instead, he planned to terminate the relationship privately and allow Mary's family—or the baby's father—to step forth and take responsibility. We should take note that Cana was just six miles away from Nazareth and understand most of the inhabitants at this time didn't live in condos or apartments. The population was scattered on acreage and had to rely on live stock for daily needs. They didn't have the convenience to drive to the store to pick up some milk. I bring this up because it's doubtful that both Mary and Joseph lived literally in town, but instead had residences which were in close proximately of the locations we are given. However since we know Mary's family had some Levite heritage we can suspect (Levites had early tradition to settle in town though this didn't preclude other tribes from living in towns *[Numbers 35:2-8]*.) that her family lived in town and Joseph being from the tribe of Judah most likely lived on acreage.

Joseph, thou son of David, fear not to take unto thee Mary thy wife: for that which is conceived in her is of the Holy Spirit *(Matthew 1:20 [KJV])*. God does things in the light, and there is no deception in anything He does, even though most of us would have brought the Son of God into the world some easier way. "What people don't know won't hurt them" is a common Western thought. **Behold, a virgin shall conceive, and bear a son, and shalt call his name Immanuel** *(Isaiah 5:14 [KJV])*. According to God's Word, the Messiah would come from a virgin. God demonstrated this to Joseph, but, of course, Nazareth did not believe Mary was a virgin when she became pregnant.

Today, we have the Internet and magazines to spread gossip. But in Joseph's time, they had only the village grapevine, and Joseph was asked by God to be on the front screen. Joseph's whole life, from the point he took Mary to be his wife, was subject to ridicule. From the village's perspective, Joseph was marrying a woman who played the whore. Some neighbors likely took pleasure in Joseph's discomfort. They didn't have soap operas or big-screen TVs, so they were entertained the old-fashioned way.

We can surmise that Joseph heard every insult imaginable about his wife and his son. Wherever Joseph went, there would always be public snickering. We know Jesus had half-brothers and sisters. "Did you hear Mary is pregnant with another child? Who is the father this time?" The depravity of human behavior hasn't changed with history; today, as well as then, people take pleasure inflicting emotional pain on others.

Joseph had the comfort of knowing God's purpose. He saw angels and was aware that his stepson was the Messiah. But the Messiah was not from his loins. He had no blood connection to the child but was tasked by God to be the child's protector and, for all practical purposes, everything an earthly father should be. Angels informed Joseph that God Himself was decreeing that Joseph wed Mary. I think we underestimate what a grievous mission Joseph was asked to carry out—to live a life of shame for the benefit of God's will.

God could have chosen a different, cleaner method for Joseph and Mary. He could have made Mary pregnant the day before the wedding so that no one would know about the Immaculate Conception. But then Mary's family and the world would lose the benefit of knowing about this great miracle, which is the linchpin of Christian faith. How anyone accepts or rejects this, today or in Jesus' time, dictates their perspective on Jesus' deity.

CHAPTER 5

Before the Wise Men Visit

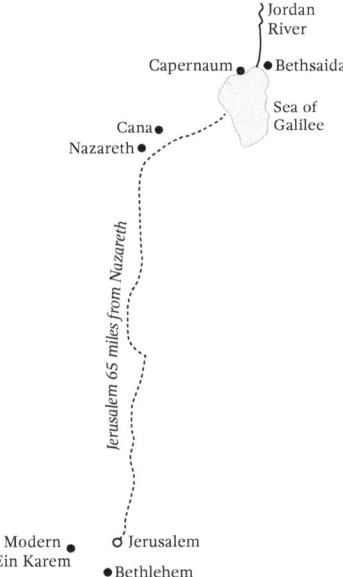

Many interpretations of the Bible have been passed down through the centuries that make it impossible for believers to connect to a comprehensible Gospel story. These teachings indoctrinate believers with knowledge of particular events, but they miss understanding the human story in the Gospels. **To be taxed with Mary his espoused wife, being great with child** *(Luke 2:5 [KJV])*. The Scripture says that Mary went to Bethlehem with her husband to fulfill Caesar's law. Mary did not go there to have a baby in a stable. And so it was, while they were there- Luke is telling the audience that while fulfilling the law of Caesar, Mary happens to go into labor and delivers Jesus *(Luke 2:6 [KJV])*.

33

Matthew 24:44 [KJV]—**for in such an hour as ye think not the Son of man cometh.** This verse is given by Jesus in relation to His second coming but probably relates to His first coming, too. Mary most likely felt she had more time until the baby came, but while she was in Bethlehem, she went into labor. Matthew will tell us indirectly that this was God's will for fulfilling an earlier prophecy of the Messiah's birth in Bethlehem. Jesus is born in a stable and given a manger as a bed, and the angels appear to shepherds near Bethlehem. Luke alone provides us with the nativity scene. The wise men were not in Luke's Gospel because they did not participate in Jesus' birth story.

John the Baptist's and Jesus' birthplaces were, interestingly, very close to each other and relatively the same distance from the Temple Mount in Jerusalem.

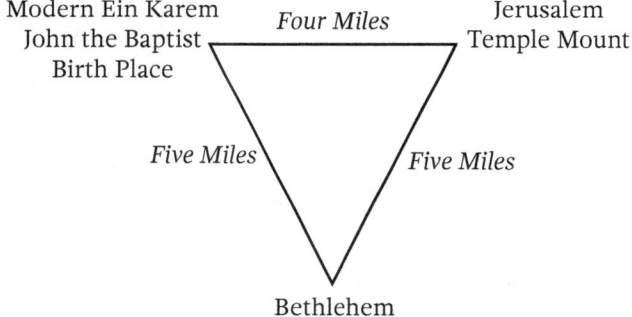

The first readers of Scripture would have understood the reason Luke told them earlier that Mary had family close to Jerusalem and Bethlehem, and they would have naturally grasped the fact that Mary would have preferred to deliver the baby there, rather than in a stable. Luke has told us that Mary had many relatives in Juda (modern Ein Karem) and would, naturally, stay with them before heading into Bethlehem (five miles away) to fulfill Caesar's law. Obviously, Mary's relatives would be quite concerned about her traveling to Bethlehem in the full term of her pregnancy. Inexplicably, believers have not been taught about them, so they will not see them here in the birth story or their appearance later in the Gospels. Of course, they would have checked on Joseph and Mary if they didn't immediately return from Bethlehem. We are not told of anyone else going with them, but early readers would have surmised this from the custom of the day, where Mary would have a female family member always with her. Perhaps Mary's younger sister or older relative travels with them to Bethlehem and is there to assist Mary in delivering the baby. Afterward, they would have informed the family near Bethlehem. Fast forwarding to Jesus' resurrection, we should note that the apostles are meeting and staying near Jerusalem for the very reason that Mary's family resides near there.

If Joseph and Mary went to Bethlehem alone, it wouldn't make any sense for the family not to check on them. Elisabeth and her household obviously were anticipating the birth of the Messiah. As soon as Jesus was born, the family would have assisted them in returning to the family residence in Juda (Ein Karem). Jesus' actual birth story is omitted in Matthew's Gospel, which explains why Luke's Gospel, written later, gives us more critical details about Mary's family. Mark and John do not tell us anything about Jesus' birth. For us to connect to Jesus' birth story, we must understand that it is only told in the Gospel of Luke. While Luke will become a companion to the apostle Paul, some Bible expositors don't connect the dots: that Mary apparently gave this information directly to him. This is important to note so that we have some understanding of Jesus' relatives' influence on the Gospels as direct witnesses.

Only Matthew recorded the visit of the wise men. The tradition celebrating the nativity scene with wise men comes to readers from wrongly assuming that Matthew was telling us the story of Jesus' actual birth. Matthew gives us details relating to Joseph and his thoughts about putting Mary away before Jesus was born. Matthew is unique in that it shares details as they relate to Joseph's contribution, which is why his genealogy is found there. Joseph lived in Nazareth, which is why the wise men's visitation is found only in this Gospel.

Now when Jesus was born in Bethlehem of Judaea in the days of Herod the king, behold, there came wise men from the east to Jerusalem *(Matthew 2:1 [KJV])*. The NIV replaces "now when" with the word "after." Let's read it again with just that change: "After Jesus was born in Bethlehem of Judaea in the days of Herod the king, behold there came wise men from the east to Jerusalem." It's my contention that Matthew is clearly telling us the next series of events happened after Jesus' birth. Early Bible expositors believed the visit from the East was a simultaneous event to Jesus' birth, which has become the tradition in our nativity scenes. **Saying, Where is he that is born of the King of the Jews? for we have seen his star in the east, and are come to worship him** *(Matthew 2:2 [KJV])*. Early Bible expositors did not notice the star appeared to men in the East two years before they made this statement. When Jesus was born, some in the East took notice that a star had appeared that had never existed before. They understood that something great had happened in the heavens, which related to the Earth, and they didn't stay home and wonder but embarked on a great journey to Jerusalem. Herod's questioning of them relates to when they saw the star. Two verses will tell us that it took the wise men over two years to arrive in Jerusalem. This was a costly enterprise, but God calls them wise, for their sacrifice was worth it, for they would gaze upon the King of Kings.

This means Jesus was over two years old when the wise men from the East came to visit. If we want to find out what happened to him before their visit, we must go back to the Gospel of Luke: **And when eight days were accomplished for the circumcising of the child, his name was called Jesus, which was so named of the angel before he was conceived in the womb** *(Luke 2:21 [KJV])*. Joseph named Jesus according to the custom, which is significant because it's found in Luke. By Joseph naming the child Jesus, he is confessing a truth to Mary's family, who would be attending this important event. He is witnessing to them that Mary had this child as a virgin and, as such, named him Jesus, as commanded by an angel. Joseph's confidence in Mary could not be assumed just because he married her. The naming of the baby is critical because it tells us that Joseph accepted the child as being virgin-born and attests to the virtue of Mary to her family. The early Gospel readers would have understood that the naming of a child was a big deal to the respective family, and knew that Mary's family was there. With no hints to the contrary, it appears that Joseph's family wasn't present at this auspicious event.

And all the firstborn of man among thy children shalt thou redeem *(Exodus 13:13 [KJV])*. After a child was circumcised, the next thing the firstborn male had to do according to custom, was go to Jerusalem. But first, they had to wait forty days until the purification was accomplished before entering the temple. **And she shall then continue in the blood of her purifying three and thirty days; she shall touch no hallowed thing, nor come into the sanctuary, until the days of her purifying be fulfilled** *(Leviticus 12:4 [KJV])*. We can infer that purification was for a woman who had brought a sinner into the world with her blood. Coincidently, Jesus would later spend forty days and forty nights in the desert, to be tempted. But the difference is that Christ would save sinners with His blood. This period didn't prevent the family from taking care of a woman and her infant.

Mary's family would naturally desire to retrieve Mary from Bethlehem to stay with them. It would be indecent for a family then, as well as today, to ignore a relative having an infant in a stable, let alone the mother of the Messiah. There could be no doubt that Elisabeth is fully anticipating the birth of Jesus, as Luke has made a point to tell us. Yet, many Bible expositors evidently believe that Mary stays in Bethlehem for two years, where there was no room for her until the wise men visit. Some Gospels' interpretations depart from common sense and miss the loving family presented in Luke. The family was overjoyed by the birth of John the Baptist, and now, the birth of the Messiah from a Virgin. Bible expositors have missed this beautiful story and the fact that Mary's relatives believed in her and were our first believers in Jesus.

And when the days of her purification according to the laws of Moses were accomplished, they brought him to Jerusalem, to present him to the Lord *(Luke 2:22 [KJV])*. The Jewish custom required families to travel to Jerusalem no matter where their firstborn son was born. Mary and Joseph took baby Jesus to Jerusalem to fulfill the law, and we should note that it was just a few miles away from Mary's family

And to offer a sacrifice according to that which is said in the law of the Lord, A pair of turtledoves, or two young pigeons *(Luke 2:24 [KJV])*. During their visit, God provided devout people who recognized the infant as the Messiah. Through the words of Simeon and Anna (*Luke 2:25-37*), God encourages Joseph and Mary.

Anna's devotion to the temple implies that she was aware of the circumstances of John the Baptist's birth. God took notice of her faithfulness, kept her alive, and put her name in Scripture for many to read. Luke is the only writer to tell us about her and the circumstances of John's birth. The detailed personal information about Anna should cause us to ask how the author knew all this about her (a relative of Mary's acquaintance). She was probably related to Zachariah or Elisabeth. She might have even been a contemporary of theirs, possibly growing up with them as a cousin. We are given her father's name—an uncommon occurrence—which is somehow significant. Luke is pointing out relationships of family members because they are central to our understanding of the Gospel story he is presenting.

Anna was apparently well over a hundred years old. Put together her seven-year marriage with the fact that she was widowed at eighty-four years of age. Twelve tribe's times seven years equals eighty-four years. I believe coincidences are God's fingerprints and have meaning in Scripture. We will see several miracles in the Gospels relating to the numbers twelve and seven. In *Luke 8:42-43*, a man asked Jesus to heal his dying twelve-year-old daughter, while a woman who suffered from a bleeding disease for twelve years touched Jesus and was healed. God was loudly telling the people to wake up and see His visitation. In *Luke 9:10-17*, Jesus used seven food objects to feed five thousand men, and twelve baskets full of food remained. In *Matthew 15:32-38*, Jesus used seven fish to feed four thousand men, not including women and children, with seven baskets left over. The number seven, in Scripture, represents completeness, and God was clearly saying that He could completely fill all twelve tribes if they would come to him. **I am the bread of life: he that cometh to me shall never hunger** *(John 6:35 [KJV])*.

That the widowed woman was over one hundred years old was a miracle. Her recognition of Jesus was God's bugle call to the people: "Hey, the Messiah has been born!" We are given no details about the effectiveness of Simeon and Anna's witness. The people were apparently asleep to the wake-up call from God, as we will see in the case of the wise men's' visitation. We are to see that God does His part, but people are too consumed with their lives to take notice.

And when they had performed all things according to the law of the Lord, they returned into Galilee, to their own city Nazareth *(Luke 2:39 [KJV])*. They returned to Nazareth, where they lived; not to Bethlehem, where there was no place to live. Luke tells us the simple story, obviously from Mary's perspective, and inexplicably, Bible expositors are confused by Matthew's Gospel. Mary and Joseph only traveled to Bethlehem to fulfill the Roman law, and then went to Jerusalem to fulfill God's law. As the Apostle Paul pointed out, we have dual citizenship. We are to obey the laws that govern us, even if we don't agree with them. **Render therefore unto Caesar which are Caesar's; and unto God the things that are God's** *(Matthew 22:15-22 [KJV])*. We should see that they were conscious of both requirements and, as such, intended to have the baby with Mary's relatives in the first place, near Jerusalem. We should see the humanity of the story. Having a child—let alone the Messiah—is a big deal. Jesus' birth story is about the importance of love in our family. Mary's family loved Jesus, and Luke gives beautiful details about why. God blessed them with a time of joy, and believers should see God's love in the story. Matthew's story is about rejection, which comes later, and the persecution of Jesus' family, that begins after the wise men's visit. In the next chapter, we will see the fact that Jesus' birth is commemorated on the wrong month by the creation of our calendar adding to Bible expositors' confusion.

CHAPTER 6

When Was Jesus Born?

And in the sixth month the angel Gabriel was sent from God unto a city of Galilee, Nazareth *(Luke 1:26 [KJV])*. This verse is referencing the fact that Elisabeth was six months pregnant with John when the angel Gabriel visited Mary. Some Bible expositors believe this is for the particular month in which Jesus was conceived. This type of logic misses the message that Luke is conveying to the readers, which is the fact that the births of John the Baptist and Jesus are both miraculous and tied together.

Jewish festivals are based on lunar months, rather than a solar year, which is why Easter varies year to year. The Jewish calendar has twelve months, but every two to three years, they had thirteen months to keep up with the solar year. We start a new school year in September, while the calendar year starts January 1. Similarly, the first Jewish calendar month is Nissan, in the spring, when the Passover occurs. But they celebrate the annual New Year in the fall, with Rosh Hashanah, at harvest time. According to articles written for Lamb and Lion Ministries by Dr. David R. Reagan *[Was it really on December 25th?]* and Dr. James Yaakov Hug *[When was Jesus Born?]*, Jesus was likely born either in late September or early October, during the Feast of Tabernacles. Reagan exquisitely points out in the article, "So, when God came to earth to tabernacle among Men it appears that He timed His arrival in the Bethlehem manger to coincide with the Feast of Tabernacles."

When Luke was written, they knew the day Jesus was born. Why does it matter? It is one of the most important events in our history, but believers don't celebrate it on the right day. Consequently, we're not connected to Mary's family participation throughout the Gospel, and Christ's resurrection appearances to them are still today ignored by Bible expositors. The first readers of Luke would have comprehended that Mary and Joseph were staying with family members, as was customary during the Feast of Tabernacles. God would want us to understand His omnipotence; that He ordained the feasts to commemorate His birth, His death, and His ascension; that we might know that the purpose of the Old Testament is not to be a historical narrative, but, rather, to foretell and announce His coming to His people. The Feast of Tabernacles was a feast of great joy and what greater joy is there that God is with us? Yet, we celebrate Christmas on a day that wasn't Jesus' birth. Why? In the fourth century, the Catholic Church was unable to get rid of a pagan holiday that occurred at the winter solstice—the shortest day of the year, which affected animals and crops. It was a favorite holiday for exchanging gifts related to the worship of the Roman god of agriculture, Saturn, who, tradition said, was bound by chains until the winter solstice.

The church concluded that they could never get rid of the holiday, so if you can't beat them, join them. They renamed Saturnia as the Festival of Nativity. They saw themselves as limiting evil, but they introduced a lie that has skewed Bible interpretations to this day. Later, the church launched a new calendar based on the birth of Christ, which was off by four to six years, confusing the dating of events to this day. But it's all based on faulty assumptions.

Behold, there came wise men from the east to Jerusalem. Where is he that is born King of the Jews? For we have seen his star in the east, and are come to worship him *(Matthew 2:1-2[KJV])*. I've read some expositors who suggest that the men were astrologers or sorcerers ("Magi," relating to magic). But Leviticus says, **Neither seek after wizards, to be defiled by them; I am the LORD** *(Leviticus 19:31 [KJV])*. The Lord of Glory would not be defiled by sorcerers, but was honored by wise men from the East. The assertions that they were sorcerers are subtle attacks on the Word of God. **Now the serpent was more subtil** *(Genesis 3:1 [KJV])*. It seems to me that Satan would want to teach the world that sorcerers know the way of the Lord.

King James Version calls the men from the east "wise," apparently because they alone were conscious of the Jewish Messiah's birth. Sorcerers were not wise in God's eyes. If these men were from Persia, it would not have taken them more than two years to get to Jerusalem, which was less than one thousand miles away.

Bible expositors get their interpretation from the Old Testament, connecting Balaam's prophecy with Persia: **There shall come a Star out of Jacob, and a Scepter shall rise out of Israel** *(Numbers 24:17 [KJV])*. The story of Balaam is about a sorcerer, thought to be from Persia, who was hired by Israel's enemies to curse Israel. God does have a sense of humor, for He made a donkey speak to Balaam, illustrating that the jackass had more wisdom than the man. **The ox knoweth his owner, and the ass his master's crib: but Israel doth not know, my people doth not consider** *(Isaiah 1:3 [KJV])*. God ordained that Jesus would ride on a donkey for His triumphal entry into Jerusalem, possibly relating back to this verse, indicating that the donkey knew who Jesus was.

We can be sure that the wise men were not magicians, but, rather, lords who had wealth and subjects. In 2016, the Chinese New Year was February 8 and the Jewish New Year was celebrated October 2. If the wise men saw an extraordinary event in the heavens in February, they might have surmised something relating to China, but they saw the star appear on the exact date of the Jewish New Year, and that is why they took notice. A friend and I once witnessed a meteor coming toward the Earth, and it seemed that it was coming right at us. It alarmed us. We were camping at a lake when the meteor hit the atmosphere and shone like a mini sun. We were both amazed. It lit up the darkness. It was the first time and last time I've ever seen anything like that. To me, it is rather obvious that something very spectacular happened at Jesus' birth and the East took notice of the implications. They had to wonder who the great One was born in an insignificant country currently occupied by Rome. Perhaps they pondered that the Jewish Messiah would no doubt overcome the greatness of Rome.

Where Is He Who Is Born King of the Jews?

Imagine you're one of the wise men from the East, and you've seen this great celestial event. You're tired from the hard travel but energized to conclude your quest. You left your home and some of your family. You sacrificed, spent money, and then the last thing you expect occurs.

When you arrive, the very people who should know have no clue what you're talking about. **We are come to worship him** *(Matthew 2:2 [KJV]).* Can you imagine their astonishment to learn that the Jews were clueless that their King had been born? From the beginning, the Jews were ignorant and resistant to God's call.

In the US, some of us consider this nation as Christian. In China, Christians are a small minority, yet it is estimated that sixty-eight million Chinese are now Christians. One of the reasons God gave light to the East was to demonstrate that He is not a Western God, but the God of all creation. **And I say unto you, That many shall come from the east and west and shall sit down with Abraham, and Isaac, and Jacob, in the kingdom of heaven** *(Matthew 8:11 [KJV]).* Therefore, I agree with some who believe that Matthew is the Gospel of the Kingdom, for this verse coincides with the fact that the wise men are only mentioned in Matthew.

Palestine rejected Jesus from the beginning, and, therefore, rejected Him at the end. Is it fair to say that the Pharisees rejected the wisdom of the East and the West, as the Middle East does to this day? Even today, the Middle East rejects wisdom on both ends, and the consequence is an insane geopolitical situation.

Let us go back to Matthew. The wise men came to Jerusalem, where they found both ignorance and insanity. Herod was obsessed with his vanity. So it is with all leaders on this planet who reject the truth of the Word of God and go after vanity. Herod was the chief of a dysfunctional family; he took his wife from his brother. He sat on his little perch and abused power at every opportunity.

When the wise men asked "Where is he that is born King of the Jews?" Fear entered Herod's heart. Why? If three people had shown up and asked him a question, he would have dismissed the issue as lunacy. But when two to eight hundred men descended upon Jerusalem, he was startled that such a number knew something he wasn't aware of. Also, the entire city was troubled by the visitation, which three people would not have accomplished (pointed out by J. Vernon McGee in His commentary on the Gospel Matthew in *Thru The Bible*). **When Herod the king had heard these things, he was troubled, and all Jerusalem with him** *(Matthew 2:3 [KJV])*.

Notice "all Jerusalem." The city was concerned when a grand caravan descended upon it. We can imagine some of the conversations: "What is the meaning of this? Why would so many come so far?" God wanted His people to know that He was walking among them. This is what is missed in many stale interpretations passed down by religion to believers. God is omnipotent and had the Eastern lords come to Jerusalem on purpose and to highlight He was rejected at the beginning.

But how do we commemorate Christmas events? Three wise men in a nativity scene, which the origination of this tradition will be explored later in the book. We don't see the wonder and magnificence of hundreds of people coming to honor Jesus from the East. The visit of the wise men may be connected to the prophesied Eastern horde of two hundred million who will come to the Middle East and usher in the return of Christ. **I heard the size of their army, which was 200 million mounted troops** *(Revelation 9:16, [NLT])*. Maybe this is the clue to the exact number of wise men who came to Jerusalem—two hundred men on camels or horses came upon Jerusalem.

The Bible informs us that in the latter days, armies from both West and East will invade Israel. Then some in Israel will understand Who the Messiah was and will start praying for His return. They will know that no army of Israel can stop two hundred million men (see *Revelation 9:16*). God will hear their prayers, and He will destroy the Eastern army.

There is a great significance in the story of the East, and while the Bible may seem scattered to some, to God, it is complete unity. The wise men's visit was a sign that should have alerted the Jewish nation to the fact that their Messiah had been born, as in the future, the Eastern army that invades Israel will be the sign of His return.

We connect to the story by understanding the size of the caravan shocked Herod, and so did their question. **And when he [Herod] had gathered all the priests and scribes of the people together, he demanded of them where Christ should be born. And they said unto him, In Bethlehem of Judea** *(Matthew 2:4-6 [KJV])*. The key word is "Christ." Herod had the knowledge of Who the wise men were asking for, and he knew who to ask about the Messiah (Hebrew) or the Christ (Greek). Probably some time elapsed, as Herod gathered all the Jewish leaders of Israel to answer the wise men of the East. Where is the King of the Jews? No doubt, the wise men from the East were puzzled and somewhat discouraged at the turn of events. The importance of their visit has several preludes to the lesson that God would have believers understand. Though the Jewish leaders had knowledge, they had no understanding. Some of Jesus' followers had no knowledge, but, yet, their understanding of Jesus was vastly more important. **Knowledge puffs up, but love edifies** *(I Corinthians 8:1[NIV])*. Knowledge creates hypocrites, but real understanding has an awareness of humility and is demonstrated with loving actions that require patience.

When Jesus started His ministry, many of those whom Herod had called were dead, but some may have been alive at Jesus' trial. The Jews may have recorded events, or the public event of the wise men's' visitation would have been remembered. Some of the Pharisees knew that Jesus was the Messiah, and they rationalized His death in their minds. They justified murder, believing that Jesus' death saved them politically. **And led him away to Annas first; for he was father in law to Caiaphas, which was the high priest that same year. Now Caiaphas was he, which gave counsel to the Jews, that it was expedient that one man should die for the people** *(John 18:13-14[KJV])*. We can infer that Caiaphas was older, giving counsel, and knew about Jesus' birth and that Jesus was the Messiah.

And one of them, named Caiaphas, being the high priest that same year, said unto them, Ye know nothing at all. Nor consider that

it is expedient for us, that one man should die for the people, and that the whole nation perish not. And this spake he not of himself: but being high priest that year, he prophesied that Jesus should die for that nation; and not for that nation only, but that also he should gather together in one the children of God that were scattered abroad. Then from that day forth they, took counsel together for to put him to death *(John 11:49-52 [KJV])*. Therefore, they rationalized that they were heroes because they were going to help the Messiah do His job. But they had no concept that Jesus was God. No matter what miracles Jesus did, their hard hearts would never understand that God would make Himself weak in love. They, therefore, were clueless about the sign of the star from the One Who created all stars. They did not understand God called them to be servants, for they sought to take from the people, not serve them. They had no interest in seeking Him out because they didn't believe God would make Himself weak (in this world's eyes) in love.

The Jewish leaders enjoyed power, even under Rome and Herod. They didn't want any trouble with Rome, so they didn't want some imagined Messiah causing problems, inviting Rome to destroy the status quo.

The Jewish leaders were devious and resourceful. If they wanted Herod dead, they could have figured a way to get rid of him. Herod would go on to slaughter innocent children, and what did the Jewish leaders do about it? They were wolves in sheep's clothing, *(Matthew 7:15)* themselves, and the murdering of innocents was not an offensive thing to their darkened hearts. They no doubt used Herod's murderous act to their advantage. It probably helped them get more control over frightened people. Out of ignorance, the Jews turned to their leaders, but the leaders didn't care, much as our politicians are detached from ordinary citizens to this day. They cared only about their power and ability to control others.

Herod asked the wise man when the star appeared—not because he loved God but to eliminate a threat to his throne. **Then Herod, when he had privily called the wise men, enquired of them diligently what time the star appeared** *(Matthew 2:7[KJV])*. The keywords here are "diligently" and "time." Herod understood that the appearance of the star coincided with the date of the Messiah's birth. Skipping ahead, we learn the answer, which the wise men gave to Herod. **Then Herod, when he saw that he was mocked of the wise men, was exceedingly wroth, and sent forth, and slew all the children that were in Bethlehem and all the coasts, thereof, from two years old and under, according to the time which he had diligently enquired of the wise men** *(Matthew 2:16 [KJV])*.

Since Herod slew all the children "according to the time which he had diligently enquired of the wise men," we can infer that Jesus was born less than three years and more than two years before He was visited by the wise men. Herod, considering himself to be King of the Jews, wanted to kill the child who threatened his rule and "diligently enquired" to know how old his target was.

The common belief of this visitation at Jesus' birth could also explain why there is debate regarding the accuracy of our calendar. Dionysius Exiguous, a Russian monk, was commissioned by the Pope in AD 533 to create a calendar with the future dates of Easter. He expanded upon the Pope's commission and established a calendar based on Jesus' birth. That's when the division of history into BC (Before Christ) and AD (*Anno Domini,* Latin for "Year of Our Lord") were established. His calculations were off by a few years, as he used the wrong year from Roman records for Herod's death. Herod died in 4 BC, not in AD 1, as Dionysius thought. Consequently, his calculations are considered to be off by four years. Yet, Jesus was over two years old when Herod died, and this means that Jesus was born 6-7 BC. This dating helps answer some contradictions raised by historians. Today Pope Benedict also disputes the date of Jesus' birth in his book. Dionysius apparently linked Jesus' birth to Herod's death, which, I contend, were not simultaneous occurrences, as he thought and as consequence, our calendar dating is off six to seven years.

And he sent them to Bethlehem, and said, go and search diligently; and when ye have found him, bring me word again, that I may come and worship him also *(Matthew 2:8 [KJV])*. Very sweet talk from

Herod, but we know from *Matthew 2:16* that his real intention was to kill the child. **When they heard the king, they departed; and, lo, the star which they saw in the east, went before them** *(Matthew 2:9 [KJV]).* Apparently, the star was hidden from the wise men as they approached Judea. Why? God's will was for them to go to Jerusalem.

Even after the wise men came to Jerusalem, apparently, no one else in Israel noticed the star. We know Herod didn't, for he desperately wanted to kill the Christ. The parallel comparison we should look at today includes the fact that our current world is blind to the true light of God. The religious believe in God's existence, but cannot see the light of Christ, even if it's in front of their eyes. This theme is presented continuously throughout the Gospels and is relevant to this day. **Having eyes, see ye not? And having ears, hear ye not?** *(Mark 8:18 [KJV]).* We should note that the political and religious powers both have no understanding of Jesus' birth from the very beginning. The only ones who did were Mary's family and the wise men, and yet, even today, their contributions are neither seen nor understood.

When they saw the star, they rejoiced with exceeding great joy *(Matthew 2:10 [KJV])* We should always pause when we read Scriptures and ask ourselves questions like what does the verse imply for us today, and what does it mean to the story? The wise men are an encouragement to all of us. They went where they were supposed to go, even though it didn't work according to their expectations. They probably assumed that they would find the King in a palace. They expected the Jews to be in a state of hope, knowing that their great King, the Messiah, was born. Instead, they found themselves in the darkness of disbelief, with no understanding of the birth of Christ.

These noble men must have recognized that Herod was not noble—a tyrant who was most likely quite pathetic to their perspective. They probably had the cognizance to understand that Herod and the Jewish people were lost and blind. Yet, they were now relying on them to point them in the direction of Christ. They departed toward Bethlehem, just five miles south of Jerusalem. Scripture has made it a bullet point to tell us that when they saw the star, they had exceedingly great joy.

Then we should stop and ponder the fact that they had no joy after learning from Herod that Christ was born in Bethlehem. Perhaps we should understand that Herod was anti-Christ and, therefore, had no light by which to direct the wise men to Jesus. We should then consider that these people had gone to great lengths to visit the child and were told by Herod that He was born in Bethlehem. Apparently, Herod knew that the Messiah's birth occurred more than two years from their visit, which is why he asks them to report back to him when they locate the child. Herod asked them "to search diligently" because he and the Jewish leaders possibly knew that the birth of the Christ coincided with the census ordered by Rome during the Jewish New Year and that the child may no longer have been in Bethlehem.

Since Bethlehem was very close to Jerusalem, the wise men most likely visited it in a vain attempt to locate the Messiah, or where He had been moved. Luke tells us that Joseph and Mary were visiting Bethlehem and clearly had no place to stay. It's obvious that they had no relatives, from the fact that Jesus was born in a stable: "there was no room for them in the inn" *(Luke 2:7 [KJV])*. If the wise men visited Bethlehem, they would find no relatives of Joseph or Mary to point them to where Jesus was. In God's providence, He protects not only Jesus but also Mary's relatives, from Herod's ensuing wrath with troops. We should suspect that Herod had spies follow the wise men's movements.

I believe the wise men were confused and disheartened, and yet Herod's spies had nothing to report back to him. I wonder if, at this point, the wise men had lost hope of finding the Jewish Messiah and pondered returning to their home, when the star suddenly reappeared. They were joyful because the star was pointing them to the north, contrary to where Bethlehem is located, south of Jerusalem. Their prayers answered; their arduous journey would not be in vain. We can all take courage from their examples when we are discouraged in the face of trials.

When they heard the king, they departed; and, lo, the star which they saw in the east, went before them, till it came and stood over where the young child was *(Matthew 2:9 [KJV])*. The light of God directs the wise men to where Jesus is. We will see the phrase "young child" repeated in another verse. Note that Jesus was not an infant. He was in Nazareth with his mother, as we see in **Luke [KJV] 2:39: And when they had performed all things according to the law of the Lord, they returned into Galilee, to their own city Nazareth.**

And when they were come into the house, they saw the young child *(Matthew 2:11 [KJV])*. Notice it was not a stable, or an inn, but a house. Whose house? The house of Joseph in Nazareth. **That I might dwell in the house of the LORD all the days of my life, to behold the beauty of the LORD** *(Psalm 27:4 [KJV])*. The wise men came to the house of the Lord and beheld the meekness of God. **Honor thy father and thy mother: that thy days may be long upon the land which the LORD thy God giveth thee** *(Exodus 20:12 [KJV])*. One reason the wise men visited was to honor Joseph and Mary. We will later see that God honored them, even at His death.

The visit from the wise men was a sign from the Lord to encourage Joseph and Mary during the many trials they would suffer. The omnipresent and omniscient God showed them a taste of the glory ahead so that when despair came upon them, they could remember this fantastic event—hundreds of men bowing to their child, laying precious gifts at His feet.

With Mary his mother, and fell down, and worshipped him *(Matthew 2:11 [KJV])*. Jesus didn't just start performing miracles when He was thirty; His whole life was a miracle, being born of a virgin. The star was a miracle, as were the wise men and their faith in following it to God's precious reward. They did not find merely an infant—they found the King of Kings. Today, some gifted children born with very high IQs can speak earlier than normal. Jesus was God, who is infinite intelligence and therefore He was the most gifted child ever born. I am confident that Jesus was talking and was able to answer questions, which could explain why they were overwhelmed at His presence.

We should also note that they found Jesus with Mary; but where was Joseph? Joseph's absence from Scripture here may be connected to his absence at the cross. Thus, one of the wise men's gifts was a connection to Jesus' purpose of dying for His people.

They presented unto him gifts; gold, and frankincense, and myrrh *(Matthew 2:11 [KJV])*. After Jesus' crucifixion, we read: **And there came also Nicodemus, which at the first came to Jesus by night, and brought a mixture of myrrh and aloes about hundred-pound weight** *(John 19:39 [KJV])*. Myrrh could be foretelling of His death and His purpose for dying for His people.

Frankincense is a spice that smells wonderful and speaks of His life. The Old Testament says that God enjoys the smell of Israel's sacrifices. **They presented unto him gifts: gold** *(Matthew 2:11 [KJV])*. Does God need gold? No, but Joseph will in order to finance the family's flight into Egypt. The wise men had gold, so let's assume they were wealthy. They brought gifts to royalty, not to a peasant in a stable. They would not have traveled so far to bring gifts not worthy of a great king. They were surprised that the Jews had no idea of His birth, for they expected Him to be in a palace, not a stable. They expected a King who would subdue all His enemies. So, they gave out of abundance, not out of poverty.

The Jewish leaders had the knowledge of the Messiah's birth, but not the understanding. Let's give the Easterners some credit where it's due. Who else noticed and worshiped Jesus as a child? We can be sure no Pharisees or Herodians did.

And being warned of God in a dream that they should not return to Herod, they departed into their own country another way *(Matthew 2:12 [KJV])*. God warns the wise men to flee from Herod. At this point, we should remember that Herod wanted to find out where the Messiah was, so he could have Him killed. Since Bethlehem was just a few miles from Jerusalem, we should consider that Herod was unconvinced that the child was still there. Since Herod and the Jewish leaders learned from the wise men that Christ was born during Rosh Hashanah, they would connect the event with Caesar's edict, over two years ago. Therefore, Herod didn't assume the Messiah was still in Bethlehem. We can surmise that Herod's spies followed the wise men's movements and knew of their visitation to Nazareth.

I picture two hundred people, all bowing to honor Jesus in Nazareth. The townsfolk were speechless and bewildered. Perhaps Joseph and Mary were blown away by the visitation from the East. Maybe now life would finally take a happy turn. I imagine Joseph going to bed on cloud nine, expecting an entirely different treatment in Nazareth in the days to come. His wishful imaginations would be interrupted by a stunning warning from God. Getting the wise men's story correct is necessary for believers to understand the hostility that Jesus' family endured in Nazareth.

The Family that Celebrated the First Christmas

Christians should see God's omnipotence protected Jesus, Mary, Joseph and Mary's family from Herod's future wrath. If Joseph was just five miles away from Jerusalem, Herod's troops would have easily overtook Him on his flight to Egypt. If Jesus was born or had moved to Mary's family in Ein Karem Herod's troops would have paid them a visit. God gave Mary's family a time to rejoice in the birth of the Messiah. Jesus' birth is a big deal to God, which is the reason He gave the Israelites a holiday called Rosh Hashanah (Feast of Tabernacles). The feast is also translated to the feast of trumpets and celebrated today by some Jewish people blowing trumpets.

Ironically Christians celebrate Christmas with family and yet they don't see Jesus family celebrating the first Christmas together. All of Mary's family may have not been at His birth but they retrieved Jesus quickly and had a time of great joy. Lifting Him up and praising God for His birth. God saw it before it happened which is why His ordained feast was over eight days and not just one day. And when eight days were accomplished for the circumcising of the child, his name was called Jesus- at the end of the feast Jesus was named surrounded by Mary's family that loved Him.

Jesus loved Mary's family before he was even born which is why He was quite content to be born in a stable so that not a hair on their heads would perish. They believed in Him before He was born and God never abandons the families that have faith in Him.

Confusion about Christmas

The Gospel writers knew the story, but, evidently, we have some confusion with it. Earlier traditions taught that the wise men visited Jesus in Bethlehem at His birth, which presents more confusion than answers. Herod is clearly paranoid and bloodthirsty. After finding out that a Messiah was born five miles away, he is seemingly content not to take any action. Supposedly, what is customarily believed is that Joseph and Mary came into Jerusalem and fulfilled the law and went back to Bethlehem, where they had no family, and stayed two years until the wise men visited. Scripture is point blank on the fact that there was no place for them in Bethlehem, and yet scholars hold onto this common belief that misses the connection to the human story. It is ironic that Bible expositors have forgotten about Mary's family, but Mary's family never forgot about Jesus. Mary's family loved her and would have immediately sought her out. Luke told us that Mary's relatives were exuberant about John the Baptist's birth, but, for some reason, Bible expositors can't extrapolate this family's reaction to finding out that one of their own was carrying the Messiah in her womb. To the family, one of their own was going to have a child, who was going to be King and would deliver Israel from the Romans' hands. Celebrating Christmas in December has led many Bible expositors to be ignorant of the importance of the Feast of Tabernacles to Jesus' family. Obviously, Mary and Joseph would have visited them, as they would during the entire life of Jesus. Mary's family was anxiously anticipating the birth of the Messiah and would have to know that Mary had gone to Bethlehem for a day. It is for that very reason Mary was staying with relatives so she could fulfill the law. God in His omnipotence uses Mary's family to make it convenient for her to have delivered Jesus in Bethlehem. As a believer, if I can't see the love in the Gospel, what do I have to share with non-believers? Therefore, I believe it's important to see the love of Jesus' family in the Gospels. It is the same love that will not abandon Jesus at the cross. Seminaries through the ages have not discerned Jesus family at the cross because they ignore them at His birth.

Jesus was born in Bethlehem. The Gospel of Luke tells us that after forty days, His parents took Him to Jerusalem and then home to Nazareth. It is my contention that the Scriptures are true, but our interpretations of them are confusing and contradictory. The scholars believe the visit occurred in Bethlehem and that Joseph fled to Egypt, thus creating a conjecture that there is something wrong with the Gospel of Luke. I believe the correct interpretation validates the accuracy of the Gospels and does not contradict them.

CHAPTER 7

Fleeing into Egypt

Behold the angel of the Lord appeareth to Joseph in a dream, saying, Arise, and take the young child and his mother, and flee into Egypt, and be thou there until I bring thee word: for Herod will seek the young child to destroy him *(Matthew 2:13 [KJV])*. Joseph wasn't even given one day to bask in the newfound respect of the town. Herod wanted to kill the child, and God told Joseph that Jesus would be safe in Egypt. There wasn't a place safe in Israel, let alone the town of Nazareth. **When he arose, he took the young child and his mother by night, and departed into Egypt** *(Matthew 2:14 [KJV])*. "When he arose" doesn't mean that he got up in the morning. The dream woke him up, for the angel commanded him to arise. Joseph didn't hesitate to follow God's command. He didn't tempt God, saying to himself, *"I can return to my sleep, for God can protect the child."*

Joseph fled the town in the dark of night, which is revealing. He didn't stop and tell a neighbor, *"I'm taking the family to Egypt."* Joseph believed the Angel and understood that Herod's men were coming to Nazareth. If he told anyone he was going to Egypt, Herod's men would have found out and overtaken him and his family.

There was another who would arise at night. Last Easter was my eldest son's birthday, and he wanted to see *The Passion of the Christ*. The end of the movie shows Jesus resurrecting at sunrise. But that's not what happened. The Light of the World and the Bright Morning Star didn't need the light from our small sun. He arose out of the death of night, as we will see later in the resurrection story.

The wise men had come, and we can imagine that Mary might have thought her ship had finally come in. She felt honored by God and must have thought her boy was going to be respected as Messiah and King. But God didn't even give her one night to live with this illusion. Suddenly, Joseph woke her and told her to get up. They had to flee for their lives. Her hopes of respect in Nazareth were obliterated. She was shocked and probably upset to hear these words from her husband. The lesson for our encouragement is God loves His children and doesn't allow them to live in drawn out illusions of this world and allows hardships, so they understand the only thing that matters is love. The rich and famous have illusions about themselves for fame has nothing to do with the enduring purpose of loving others. Their mirages of vanity they hold tightly to always come to an abrupt collapse because they are not built on the true foundation of love.

If a woman ever had implied authority over her husband, I would think it would be Mary. But Mary did *not* reply to Joseph: "*Who do you think you are? Do you not know I am the most blessed among women, that angels have appeared to me and God Himself highly favors me? I am the mother of the Messiah. And you are not His father. Surely, if God wanted to uproot us, He would have told me, not you. I have finally been invited for lunch . . . every day this week. Besides, God told our forefathers in His Word never to return to Egypt, so I am not going.*" Mary was blessed, in part, because of her willingness to obey God, for she believed her husband's words and got the family ready for the trip.

When he arose, he, took the young child and his mother by night, and departed into Egypt *(Matthew 2:14 [KJV])*. Even though this was terrible news, Mary didn't resist the unwelcome reality. This does not mean she was a doormat, for later in the story we will see that she has the boldness to instruct Jesus. She had work to do. They didn't have a sport utility wagon or a nearby airport. They traveled by foot or by livestock, most likely three hundred miles. There were no motels or rest stops. They had to gather provisions quickly.

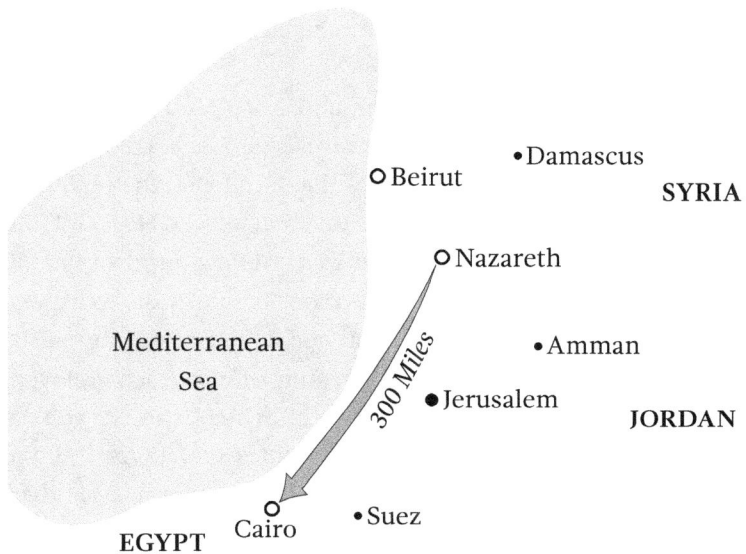

The angel's order was also terrifying because Jerusalem was in the direction of Egypt. Joseph would take alternative routes to avoid Jerusalem, where Herod was seeking to kill the child. Mary and Joseph were heading directly into danger, not away from it. Mary listened to her husband and together they obeyed God faithfully. It is a testament to wives to understand that God may ask godly men to walk a path that doesn't seem expedient. God may sometimes ask a man to surrender and put God's will ahead of the family vacation or financial benefit. The world and Satan attack marriages mercilessly, for the division between spouses, can be detrimental to children, godly purpose, and psychological health.

God the Father, God the Son—Jesus Christ—and God the Holy Spirit are One. God is never divided, nor can any house that splits into two halves stand. The worst thing we can do is turn our marriage into a constant battle between the genders and play a blame game that is destructive emotionally. Joseph and Mary seemed to understand this. God respected purpose and gave it to Joseph by giving him the word to leave. Joseph wasn't left out in the cold, following Mary with a boy who wasn't his. Joseph knew his purpose, and that God was making him accountable for the protection of this family. Through the wise men's gifts, God had provided gold and other valuables which Joseph could trade in Egypt to support the family.

Why did God bother to do this? After all, He was God and knew He would eventually kill Herod. God never reveals all His reasons, for we can't comprehend the infinity of timelines that He alone can see. But all Scripture is profitable for us, that we might understand who He is and find our purpose in Him in this life. God wants us to know our own unique life story. Wisdom understands that part of our life purpose, to experience peace during adversity. We will always be directed into storms, for there is little adversity to overcome while resting on the beach. **Beloved, think it not strange concerning the fiery trial which is to try you, as though some strange thing happened unto you** *(Peter 4:12 [KJV])*. We are not to resist trials by mourning their appearance in our lives. Rather, we are to accept them, knowing that God can easily overcome them in our lives. **In the world ye shall have tribulation: but be of good cheer; I have overcome the world** *(John 16:33 [KJV])*.

God chose Joseph and Mary and prepared them for all their undertakings. They were faithful and walked in humility and obedience to God. I suspect they may have both endured some childhood hardship. They looked to God in faith to overcome the threat from Herod.

And was there until the death of Herod: that it might be fulfilled which was spoken of the Lord by the prophet, saying, Out of Egypt have I called my son *(Matthew 2:15 [KJV])*. In his "Thru the Bible" commentary on the book of Exodus, J. Vernon McGee suggested that Egypt symbolizes this world. We are all called out of this world. It started with Abraham, who was called out of Syria to be a pilgrim in a land promised to his descendants. God then called Israel out of Egypt. He gave them laws, instructing them to be nothing like the world power of Egypt, such as multiplying horses. **But he shall not multiply horses to himself, nor cause the people to return to Egypt, to the end that he should multiply horses: forasmuch as the LORD hath said unto you, Ye shall henceforth return no more that way** *(Deuteronomy 17:6 [KJV])*. Tragically, not even David obeyed this command, and, hence, kings who followed him put their trust in alliances with Egypt, rather than in God Himself.

According to Jeremiah and the book of Kings, the remnant fled into Egypt after directly disobeying the Word of the Lord from Jeremiah. We never hear anything about any of them returning to Israel, because God told them they would all be consumed in death for returning to Egypt (Jeremiah *44:1-30*).

God wants to get our attention in this verse: *He sent Jesus to Egypt, a place that was forbidden and led to the destruction of the Israelites*. How does this apply to us? God is calling believers out of the world. The word *church* comes from the Greek *ekklesia*, which means "called-out ones." The church has become associated with buildings, and so has believers' practice of Christianity.

Egypt represents slavery, this world, and death. Jesus preached that the Kingdom of Heaven was at hand, to lead believers from attachments to this world and show us the way to connect to the giver of life, God. **If the Son therefore shall make you free, ye shall be free indeed** *(John 8:36 [KJV])*. We are called out of Egypt so that we won't experience the plague of sins and dysfunction in our lives. In today's society that is abundant in riches many Christians cannot help but be intertwined with this world and suffer its plagues. And why did He call sinless Jesus out of Egypt? Jesus could have remained on His throne in Glory, but in love for us, He came to be like us, so we could be like Him. **We shall be like him; for we shall see him as he is** *(I John 3:2 [KJV])*. At the Resurrection, God would later call Jesus out of death. And our hope is that we, too, will arise from death. **Knowing that Christ being raised from the dead dieth no more; death hath no more dominion over him** *(Romans 6:9 [KJV])*.

Then Herod, when he saw that he was mocked of the wise men, was exceeding wroth, and sent forth, and slew all the children that were in Bethlehem, and all coasts thereof, from two years old and under, according to the time which he had diligently enquired of the wise men *(Matthew 2:16 [KJV])*. We should take a pause and ask why Herod was so angry and felt mocked by the wise men. According to what is customarily believed, Herod surmised that the wise men had stood him up, and in his wrath, he sent troops to Bethlehem to kill a baby, Jesus, but the family had escaped. Yet, the verse tells us more than just that. For one thing, it tells us again that "according to the time he had diligently enquired" and that the answer was "two years old." We should notice that the troops didn't just go to Bethlehem, but also "all the coasts." We should note that Herod wasn't confident that the Messiah was in Bethlehem. We should also note his "exceeding wroth." Perhaps he was just mad because the wise men didn't comply with his wishes. More likely, the fact that Herod knew the Messiah had escaped him is what drove him to slaughter infants that he, in fact, knew were innocent. If we use a little imagination from the movies, which imitate human behavior, it's not hard to see what the troops were trying to accomplish. They went to Bethlehem to intimidate the townspeople, to find relatives of the Messiah. Surely there isn't anything lower than killing babies, and the troops demonstrated a zealous fury in accomplishing their mission.

It's probable that Herod had spies following the wise men, or was alerted that they had turned north, in the opposite direction of Bethlehem which was south of Jerusalem. If Herod's troops visited the townsfolk of Nazareth, they would inform them that the wise men had visited the town and would have pointed them to the house of Joseph, who had fled. This is one way Herod would ascertain that the Messiah had indeed escaped, inflaming his anger. It would have taken a significant amount of time for spies to travel sixty-five miles from Nazareth to Jerusalem to inform Herod. It was much farther than Bethlehem, which was just five miles away, allowing both the wise men and the family to escape. One hundred and thirty miles round trip was not a short distance, at that time. Most probably, Herod surmised that the family had gone north, in a direction away from Jerusalem and into Syria. This also explains why Herod sent troops throughout the coasts because there was a route to the north. It should not surprise us that God commanded Joseph to do the opposite of what His enemy thought.

Saying, Arise, and take the young child and his mother, and go into the land of Israel: for they are dead which sought the young child's

life *(Matthew 2:20 [KJV])*. Once again, God spoke through an angel. Joseph left Egypt immediately but then pondered about not returning to Nazareth in Galilee.

But when he heard that Archelaus did reign in Judaea in the room of his father Herod, he was afraid to go thither: notwithstanding being warned of God in a dream, he turned aside into the parts of Galilee *(Matthew 2:22 [KJV])*. Can we blame Joseph for being afraid? If Nazareth weren't dangerous, God wouldn't have told him to flee to Egypt. Joseph understandably didn't want to return to Nazareth. He understood that Herod was informed of the wise men's visit, and knew the Messiah was in Nazareth. Therefore, Joseph reasoned that Herod's son, who succeeded him on the throne, would also know. Joseph, therefore, thought it wiser to avoid Nazareth altogether. Many of us would have agreed with him. But God visited him in a dream and made it clear that he was to return to Nazareth. Joseph obeyed God, despite his fears, and returned to Nazareth.

Why Did God Allow the Babies to Be Killed?

It's hard for us to comprehend why God allowed such evil. In fact, He still allows babies to be killed every day all over the world. We can take comfort in Jesus' assurance that children who die have souls that go to Heaven: **But Jesus said: Suffer little children, and forbid them not, to come unto me: for of such is the kingdom of heaven** *(Matthew 19:14 [KJV])*. King David mourned and wept as his sick infant son was near death. When the baby died, his servants were astonished that the King was at peace. So, being perplexed by the king's behavior, they inquired of him. He answered them: I shall go to him, but he shall not return to me *(2 Samuel 12:23 [KJV])*.

The devil wants everyone to blame God for evil. From the very start, he convinced the first parents and their subsequent children that we're all victims of God's mismanagement: **Yea, hath God said, Ye shall not eat of every tree of the garden?** *(Genesis 3:1 [KJV])*. Even today, Satan deceives this world into believing that God is incompetent and helpless.

The truth is this world rejected God from the beginning which had consequences. There is a tendency to blame God for all the consequences and be blind to the rejection of His grace. It's critical that believers see the rejection of Jesus' birth from Herod, Jewish leaders, and Nazareth. This refusal set off a chain reaction throughout the Gospel. The Jewish leaders were not thrilled about learning of the Messiah's birth, nor did they show the same zeal for opposing Herod as they did for turning Jesus over to the Romans.

But this is your hour, and the power of darkness *(Luke 22:53 [KJV])*. The infinite wisdom of God has allowed evil to have its hour. God works in spite of it, and evil is being used by God to bring about redemption for His creation. God uses evil to destroy evil. Evil is no match for the wisdom of God, so we are not to glorify it by being afraid of it or by judging God for not getting rid of it. The world will never understand God's wisdom. Almighty God uses evil to usher in salvation for lost souls.

Jesus answered, Thou couldest have no power at all against me, except it were given thee from above *(John 19:11 [KJV])*. God allows evil power, but its path is still under God's rule. God will fulfill His own purpose and then remove all evil with one stroke. **Lest while ye gather up the tares, ye root up also wheat with them. Let them both grow together until the harvest** *(Matthew 13:29-30 [KJV])*.

For whom he did foreknow, he also did predestinate to be conformed to the image of his son, that he might be the firstborn among many brethren *(Romans 8:29 [KJV])*. God wanted us to be born so we could have eternal life. That is why evil is permitted its hour. We need to learn that He reigns supreme and be thankful that evil has but an hour and that it will not even be remembered. **For, behold, I create new heavens and a new earth: and the former shall not be remembered, nor come to mind** *(Isaiah 65:17 [KJV])*.

And the cares of this world, and the deceitfulness of riches, and the lusts of other things entering in, choke the word, and it becometh unfruitful *(Mark 4:19 [KJV])*. When we become concerned with the happenings of the world, we are unconsciously judging God. The Lord knows what is going to happen tomorrow, and we should trust

Him. **Blessed is the man that trusteth in the LORD, and whose hope the LORD is** *(Jeremiah 17:7 [KJV])*. Many of us are astonished by how countless evil acts occur daily in the world. We wish we could do something about it. God does not need our wisdom, but, instead, asks us to trust Him. **Who hath directed the Spirit of the LORD, or being his counsellor hath taught him?** *(Isaiah 40:13 [KJV])*.

Our attention should be on God's goodness so that we glorify His acts of light. Despite evil, God continues to usher in salvation and goodness in this world. **Ye are the light of the world** *(Matthew 5:14 [KJV])*. We cannot be the light of the world if our attention is consumed with acts of darkness.

God uses the ungodly, like Herod and Pharaoh of Egypt: **For this cause have I raised thee up, for to shew thee my power** *(Exodus 9:16 [KJV])*. Pharaoh was under the impression that he was king of kings, ruler of the world. God thought differently and let Pharaoh know that he was nothing but a pawn fulfilling the purpose of Almighty God. **We remember that the deceiver said, while he was yet alive, After three days I will rise again** *(Matthew 27:63 [KJV])*. Jesus' enemies give testimony of the Gospel. The disciples are hiding in fear, so God uses His enemies to testify of Jesus' words. **So they went, and made the sepulchre sure, sealing the stone, and setting a watch** *(Matthew 27:66 [KJV])*. We might judge God's enemies in the Bible, but the truth is God uses them to bring us the Gospel.

If God be for us who can be against us? *(Romans 8:31 [KJV])*. God's enemies believe they can win. **But we speak the wisdom of God in mystery, even the hidden wisdom, which God ordained before the world unto our glory** *(I Corinthians 2:7 [KJV])*. God's enemies are used for believers' glory. Our struggles are not because God is angry with us. Some of them are blessings so that God's glory is revealed in us when He overcomes them in us. **Which none of the princes of this world knew: for had they known it, they would not have crucified the Lord of glory** *(I Corinthians 2:8 [KJV])*. God used death to overcome the father of death: Satan. **The last enemy that shall be destroyed is death** *(I Corinthians 15:26 [KJV])*.

In the Gospel, Jesus' enemies lose. They crucified Jesus, but they accomplished God's purpose. Understanding this can give us peace in an insane world. Evil has one agenda: to destroy the meaning of life. This insanity plagues our world and yet, God is eternal and will put an end to evil. **This is your hour, and the power of darkness** *(Luke 22:53 [KJV])*.

Joseph and Mary didn't blame God for Herod killing babies in Nazareth. I ask the reader to be open to the possibility that some did blame them and, therefore, Joseph and Mary suffered immensely, but will be mightily used by God for the salvation of their family and our own. They humbly obeyed God, despite the consequences awaiting them in Nazareth. What a testimony they provide us.

CHAPTER 8

Growing Up in Nazareth

And he came and dwelt in a city called Nazareth: that it might be fulfilled which was spoken by the prophets, He shall be called a Nazarene *(Matthew 2:23 [KJV])*. Then Mary and Joseph lived happily ever after. No, unfortunately, their initial suffering and hardship were just scratching the surface. They came home to a community where some would despise them all their days.

We should surmise that Nazareth had earthly justifications to be hostile towards Mary and her child. From the town's perspective, Mary had invented a clever lie to get Joseph to marry her. However, the ingenuity of her deception generated a chain reaction that brought great harm to the town. She admitted to being pregnant before marriage, and Joseph was not even the father. Then her insistence on spreading an imaginative story attracted attention from foreign dignitaries to recognize her illegitimate child as the Messiah. This apparently provoked a response from Herod, who took Mary's inventions as a threat to his rule. Then, compounding her transgressions to Nazareth, she escapes with the child who caused the entire disaster to the town. Now she returns to live among them and later brainwashes the child, Jesus, into believing that he is the Messiah. Then he will cause trouble with the Jewish leaders in Jerusalem, and possibly another Herod who is on the throne. The entire town suffers because Mary lied to cover up her infidelity.

I picture a mother with a toddler and a newborn baby. A huge entourage visits Mary and Joseph in town and gives them presents. The next day, they're gone, and no one knows their whereabouts. Rumors fly. After a week, the townsfolk are still talking about it when another two hundred men approach the town. "It appears to be Herod's men." Some relax. "Maybe it has something to do with that other caravan." But the soldiers come into every house, killing every infant. A soldier barges into a mother's house and slaughters a baby. Another soldier kills the sibling, a toddler. The mother is speechless and has no breath, no strength. She then prays, *"Just kill me."* But the soldiers don't answer the prayer. She wails, *"Why, God Why, God? How can you let this happen?"*

I wonder what some of the mothers in Nazareth thought when, after a period of time, Joseph and Mary strolled back into town as though nothing had happened. Their three-year-old son, Jesus, who was conceived by fornication, seems healthy. Maybe Mary appears to be pregnant again. A childless mother's reaction might be to walk over and slap Mary. They fled and didn't tell anyone about the danger, but, apparently, they knew something. Some of their relatives might have surrounded them, asking, *"Where have you been?"* Mary may have even said, *"Hello"* to another mother whose child had been murdered, only to receive spit on her face as a reply.

Guilt

The town of Nazareth was blind to the greatest blessing that ever came to a community. In our time, celebrities have hometowns that take great pride in their accomplishments and customarily give them a key to the city or a parade or some other honor. Conversely, when Jesus became famous, He returned, and the people's hostility was so great, they attempted to kill Him. This is a somber commentary on human nature and how distorted it is to the blessings of God.

Consciously, the best decision for Joseph and Mary was to stay far away from Nazareth, yet the Creator considers a spectrum of consequences, including their unconscious guilt complex. In Leviticus, God instructs the Israelites to give a guilt offering in addition to the sin offering. The reason is that we may be conscious of some sins, but unconscious of many more that cause guilt (i.e. separation from God). God's will was for them to be free of its lingering shadow so it would not guide their path. I believe it's important for us to see their testimony: that obedience to God doesn't necessarily equate to what is easy for us consciously, but what is freeing from the unconscious guilt complex that is detrimental to our purpose.

God's command was for Joseph and Mary to flee Nazareth immediately, not to go and warn the townspeople. Their conscience was clear for obeying God. We should understand the tragedy was caused by the rejection of the Christ. The town rejected Jesus and therefore the light of the world. Obviously, God could wipe out a small band of Herod's soldiers, as He did with Egypt's army in Genesis, but this was not His will. Nor was it His will for Nazareth to reject Mary or for Adam and Eve to reject His Word.

Satanic forces were always opposed to the Christ *(see Genesis 3:1)* because God allowed it. Otherwise, Jesus would never have been crucified.

God always commands us to let go of our understanding, or what others think, and just obey (do the right thing). More than once in my life, I have found that it's healthy just to start over and move on from the past. Yet, God sends Joseph and Mary back to Nazareth to face horrendous conditions. Upon returning from Egypt, the easiest life for the family was to settle near Mary's relatives, who would have accepted them. God purposely brings them back to face relationships, despite the more comfortable route of avoiding them. We should consider that Joseph and Mary had no reason for shame, for they'd only obeyed God. Living somewhere else would have made them look—and probably feel—guilty. They had relatives in Nazareth and had to face them sooner or later. Since Mary's family lived elsewhere, we can surmise that Joseph's relatives lived in Nazareth (he surely had none in Bethlehem). Joseph probably learned his trade as a carpenter from his father and may have even had a family obligation. We don't know, but we should recognize that God's will is for all of us to be free of guilt.

Salvation is freedom from the bondage of shame. A guiltless life can only be found in the truth of grace. Guilt is a subtle lie which insinuates that God's grace is not good enough. Judas apparently believed this lie that led him to commit suicide, as many tragically do to this day. Guilt can be blasphemous, for it implies that Christ's work on the cross was not complete. That is a lie! "It is finished" *(John 19:30 [KJV])*.

If Christians were asked if they were perfect, they would say *"no."* If they were asked if God expects them to be perfect, they would have the same answer. Yet, many a believer's consciences make them feel bad about falling short. **There is therefore now no condemnation to them which are in Christ Jesus** *(Romans 8:1 [KJV])*. God is aware, and His Word is for our encouragement and freedom, not for guilt accusations. The subtle destructiveness of guilt is the unconscious arrogance that it creates.

Eve's children inherited her nature; that believed the serpent told her the truth. **"...ye shall be as gods, knowing good and evil"** *(Genesis 3:5 [KJV])*. Human beings believe wholeheartedly that they know what is good, and they judge according to their perception. When we search the Internet, we find that there is no shortage of experts who are convinced they're correct about a given subject. They judge and sincerely believe others should feel guilty when they don't measure up to them. Our world is nothing more than a giant blame game in which a guilty perpetrator causes all the problems. It keeps the world unconsciousness of its sinful nature. Many people are unable to see its invisible chain, which guides this world to constant dysfunction. The lie is that humanity should be better as if he could achieve anything good without God. The truth is we are nothing without Him. We can't even take a breath of air without His permissive will.

And Jesus said unto him, Why callest thou me good? none is good, save one, that is, God *(Luke 18:19 [KJV])*. From God's perspective, there is nothing good about this world because it's not perfect and eternal. The trap is that we inherently want ourselves and this world to be perfect. Our carnal nature vainly strives to measure up to God's standards. We cannot help but judge and make comparisons about things in this world that are important to us. Yet, our narrow view has no capacity for that which is eternal: the Kingdom of God.

Many Christians are aware of the apostle Paul's writing in Romans, where he inexplicably states that carnal nature is at war with God and has no capacity to serve Him. Yet, I wonder if many understand that this applies to the ego; that the human brain will never be Christian. **God is a Spirit: and they that worship him must worship him in spirit and in truth** *(John 4:24 [KJV])*. Our finite minds in this world are not eternal and therefore cannot comprehend an infinite God. Yet, our soul can because it's attached to the infinite God that created it.

I've shared this with believers before; some of whom immediately became indignant and said something like, "Well, I use my mind to serve God," or they quote *Romans 12:2*. From my perspective, vain interpretations are a huge problem in many churches. It sets believers up for eventual failure with the expectation that they should be perfect. That's the attitude of a Pharisee, which non-believers will repel because they sense it judges them. The "way" that is simply freeing is to accept the grace of God, as Jesus says in *Matthew 11:30 [KJV]*, "For my yoke is easy, and my burden is light."

If a person is not accepting of other people, that person is most likely arrogant. The Pharisees will be shocked by the people with whom Jesus hangs out. They will be angry at His personal choices because they think they are righteous to judge Him. They demonstrated today's human propensity to judge God Himself. The Scriptures are not for us to judge the Pharisees, but to see that we all have the nature that wants to follow their example. The accusing nature of guilt led to accusations against Jesus because they rejected His Spirit of grace.

God calls believers today to see His grace; not to strive against Him, judging Him or His creations. He doesn't need believers to judge the world, but, rather, He asks them to reflect His mercy. Are we attentive to the ego, which immediately wants to defend us and then accuses the other party who dared to accuse us? If we accept we're not perfect, *then why do most of us have a problem with someone who accuse us for making mistakes?* The human emotional complex is not spiritual; it's carnal. It does what it's supposed to do and denies our faults and uses emotional triggers to defend itself. God sent Jesus because His will is we don't defend ourselves. Jesus did not deny His deity at the trials, but he did keep silent because we are guilty of not being perfect (*Matthew: 12-14*).

The bottom line is:

> *Our guilt complex is caused by*
> *the inherent belief we should be perfect.*

All of this world's problems are caused by a carnal nature that is afraid. It's anxious because of its separation from God. It denies this truth and over compensates by having the arrogance to accuse others for not being perfect. The entire dysfunctional cycle that drives the planet is caused by not accepting the grace and omnipotence of God.

The lie of guilt says I must *be* something. Instead, our call is to be attached to the only thing that matters: His Spirit. The carnal nature is empty, and anxiously wants to be something, yet it always feels inadequate, no matter what it does (see the Epilogue in back of the book). We enter communion with the Prince of Peace when we allow the grace of His perfection to accept us completely, despite our countless imperfections.

Hostile Environment

For thy sake I have borne reproach; shame hath covered my face (*Psalm 69:7 [KJV]*). No one has ever been as hated as Jesus. The hatred didn't start at the cross; it started at His birth. Nazareth rejected His immaculate conception, and then Herod tried to kill Him. Jesus was perfect, which means He was a perfect brother, cousin, neighbor, nephew, and a perfect son. **And he went down with them, and came to Nazareth, and was subject unto them** (*Luke 2:51 [KJV]*). In other words, we might assume that He submitted to their will and the order of the town. We will see that it pays Him no dividends.

They that sit in the gate speak against me; and I was the song of the drunkards (*Psalms 69:12 [KJV]*). Jesus was the talk of the town.

He overcame it, as He overcame all things. God did not sweep anything under the rug when Mary and Joseph returned to Nazareth. Since Joseph wasn't Jesus' biological father, Jesus did not resemble Joseph at all. We know that the rumors were partly correct: Jesus wasn't Joseph's son, and Mary may have confirmed this to her other children. Jesus' siblings would then have been indoctrinated by their own parents, and by the town, that Jesus had a different father. The point is that Jesus' siblings were faced with doubt about who Jesus' father was. **We be not born of fornication, we have one Father, even God** *(John 8:41 [KJV])* was the Pharisees' response to Jesus about His lineage. They apparently knew about the claim of the virgin birth and were insulting Jesus' parentage. That Jesus was either Joseph's or any other man's son insinuated that Jesus had two fathers. They just missed an important point: that Jesus' Father was God.

I am become a stranger unto my brethren *(Psalm 69:8 [KJV])*. This verse may refer to cousins, aunts, uncles, and grandparents on Joseph's side, for if we see that Mary's family supported Jesus, and then we know this speaks of Joseph's family, who lived in Nazareth. Let's try to put ourselves in Joseph's relatives' minds, who had to wonder which assessment was true about Joseph's involvement with Mary's pregnancy. Either Joseph marries an unfaithful woman and believes her ridiculous story or Joseph helped make up the story to cover up his sin. In either case, it's hard to fathom that they supported the family in Nazareth. Then he disappears with Mary, the child, and soldiers come seeking him. The townsfolk believe Joseph was warned by the men from the East and perhaps warned Joseph's relatives. As a result, the town looked down upon Joseph's relatives. In summary, Joseph's insistence on lying about his sin and marrying a wayward woman brought trouble to the family. Now he returns, likely only to bring more trouble to the relatives he once abandoned. Therefore, Joseph's relatives had no understanding of the blessing of Jesus, her son, and would come to despise Him, also.

In the world ye shall have tribulation: but be of good cheer, I have overcome the world *(John 16:33 [KJV])*. Jesus overcame the world, but He first overcame the dysfunction of His childhood. This is an encouragement to us that we, too, can overcome the wounds of our childhood, because He did it before us. We are not to judge the people of Nazareth, but be thankful for them, so we might learn not to be like them. The lesson of Nazareth is for believers to see that the door of judgment always leads to suffering and misses God's best. There is only one door to God's will, and that is His grace through His Son, Jesus Christ.

Jesus' Siblings

Is not this the carpenter, the son of Mary, the brother of James, and Joses, and of Judah, and Simon? Are not his sisters here with us? *(Mark 6:3 [KJV])*. This verse gives us the names of Jesus' half-brothers, probably in chronological order, which would make James the next oldest after Jesus. "Sisters" is plural, so Jesus had at least two sisters.

The family is a blessing from God, and division within it is the work of the enemy. The first family was Adam and Eve, and it was so dysfunctional that the first brother slew his younger brother. Then we shouldn't be surprised that within Jesus' family, as with all families, there was also dysfunction and division. My hope is that readers understand how oblivious some religious dogma is to parts of Jesus' life; one being His brothers. What should be crystal clear is that Jesus' will for all of us is the same as for His brothers: that we follow Him. We should note that none of them do. We will repeatedly see in the Gospels (eleven times in NIV translations, to name a few, including *Matthew 4:19*, *16:24*, and *19:28*; *Mark 1:17*, and *10:21*) that Jesus tells others to "Follow me." It should be obvious to us that Jesus loved His brothers, and yet, they refused to follow him. Their rejection of Him has a great lesson for us today. Understanding this, we can connect to the heartwarming conclusion of the story.

Growing up as a sibling of Jesus was no picnic. It began with taunts from other children. Jesus' appearance might have been strikingly different from that of His siblings. I picture a pair of Jesus' siblings walking through town, listening to wisecracks about Jesus. Their claims of His virgin birth resulted only in scorn. This type of psychiatric suffering likely made Jesus' siblings so angry that they wanted to blame their pain on someone.

Some of the parents who lost children hated Joseph and Mary and showed their contempt by telling their children that Jesus was illegitimate, or Mary was a whore. If we figure out why Jesus' siblings grew up in a hostile environment, then we can understand why none of them wanted to believe in Him.

For neither did his brethren believe in him *(John 7:5 [KJV])*. Peer pressure isn't just in schools; it's everywhere in our society, so we should understand that Jesus' siblings were under duress. Jesus' siblings apparently took the easier path, not defending Him, especially when you consider the fact that Joseph's family rejected Joseph, Mary, and Jesus. If Jesus' siblings had been brought up with support from Mary's family, we might see a different outcome, for we will see that Jesus later went to their region to start His ministry. They accepted Mary's version of the truth. Jesus' siblings likely understood that, but under the daily onslaught, it was too much for them to overcome.

An alien unto my mother's children *(Psalm 69:8 [KJV])*. What rationale would His siblings have for rejecting Him? Their eldest brother showed them love and told them the truth from the day they were born. He never picked on them and knew them better than they did themselves. They could have asked Him any question, and He'd have the answer. So, we can conclude that they rejected His wisdom and His example. Jesus overcame this adversity, but His siblings refused to recognize that this was God before their eyes. **And ye shall know the truth, and the truth shall make you free** *(John 8:32 [KJV])*. If they believed in the Truth, the Truth would have set them free from the torment of the town.

Mom and Dad Lied to Us

For neither did his brethren believe in him *(John 7:5 [KJV])*. Jesus' brothers did not believe He was divine. That means that Jesus' brothers thought either Mary was a liar or both parents were in on the lie. But because they believed a lie, they embraced pain unconsciously. They chose the town over their own parents. This choice only brought them more grief, for they held contempt for their parents. For they did not heed God's commandment: **Honour thy father and thy mother: that thy days may be long upon the land which the LORD thy God giveth thee** *(Exodus 20:12 [KJV])*.

If Jesus' siblings embraced their parents for telling the truth, they would have understood how favored by God their mother was. **Blessed art thou among women, and blessed is the fruit of thy womb** *(Luke 1:42 [KJV])*. They should have walked with heads held high with confidence in God's blessing on their family. As it is with all believers, it doesn't matter what this world says about us—we are blessed who are in Him.

This means they didn't respect Mary. They didn't believe her story: that she was a virgin when she conceived Jesus. *"I'm so tired of Mom making up that story. The whole world knows that Dad got Mom pregnant, but persists in telling some fantastic story of being a virgin."* At some point Joseph was dead and he wasn't alive to back up Mary's story. This likely caused Jesus' siblings to feel contempt toward both their parents and Jesus. This would have caused them a negative self-image and further unconscious suffering.

It is very likely that they were also jealous of the fact that He might have appeared to be His mother's favorite. After all, she is the one who told Jesus he wasn't illegitimate, but the Messiah.

We should suspect that Mary was proud of Jesus and told her children to follow Him. No doubt His siblings got tired of Mom talking about Jesus. I kind of laugh when I ponder this: James says to Jude, his brother, *"I wish for once mom would stop talking about Jesus."* When most of Jesus siblings became teenagers and they didn't have a father to tell them his side of the story. They looked at Jesus and had to ponder He was misguided for believing Mary as was her relatives. John the Baptist's miraculous birth wasn't relevant to them, for they weren't alive to witness it. Their perspective could have been that their mom's side of the family was crazy for believing her. Some considered John a prophet, but they saw an embarrassing cousin further undermining their reputations and prosperity in Galilee. After all, John ate locusts for meat and wore camel's hair and didn't respect the Jewish leaders. Their cousin made an enemy of Herod and was eventually beheaded. Especially once Joseph had died; it was left in their hands to do what would serve the best interests of the family.

CHAPTER 9

Joseph is Dead

It is painful when well-wishing friends flee, especially when we could use them the most. Yet, **There is a friend that sticketh closer than a brother** *(Proverbs 18:24 [KJV])*. The apostle John was the one friend who never left Jesus' side, even at the cross, while Jesus' brothers, sisters, and other disciples were apparently nowhere to be found. Though John was just a boy, he was Jesus' best friend (for John the Baptist was dead), and Jesus would give him the highest honor at the cross: **Behold thy mother! And from that hour that disciple, took her unto his own home** *(John 18:27 [KJV])*. John would have never taken Mary home if her husband was alive. So, it's obvious that Joseph was dead. The verse should also quicken believers to understand the break in Jesus' family. The culture of the day was that parents—especially widows—lived with their adult children. John's own mother and father were probably still alive, which makes sense if we picture John standing by his mother, Salome, and accept the assumption that she was Mary's sister. It makes sense that Mary would come and live with her sister, for it appears that Mary's children were nowhere to be found and have abandoned her. None of the rest of her children—not even her daughters—are mentioned as standing by her in any of the lists of those watching Jesus' crucifixion. It was the duty of the daughters to comfort their mother, and a huge taboo if they were not there. My purpose in expressing this opinion is not to judge them, but, rather, to connect to the great ordeal the entire family went through, to understand that God had plans for them as He does for all of us and that they resisted those plans, as we all do. We resist because of disbelief. Yet, God, in His mercy, worked out salvation for this family, as He does for believers to this day. God would keep His promises, despite the circumstances that appeared to the contrary.

And Jesus himself began to be about thirty years of age *(Luke 3:23 [KJV])*. It's important that believers know some of what Jesus did before he was thirty. **Ye shall not afflict any widow, or fatherless child** *(Exodus 22:22 [KJV])*. Jesus did the will of His Father: He cared for his household. My guess is Joseph died when Jesus was around seventeen years old. Jesus, the eldest son, became the head of the family. He was a fulfillment of His own law that required men to provide for their households. He demonstrated hard work is nothing to be ashamed of, a fact many believers need to hear. Family comes ahead of selfish ambition. Families come before religion, for Jesus put His household before His ministry. **Father of the fatherless and protector of widows is God in his holy habitation** *(Psalm 68:5 [KJV])*. Jesus lived this out and provided for His mother until His siblings came of age. Even though He set a perfect example, His siblings did not follow it, so He gave John charge of His mother. It is very likely that He did this because Mary already lived with her sister before Jesus was crucified, because of the sharp division in the family.

God is sending a clear message that a believer should follow Him by first taking care of their household because in so doing, they do God's will, and only then will God add to their responsibilities for him. **For unto every one that hath shall be given, and he shall have abundance; but from him that hath not shall be taken away even that which he hath** *(Matthew 25:29 [KJV])*.

God invented families, and they provide purpose and loving security which is critical to our wellbeing. In godly families, we see the love of Christ. Joseph died, and Jesus set an example for us to follow in our families. **But if any provide not for his own, and especially for those of his own house, he hath denied the faith, and is worse than an infidel** *(I Timothy 5:8 [KJV])*.

When Joseph died, Jesus likely subjected Himself to His uncles (Joseph's brothers) or cousins and worked as a carpenter. He is portrayed in some movies as a loner, but we should understand that this period required families to work together in occupations. It's not like they had F-350 trucks to go to Home Depot and get lumber or concrete. Work back then took much more cooperation and coordination than what we could do easily today.

Jesus did it well, yet He was treated like an outsider by His brethren. He worked alongside them, to their disgust, as they witnessed their older cousins and uncles mistreating Him. A parallel to His family experience was how Joseph of the Old Testament was despised by his brothers, favored by his father, delivered to the Gentiles, and yet rose to be a prince of all the people, not just the Israelites.

His brothers knew that following Jesus would bring severe consequences to their respective families: Total separation from their father (Joseph)'s family and choosing Mary's family over them. Jesus' brothers likely had wives and children and wanted to support them, which was the right thing to do. Rejecting Jesus has consequences, as it does for all believers. Some of us believe in Him and want to serve Him, but many of us have rejected His calls because they require us to go far outside of our comfort zones. His work always requires us to leave some of our attachments because HE is always to come first. When we reject the call, the attachments will become a snare. We will attempt to hold them even tighter, and the result can be stress and anxiety. After all, we are just trying to hang onto what we see is best for us and our families. The problem is that it's not God's will. It's never His will that we have stress; we bring this on ourselves due to how we judge our life experience, which is the norm in this world. **My peace I give unto you not as the world giveth, give I unto you. Let not your heart be troubled, neither let it be afraid** *(John 14:27 [KJV])*.

Nazareth was a snare to Jesus' brothers, but it was they who chose to remain in it. They blamed Jesus for the complications in their lives. Yet, it was their choice, as it is always our choice to have a given response to a particular situation. We can lay it down to Him or we can own the situation. It is on all of us. His choice is for us to understand that whatever hardship comes, we are to see something greater than the hardship. God never creates problems and is the only problem-solver Who walked this world. This world is an expert on problems because it's blind to the truth that the problems are the same as in the beginning. This world bases its truth on lies and tells itself that it's making progress on being good. It is true that technology has improved, but the sinful nature of humanity will never improve. A great challenge for believers lies in experiencing the problems of this world and seeing our motives as good, trying with our might to solve those problems out of love for others. God's solutions are usually something we don't think of and, as such, can give us more stress than our problems. When I reflect back on many past decisions in my life, I see they came from choices that I believed had fewer negative consequences, but that was fear based. This is the reason God calls us to walk by faith, not by our sight which is fear based.

Be Still, and Know That I Am God.

Be still and know that I am God *(Psalm 46:10 [KJV])*. There is a great lesson in the humanity of Jesus. "And the word was made flesh." Our God, Jesus Christ, Who spoke the universe into existence, at times in His life was silent toward giving God's Word. God doesn't call us to jeopardize our jobs because of religion. There is a time to be still and a time to share His Word. Jesus had been the family breadwinner, and He did not jeopardize that purpose until the proper time; one being when others invited Him to or asked Him. Some believers carry an unnecessary burden of guilt because they feel responsible for their family or others' salvation. We are called to experience the peace of salvation in our lives. God is in control, and He doesn't need us. We need Him, and we can only be useful to Him when we trust Him. We need to avoid a sense of self-importance in our minds. We will later see that He chose, at times, to speak with power and authority in Capernaum, but not in Nazareth, until the proper time.

Nazareth is best understood as a small town in relation to a county. The county and capital at one point welcomed Jesus—except Nazareth. **And** when he was come into his own country, he taught them in their synagogue, insomuch that they were astonished, and said, Whence hath this man this wisdom, and these mighty works?* (Matthew 13:54 [KJV]).* This was apparently Jesus' first time bringing His teaching ministry to Nazareth. Prior to this, the Lord fulfilled the law by first taking care of His family before pursuing His call to spread the Gospel. And we now see why. He knew the consequences. **But Jesus said unto them, A prophet is not without honour, save in his own country, and in his own house** *(Matthew 13:57 [KJV]).* God understands that family members do not always see eye to eye. Even Jesus didn't take it upon Himself to preach to His kin until the proper time for His ministry. He knew that His rejection by His hometown was not about Him, but about them. When the time comes for us to speak hard truth to those who are familiar with us, if we experience rejection, we can be comforted by Jesus' example. It's not about us, so we can choose not to take it personally. We are to avoid drama, not embrace it. It's critical that believers know that God's priority for them is not to preach to others, but to love Him. They are taught dogma and given counseling but are not instructed how to avoid the drama that leads to dysfunctional consequences. None of us can give every second of our lives to Jesus, but we can surrender moments. Learning to surrender is difficult for us. It's a process and does not happen overnight. "Born again" is a good term, but only when it's understood as growing from infancy, and that God has a different view on what we judge to be failures. His will is we see His mercy in a new day, leave yesterday in the past and enjoy His grace.

I have found that Christians who believe they have given their entire life to Jesus are delusional with some of their perspectives. Some tend to feel they are a victim who is bearing the cross for Jesus in the midst of attacks from this world. Tragically, they don't see their own contributions to embracing drama in their lives. The truth is, no matter how troubled we see this world, it's a much easier life to deal with than what Jesus and His contemporaries dealt with: "the Son of man hath not where to lay his head" *(Matthew 8:20 [KJV]).*

Why Did God Let Joseph Die?

To everything there is a season, and a time to every purpose under the heaven: A time to live and a time to die (*Ecclesiastes 3:1-2 [KJV]*). Every person is born with an appointed time of death. All the days ordained for me were written in your book before one of them came to be (*Psalm 139:16, [NLT]*). God had a purpose for us even before we were born. Joseph was not perfect, but he suffered for the sake of Jesus, and no doubt God took notice of it, for we will see God honor him later in the story. There is a sin unto death (*John 5:17 [KJV]*). Some cut their physical lives short by sin, as in Acts 5:1-10. But for some, suffering serves other purposes: This sickness is not unto death, but for the glory of God (*John 11:4 [KJV]*). Joseph died for the glory of God. We can have peace that the Creator is the only One Who gave us our days. Can any of you by worrying add a single hour to your life? (*Matthew 6:27 [NIV]*). In all three synoptic Gospels, there is what is called the Transfiguration where Jesus speaks with Moses and Elijah. What we should notice is they are not dead. They are not playing a harp but actually working and carrying out God's purpose for them on earth. Interestingly, Jesus tells us in the same three synoptic Gospels, that God is the God of the Living, not the dead (*Matthew 22:32, Mark 12:27, Luke 20:38*). How I wish our funeral service would reflect this truth. God has eternal purposes for all of us and they start after our deaths.

Interestingly, John doesn't have the transfiguration in his Gospel but uniquely has the raising of Lazarus from the dead (*John 11:17:44*). Most believers are aware that Jesus cries right before He raises Lazarus to life. There are many that have theories as to why Jesus weeps. Some say it's because the family doesn't believe him when He says" I am the resurrection and the life." What I have pondered, if Jesus knows He is going to raise Lazarus from the dead, and Lazarus' family's mourning will turn to joy, why is He so distressed? His remorse has nothing to do with Lazarus but with us all. In God's mind He isn't doing Lazarus any favors raising him from the dead and returning him to this world

(Lazarus will go on to see the resurrected Christ and was a great blessing). Do many of us really want to live in bodies for a thousand years let alone eternity? God sees the big picture, eternity, and wants all to choose eternal life, and He knows many will not make this choice, and it deeply grieves Him. For He loves all souls that were born in this world and some will go on to life, and some will choose not to.

A good friend of mine passed away, and some wondered why God took her home after all she was so effective serving the Lord feeding the homeless. The Pastor who gave the eulogy spoke of her being joyful in heaven while her family remained here. This universal concept is given at funerals that people go to heaven and worship the Lord. Apparently many Christians believe this is a great concept of faith. My view is it is a depressing teaching that we die and basically, do nothing but play the harp. As the Pastor was talking about Teri's work being done, it was as if I could hear her voice "Leonard I love you, but don't tell my family I left them because I will never leave them! Don't say my work is finished; I'm just getting started!" Teri was honored at her service for being an advocate for the homeless. Many call these celebrations of life, and yet they don't seem to acknowledge God is just getting started with those who die. Mostly what grieves me is they don't seem to acknowledge that they don't leave their loved ones in spirit. In my way of thinking, God turned Teri from an advocate of the homeless to an Angel of the homeless, and she is going to watch over them and her family. Teri worked tirelessly helping the homeless but now she doesn't have to sleep, and she is going to do even greater things for them.

There is a great lesson in Joseph's death. That God doesn't raise him from the dead to impress Jesus' half-siblings. That He didn't keep him alive to spare Mary's, broken heart. Our God does not have the sentimentality over our lives in this world as we do. He has something so much greater. An eternal purpose that doesn't mourn its birth that begins at our death.

Joseph's death was no doubt devastating to Mary. Angels visited Joseph in dreams, and he knew that Jesus was God's Son, but besides Jesus, none of her sons believed her. It's possible that her daughters could have, but we find no evidence of them in the Scriptures, whereas we find the cousins of Jesus on Mary's side. We have evidence of their associations, but no daughter was standing next to Mary at the cross.

Mary will go through a great trial because of Joseph's death because after Jesus leaves Nazareth, there is none who believes in her integrity. Jesus doesn't spare her, and He could have easily not allowed it to happen, or raised Joseph from the dead. Unlike our world, which is full of show-offs, God is infinite power, and He uses it with discretion. We will see the devil bait Jesus into using His power, and we should pay attention to the fact that He doesn't. Jesus wasn't going to do miracles to impress people, let alone His siblings. It is the same today, which is why we are in this world. God allows evil its hour. By His permission, time will play out until God ends it. God's power doesn't win recruits with His miracles, as the Gospels will show us. The mob that cheers will be the same that sneers at Him.

This is human nature, and we see it play out in today's world, such as at sports events, where the same crowd either cheers or boos their own team, depending on how well (or not) they're playing. God is opposite to the world's ways and doesn't desire this world's glory. God had all power, and He laid it down before He came to be on Earth as Jesus. Instead of using His power, He submits to the power of death to overcome it. He will later demonstrate this to His family in His glorious resurrection. Satan, however, thirsts for power and to be the center of attention, and God would have His children to be different. He demonstrates that serving Him requires the patience in a faith of His higher purpose for our lives. Our lives are not about accomplishing our agendas. If they are, we will not experience peace. We are not to judge events as being bad, as this world does, but to give thanks to God for all things. The Lord gave and the Lord hath taken away *(Job 1:21 [KJV])*

Why Hasn't Religion Noticed Joseph's Death?

Many of the Jewish leaders of Jesus' day couldn't care less about teaching about loving one's family. They cared about lining their pockets. So, they invented a religious way for people to abandon their aging parents by pledging their estate to the temple, giving the leaders a piece of the action. **Why do ye also transgress the commandment of God by your tradition?** (*Matthew 15:3 [KJV]*). Jews could pledge all their assets to the temple and then be free from supporting their parents. **But ye say, Whosoever shall say to his father or his mother, It is a gift, by whatsoever thou mightest be profited by me** (*Matthew 15:5 [KJV]*).

Religion today has missed what is important: family. Muslim extremists use religion to manipulate boys to kill themselves, rather than aspire to be good fathers. A martyr claims to make a sacrifice, but it is just a onetime act, whereas being a parent requires a lifetime commitment. God offers an eternal commitment to be Father to those who wish to be His children. Satan offers this world death, and tragically we see many gravitate to murder and kill themselves and as many others as they can. It takes nine months for a fetus to mature and eighteen years usually to be physically an adult. Tragically in just a second many throw their lives away. Why is it escalating? Look at today's headlines on the internet, and what you will see is anger, and none of it has anything to do with loving one's family. The largest religion today isn't Christianity, Muslim, Judaism or Buddhism. Today the world's largest religion is politics, and it's always ramped up about something. It has no interest in peaceful purpose (creating the healthy environment for today's families). This world is insane with drama; its propensity is demanding individual rights that are in direct opposition of being a grateful steward of what you have been already given. Quite the contrast of Jesus who had the right to do anything and yet He laid all His rights down to love His earthly family and all of us.

God holds us accountable to our family ministry first and by not knowing Joseph was dead believers have not been taught Jesus' example. Consequently, we are not taught how important family was to Jesus and what lessons we can apply to empower our relationships with them. Then we also miss the beautiful family associations Jesus had with Mary's family, that bring us the Gospel.

It's my suspicion that at some point Christianity turned into a religion. The religion was quite aware of Joseph's death but because it's religious, it doesn't believe in the power of God. Instead, it felt it had to cover it up by keeping it at a low key. The judgment might have been if Jesus didn't raise Joseph from the dead than heretics would have ammunition to attack His deity.

Adam's son, Joseph, was dead because he was the son of Adam. God's Son died for all of Adam's sons. When Jesus cried out on the cross, "Father!", if Joseph had been alive, we might have mistaken who he was calling to. Adam's sons were dead, and God's Son died so that all of Adam's sons might live with Him. Jesus did die, but He lived anyway so that death would no longer have dominion over all of Adam's children. Knowing that Christ being raised from the dead dieth no more; death hath no more dominion over him (*Romans 6:9 [KJV]*).

CHAPTER 10

John the Baptist

One Bible character that perplexed me in the past was John the Baptist. He seems to have great importance, but in the past, I was mystified what that was. **And he shall go before him in the spirit and power of Elias, to turn the hearts of the fathers to the children, and the disobedient to the wisdom of the just; to make ready a people prepared for the Lord** (*Luke 1:17 [KJV]*).

John is near the beginning in all four Gospels, and his work was preaching the coming Kingdom and baptizing. Jesus didn't start His ministry until John baptized Him. And yet, John had little to do with Jesus' ministry. Apparently, he didn't directly follow Jesus, and he didn't become one His apostles. He didn't write any epistles, nor do we hear of him performing any miracles. Jesus said: **Among them that are born of women there hath not risen a greater than John the Baptist** (*Matthew 11:11 [KJV]*). What did he do that was so great? And how did he prepare the way for the Lord?

John naturally became an orphan early in life, having elderly parents. His habits were strange: **John had his raiment of camel's hair, and a leather girdle about his loins; and his meat was locusts and wild honey** (*Matthew 3:4 [KJV]*). It appears that, at an early age, John went out to live a solitary life in the wilderness.

How did he gain followers after withdrawing from society? Remember the story of Elisabeth's pregnancy? Many relatives visited her and believed in John's miraculous birth. They probably spread the news about John's miraculous birth throughout Israel, together with the angel's promise: For with God nothing shall be impossible *(Luke 1:37 [KJV])*. Mary and Elisabeth's relatives were well prepared for a virgin conceiving and giving birth. They embraced the honor of being related to the Messiah. These relatives— Levites— together with their families and some of their friends and neighbors— became the first believers in John and the Messiah he foretold.

The funny thing is if you ask a Jew of Christian, how many tribes are there in tribes of Israel? They will answer twelve, but there is actually thirteen. God never had the Levites counted *(Number 1:47-49)*, and that tradition has been passed down to us today. Even though there are thirteen tribes, they're always listed as twelve in the Bible. Sometimes the Levites are listed, and another tribe is omitted which is a different story. J. Vernon McGee explained this well and believed Levites (they were given the purpose by God to be priests) exemplified future Christians that were under grace, and as such, they and our sins, are never counted because they are not under the law. That so many of them would come in the future, and that's why God ordered Moses never to count them.

Then went out to him Jerusalem, and all Judaea *(Matthew 3:5 [KJV])*. John's father, Zacharias, was a Levite as were relatives who also served as priests in Jerusalem. They all were aware of John's birth as a sign from God that a great prophet was born. Not even the highest Jewish leaders ever publicly challenged this belief. **All the people will stone us: for they be persuaded that John was a prophet** *(Luke 20:6 [KJV])*. The reason for this was the public pregnancy of an elderly woman. This miracle couldn't be denied, whereas the pregnancy of a virgin required faith, which is why John's testimony was so paramount to Jesus' ministry.

John could have become a priest like his father, but we might surmise that he rejected the priesthood because of the hypocrisy among Jerusalem's leadership. **But when he saw many of the Pharisees and Sadducees come to his baptism, he said unto them, O generation of vipers, who hath warned you to flee from the wrath to come?** *(Matthew 3:7 KJV])*. He called them what they were. John was the only one besides Jesus who spoke to them with such authority and truth. He saw through them because he was the only man who saw clearly that Jesus was God. John understood that the temple was governed by human-made tradition, not as instructed by God's Word.

I baptize with water: but there standeth one among you, whom ye know not; He is, who cometh after me is preferred before me, whose shoe's latchet I am not worthy to unloose *(John 1:26-27 [KJV])*. John performed a priestly function, baptizing people in the Jordan River. His cousin, Jesus, would later perform the ultimate priestly function: becoming a propitiation for sin.

John bare witness of him, and cried, saying, This was he of whom I spake, He that cometh after me is preferred before me: for he was before me *(John 1:15 [KJV])*. When Joseph died, Jesus took care of His mother and siblings until He was at least thirty. Meanwhile, John was building up followers for the Messiah, not for himself: **I am not the Christ, but that I am sent before me** *(John 3:28 [KJV])*. Many wondered if John was the Messiah and when the King was going to appear. I can understand John's disciples starting to wonder after five or ten years under John's leadership. **And as the people were in expectation, and all men mused in their hearts of John, whether he were the Christ, or not** *(Luke 3:15 [KJV])*.

The next day John seeth Jesus coming unto him, and saith, Behold the Lamb of God, which taketh away the sin of the world *(John 1:29 [KJV])*. John knew Jesus' purpose was to be God's ultimate sacrifice.

And I knew him not: but that he should be made manifest (John 1:31 [KJV]). The movies portray John the Baptist meeting Jesus for the first time as if he had never met Jesus before. The one thing they get right is John's shock at Jesus' request to be baptized. Verses such as *John 1:31* lead to wrong interpretations because Bible expositors are preoccupied with syntax, rather than understanding the story to interpret the verse correctly. Here are a couple of versions of the verse:

> *New International Version John 1:31 (NIV)*
> "I myself did not know him, but the reason I came baptizing with water was that he might be revealed to Israel."

New Living Translation John 1:31 (NLT)
"I did not recognize him as the Messiah, but I have been baptizing with water so that he might be revealed to Israel."

This horrendous error in our translations has led many Christians to miss connecting to the beautiful story of Jesus' family. Horrible is an understatement for many reasons, one implication being that you can be a man of God and the greatest in the Kingdom of God and not recognize Jesus. With so much evidence of connections between the Baptist and Jesus in the Gospel's its mystifying how this error has not been corrected in an updated translation.

John the Baptist gave this verse to this book's author: John, son of Zebedee ("little John" is a nickname I give him to avoid confusion with the other Johns), who was a disciple of the Baptist and would become a follower of Jesus. Little John was probably around twelve, yet acutely aware that the Baptist knew Jesus, his cousin. Both Johns were blood-related to Jesus, and Jesus could only be the Messiah if Mary told the truth. Mary's family likely accepted her story of the Immaculate Conception because they witnessed the miraculous birth of John the Baptist. The family had only Mary's word about Jesus' birth, whereas many eyewitnesses better attested the Baptist's birth.

And I knew him not: but he that sent me to baptize with water, the same said unto me, Upon whom thou shalt see the spirit descending, and remaining on him, the same is he which baptizeth with the Holy Spirit *(John 1:33 [KJV])*. I believe the Baptist was saying to little John, "I knew him not as my kin, but as the one who commissioned me to baptize with water. He is the same one who told me that I would see the Spirit of God descend upon him who baptizes with the Holy Spirit. And I saw and bear record that he is the Son of God."

For, lo, as soon as the voice of thy salutation sounded in mine ears, the babe leaped in my womb for joy *(Luke 1:44 [KJV])*. As a fetus, John the Baptist, filled with the Holy Spirit, leaped at the sound of Jesus' mother's voice, because he knew the Son of God. We know that Joseph and Mary traveled with family each year to Passover (see *Luke 2:41-44*) and probably visited their extended family near Jerusalem. From the

Gospel of John (see *John 7:2-11*), we know Jesus customarily attended both feasts, which prophesied of His birth and death. Then it's obvious that Jesus and John the Baptist probably saw each other twice a year: at Passover and the Feast of Tabernacles.

Is it a stretch that while these boys were growing up, the one person John wanted to see was Jesus? I imagine John asking Jesus every question imaginable. They loved one another because they were the only two people on the planet filled with the Holy Spirit before they were born! **And thou child, shalt be called the prophet of the highest: for thou shalt go before the face of the Lord to prepare his ways** *(Luke 1:26 [KJV])*. John knew Jesus was the Lord because Jesus was his Lord! We cannot know Jesus unless He is our Lord. **I never knew you: depart from me** *(Matthew 7:23 [KJV])*. Unlike Jesus' apostles, who were clueless and didn't understand what Jesus taught, John the Baptist did. **And they understood none of these things** *(Luke 18:34 [KJV])*.

John the Baptist was the only person in the Gospels who sounded like Jesus—because he spent time with Jesus. He spoke with authority because he knew Him Who is the only authority. **And think not to say to within yourselves, We have Abraham to our father: for I say unto you, that God is able of these stones to raise up children unto Abraham** *(Matthew 3:9 [KJV])*. John did not speak with flattering words. He was not out to win a popularity contest. The people knew he was talking from God.

> John answered and said, A man can receive nothing except it be given him from heaven *(John 3:27 [KJV])*.

His words are strikingly similar to what Jesus would tell Pilate:

> Thou couldest have no power at all against me, except it were given thee from above *(John 19:11 [KJV])*.

How the Baptist spoke is evidence that he spent time with Jesus. Bible expositors explain this away, believing that little John witnessed, but is the same writer and, as such, uses the same words. Tragically, this is my point with this book: They entirely miss why Jesus said John was so great, and his contribution to Jesus' family.

We all need time with Jesus, in His Word, if we hope to speak as He wills us to speak. We cannot be strangers to Jesus and believers in Christ. **And I saw, and bare record that this is the Son of God** (*John 1:34 [KJV]*). John was saying, "Jesus tells me things, and they happen, not because He is my cousin, but because He is God."

He that cometh from above is above all: he that is of the earth is earthly, and he that cometh from heaven is above all (*John 3:31 [KJV]*). Because of Baptist's testimony, some of his disciples followed Jesus. Most of these disciples were probably younger family members who knew about John's miraculous birth from their parents. These examples highlight the powerful testimony parents have towards their children in not just preaching words but what they willing support with sacrifices.

John the Baptist and Mary's families were Levites and the first Christians, but many great Bible expositors seemed to have missed that fact. J. Vernon McGee did know the Baptist was Levite and suspected that the author of the Gospel of John was Levite which aided me in putting some family connections together. I believe we miss a great spiritual lesson not connecting to the first Christians and seeing them coming from the priestly tribe. *First Peter 2:5* calls believers to be of the priesthood and it grieves me that believers don't connect the dots of an important purpose.

I believe the resurrection interpretations are confusing to believers today because Bible expositors have not identified that God used Levites to give us the Gospels. One of the Levite's functions was also to be scribes. It's my contention three of the four Gospel writers were Levites, and we connect to the story by recognizing that. It's my belief Christians are under grace, and God may not count our sins but has indeed blessed those who acted as priests of His grace.

Jesus is Baptized

For several years, John was waiting for Jesus to start His ministry. Then Jesus came and asked the unthinkable: to be baptized. John was shocked because the One who commissioned him to baptize and had no sin was now asking to be baptized. John knew the Son of God didn't need to repent. John knew Jesus was God's ultimate High Priest, yet He was asking John to perform a priestly function on Him.

But John forbade him, saying, I have need to be baptized of thee, and comest thou to me? And Jesus answering said unto him, Suffer it to be so now: for thus it becometh us to fulfill all righteousness. Then he suffered him *(Matthew 3:14-15 [KJV])*. John had been fulfilling his purpose in preaching and baptizing, and now Jesus was fulfilling His purpose. In part, the Lord was honoring John's years of work

Jesus' First Disciples

There was a man sent from God, whose name was John *(John 1:6 [KJV])*. The reason we have John the Baptist's words is that the Apostle John (little John) was one of his disciples. Little John admired his cousin and as such gave particular attention to his words. **The same came for a witness, to bear witness of the Light, that all men through him might believe** *(John 1:7 [KJV])*. Apparently, John knew the purpose of the Baptist.

Again the next day after John stood, and two of his disciples *(John 1:35 [KJV])*. Little John never referred directly to himself in the first person, but as a third-person narrator describing himself as another character in the story. **And looking upon Jesus as he walked, he saith, Behold the Lamb of God!** *(John 1:36 [KJV])*. The Baptist reiterated to his disciples— many of his younger cousins—that it was time for Jesus' ministry to begin, and they were to follow Him. **And the two disciples heard him speak, and they followed Jesus** *(John 1:37 [KJV])*. Jesus turned and asked them what they wanted. They asked, **Where dwellest thou?** *(John 1:38 [KJV])*. Jesus had been living in Nazareth His entire life, and now He had left the family carpentry business and was homeless. As relatives, they were aware of this and curious about His plans. What believers need to keep in mind reading scriptures is the writers give us a condensed form of witnessed conversations. The scriptures are commonly interpreted as if the discussions lasted fifteen seconds and that's all that was spoken. At times that may be accurate, but we should understand human beings' conversations are more in depth.

It's rather evident; some Bible expositors have missed this obvious truth and further misinterpreted the context of the communications. That's why some of the interpretations passed down are so skewed and miss some essential truths in the Gospel. Jesus' response to them is the same as Philip's words to Nathaniel later found in the Gospel of John. Jesus is not just showing them His sleeping bag but invites them to spend time with Him. When we read *John 1:35-41*, and desire to connect to the story, we should notice in a few verses they went from being near Jerusalem to arriving at Capernaum. A distance of eighty-five miles and would have taken them some days to walk. Naturally, they conversed about many things, and it's my interpretation after hearing Jesus left Nazareth, they were curious about His plans and invited Him to their homes in Capernaum.

I realize many Bible expositors will disagree with my assertions. I ask the reader to notice some scriptures that are emphatic who comes to Jesus and who doesn't. I ask them to ponder who knew Jesus left Nazareth? His Family! We should notice no brother is accompanying Jesus to visit John the Baptist. We don't hear about them because they didn't care if Jesus left without a pillow to lay His head.

One of the two which heard John speak and followed him, was Andrew, Simon Peter's brother *(John 1:40 [KJV])*. We should notice that John makes a point to identify Simon Peter as Andrews's brother because he is paramount to the Gospel story.

Why were Andrew and little John so tight together? Why did they follow the Baptist and then make a sudden course correction and follow Jesus together? **And so was also James, and John, the sons of Zebedee, which were partners with Simon** *(Luke 5:10 [KJV])*. Why were the children of Zebedee partners with Simon? I think most likely they were family. In fact, I think Peter was probably Zebedee's brother.

He Must Increase, but I Must Decrease

John was not immediately taken by Herod but continued to baptize and prepare followers for Jesus. **For John was not yet cast into prison** *(John 3:24 [KJV])*. Some of John's disciples were still with him when Jesus and His disciples came near them in Judea to baptize people. Jesus' disciples baptized people because they did the same thing when they followed the Baptist. John's disciples became irritated out of a competitive spirit. I don't picture the Baptist having hundreds of followers, more like a dozen. **Rabbi, he that was with thee beyond Jordan, to whom thou barest witness, behold the same baptizeth, and all men come to him** *(John 3:26 [KJV])*. John's disciples didn't understand that Jesus was going to die for their sins, and had worldly thoughts of hitching their wagon to a winner. Throughout the Gospels, some Jesus followers will leave Him because of this particular reasoning: *What's in it for me?* **John answered and said, A man can receive nothing except it be given him from heaven** *(John 3:27 [KJV])*. I hope I'll always remember this: not to react to the world's chaos. Whether it's our bosses or the government, no one has authority unless God gives it. That is why we are not to resent it or rebel against legitimate authority. We are not to use this world to be a scapegoat for our problems and be ungrateful for God's grace. **Ye yourselves bear witness that I said, I am not the Christ, but that I am sent before him** *(John 3:28 [KJV])*. No matter how many times John said it, some of his hearers refused to understand because they didn't hear what they wanted to hear.

He must increase, but I must decrease *(John 3:30 [KJV])*. God appointed a period for John's followers to come to Jesus. One of those followers was the one recording these words for us. **He that cometh from above is above all: he that is of the earth is earthly, and speaketh of the earth: he that cometh from heaven is above all** *(John 3:31 [KJV])*. John attested to Jesus' deity. **The Father loveth the**

Son, and hath given all things into his hand *(John 3:35 [KJV])*. John further attested that Jesus' Father was God, akin to Jesus' own later claim: **For the Father loveth the Son, and sheweth him all things** *(John 5:20 [KJV])*.

He that believeth on the son hath everlasting life: and he that believeth not the son shall not see life; but the wrath of God abideth on him *(John 3:36 [KJV])*. The Baptist gave us the Gospel, and its paramount believers understand, he received it from Jesus. John humbly said that he was unworthy to untie Jesus' shoes. Jesus stated that John was the greatest. And that's saying a lot, when we consider other heroes like Moses, David, Abraham, Daniel, and Joseph.

Let us look at how similar these two verses are:

> Whosoever believeth in him should not perish, but have everlasting life *(John 3:16 [KJV])*.

> He that believeth on the son hath everlasting life *(John 3:36 [KJV])*.

The first verse was given by Jesus, and the latter by John. The Baptist was a man of God from birth. I believe this is evidence that he spent a great deal of time with Jesus, for he gave the Gospel before Jesus went to the cross.

The Truth Exposes Darkness

The Jewish leaders were well acquainted with Baptist and knew his story. Many people heard John when he said Jesus was the Messiah. When Jesus taught in the temple, the chief priests, scribes, and elders became indignant and jealous and asked Jesus by what authority He taught. Jesus responded by, saying He'd answer them if they would answer one question: **The baptism of John, was it from heaven, or of men? And they reasoned with themselves, saying, if we shall say, From heaven; he will say, Why then believed ye him not?** *(Luke 20:4-5 [KJV])*. This verse has much greater meaning if we comprehend the Baptist told his followers he was doing what Jesus instructed Him to do. Since the Baptist knew Jesus was the Messiah, we should understand he did what God's Son commanded him to do. The Jewish leaders did not want to accept Jesus, but they dared not call John out for claiming Jesus was God's Son whom he followed. **But and if we say, Of men; all the people will stone us: for they be persuaded that John was a prophet** *(Luke 20:6 [KJV])*. It's my view John was alive when this event transpired. The people knew the extraordinary story, and the Baptist was accepted as a prophet. The Jewish leaders feared the people who gave them power by trusting them.

Many knew about Jesus even before He declared Himself publicly. The Jewish people had been prepared for Jesus by John. The Gospel of Matthew states that the Jewish leaders were alerted of the Messiah's birth. Further, they knew of Jesus because of John's witness. There was a time Jesus had not spoken out, which is why they initially tried to attach to Him when he began His ministry while John still lived. They were afraid of John, and they hoped Jesus could be controlled. If Jesus had been speaking out earlier in His life, they would have known this was not possible.

God sets the stage so that we can see why they reject Him. The Lord's purpose doesn't align itself to worldly objectives that are based on fear. The Jewish leaders had no problem with the idea of Messiah who could suddenly vanquish Rome. They did have an issue with someone Who said: **Render to Caesar the things that are Caesar's and to God the things that are God's** *(Mark 12:17 [KJV])*. They vehemently were against the dual ideologies Jesus presented. Their purpose was to be leaders of frightened people who hated Rome. The leaders used Rome (scapegoat of the blame for the people's problems), but their agendas were exposed by the way, the truth and the light. They believed if Jesus was as politically crafty as they were, He could dispose of them quickly. Hence, they felt threatened by Him and were desperate to dispose of Him.

And beheaded him in prison *(Mark 6:27 [KJV])*. When we see the power and reputation that John the Baptist had with the Jews throughout Judea, it becomes more understandable why God allowed his death and took him home. When John was alive, the Pharisees feared to make a move against Jesus. If John spoke against the Jewish leaders, the people would have moved on them and would never have allowed Jesus to be crucified. But it was God's will for Jesus to be crucified.

Jesus' ministry had a beginning. He didn't start with twelve apostles on day one. The Gospel of John fills gaps left by the other three Gospels, clarifying how Jesus' ministry began and grew, while John's purposefully shrank. John felt nothing but love toward Jesus because he understood His purpose. Ultimately what matters is God's purpose for our lives and the fruit of loving others that comes from embracing it. John the Baptist had a special bond with Jesus that no other apostle had, starting in their early childhoods. His importance has been diminished by Bible expositors because they have neglected the magnitude of His birth story being connected to Jesus.

CHAPTER 11

Jesus Moves Out

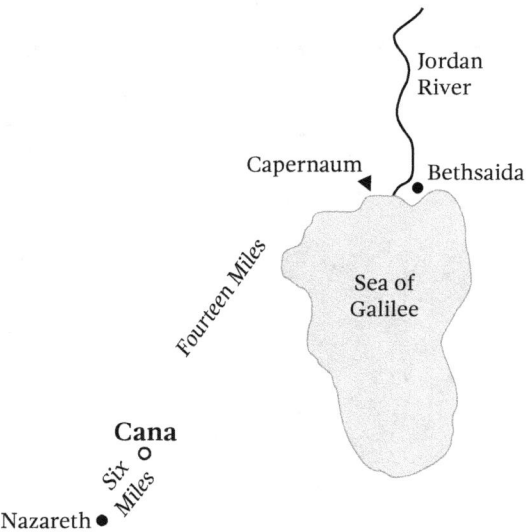

The movies present a Jesus Who walks by strangers and says, "Follow Me." They immediately leave and instantly become apostles. There is much more to the story than that. For one thing, some people who knew Him best would reject Him, so we should understand that he didn't use magical powers or was immediately embraced. I hope to present a more accurate picture of these relationships, and of who Jesus was. If I'm successful, believers will have a deeper connection to Him, and to the Gospels. Knowing more Who He was allows us to see how far we all fall short of Him, motivating us to connect His life into our own lives.

Jesus was Homeless

The fact is Jesus had no possessions and was homeless. He overcame great tribulations that we might know He will never leave us in the midst of our own. In this life, we may lose things or people we cherish, but His will is we know we can never lose Him.

One branch of His family hated Him the other loved Him. **Take my yoke upon you, and learn of; for I am meek and lowly in heart** (*Matthew 11:29 [KJV]*)—many believers today have not heard the compelling story of His meekness and humility. Jesus did go to the desert to fast, but we should consider He didn't have any money to buy food. In the Gospels of *Luke 21:21* and *Mark 10:21*, Jesus looks at the young man and, out of love, tells him the one thing he must do to be perfect: Sell all that he has and give it to the poor. Jesus did not ask the young man to do what he hadn't already done. When Jesus left Nazareth, He had no possessions besides His garment. We should be aware He didn't squabble over anything, in fact, He allowed His brothers to judge as Abraham did towards Lot (see *Genesis 13:8-11*). Instead of being convicted by His grace, His brothers became tainted with arrogance towards Him. Whatever inheritance there was from Joseph, Jesus gave it to His half-brothers, for He did, in fact, have a different Father. Jesus had no money saved up and didn't rely on a 401k retirement plan to dip into. **For I was hungered, and ye gave me meat: I was thirsty, and ye gave me drink: I was a stranger, and ye took me in. Naked, and ye clothed me: I was sick, and ye visited me: I was in prison, and ye came unto me** (*Matthew 25:35-36 [KJV]*). Lost in the dogma of our translations is the fact that some in Mary's family did just that in His life. Some took Him in their arms at His birth and some took His naked body down from the cross. Believers are disconnected to this amazing story of love and rejection of Him presented in all the Gospels and especially Matthew. Some may object to my claim and say: "*Jesus never got sick*" I don't know if He ever got a cold that's an interesting question of which I wouldn't be surprised that He lived out His life as we did.

That's why He was here, and believers don't see that many of the scriptures *(Matthew 25:35-45)* were not just about the future but about how he lived His life. He was beaten to the point of death (sickness), He was visited in prison and the ones who never abandoned Him were his family. It's critical that believers recognize the bonds of some of Jesus' family were never broken per God's will for us in heaven and on earth.

About fifteen years ago, during a rainy day in Oregon, I was at a food bank for low-income families. A girl in her twenties came in barefoot and asked a volunteer: "Do *you have any shoes?*" He said: "*I will check*," He came back with men's' dress shoes twice the size of her feet. She proceeded to put them on and walked out in the rain without a coat. I couldn't help but weep at the sight of her walking with no socks in those oversized black shoes. I didn't have any cash, so I asked an acquaintance: "*Do you have any money*?" He told me he had some, and I borrowed it and gave it to her.

After this event, I went looking for homeless charities, and I came to know a lady named Teri Gant. A few days ago I was heartbroken to find out she passed away suddenly from complications from the flu. She started a homeless mission out of her garage, and it grew to have many volunteers with a building. I loved her like a sister in my family for she was beloved by many as such. Teri loved with the Father's grace and treated strangers like family. She blessed hundreds of homeless people with the encouragement of human dignity and led some ultimately to the Lord. Her charity was called *The Father's Heart,* and the verse that inspired her was *Matthew 25:35*. Teri knew the opportunity we have as believers to be blessed in Christ.

Jesus' brothers had a chance to be kind to Him as many people did when He walked this Earth. He didn't take their rejection personally and in fact, He is more concerned with how believers treat others today. Everyone will meet Him (Face to face) someday, and many will be surprised that their lives were not about them and how others treated them. It will be all about Him and what we did to others, we did to Him.

Jesus Goes into the Desert

Three of the four Gospels mirror each other and are called the Synoptic Gospels. The Gospel writers all have a beginning and an end. They're not the same, but they intersect at critical points, thereby emphasizing key events, including John baptizing Jesus, Jesus' temptation in the desert, the beginning of Jesus' ministry in Capernaum, certain miracles, and events leading up to His crucifixion and resurrection.

After Jesus was baptized, all four Gospels tell us that He went into the desert to be tempted by the devil. One season in His life ended, and a new season began. Change is scary and the very time in our lives when our enemy likes to sow seeds to stir up fear inside of us.

The prince of this world cometh, and hath nothing in me *(John 14:30 [KJV])*. When the devil came to Jesus, there was no grievance that Jesus bore that the devil could connect with. Our childhood is in our past, and the best way for the devil to steal our future is for us not to attend to our present. The devil could not latch onto any resentment from Jesus' past because He forgave all the cruelty He received in Nazareth.

Jesus' childhood was, from our perspective, horrible. Then life got worse when He became an adult and received more hate from His own kin. **Because for thy sake I have borne reproach; shame hath covered my face. I am become a stranger unto my brethren, and an alien unto my mother's children** *(Psalm 69:7-8 [KJV])*.

He had forgiven those who tried to destroy Him emotionally, as we must forgive those who have sought to hurt us so that we may live and love in the present. **But if ye forgive not men their trespasses, neither will your Father forgive your trespasses** *(Matthew 6:15 [KJV])*. If this verse had to do with eternal salvation, no one would find it. But it's about experiencing salvation after its beginning. If we do not forgive others, we don't forgive ourselves, and so we carry the fruit of resentment.

Then was Jesus led up of the Spirit into the wilderness to be tempted of the devil. And when he had fasted forty days and forty nights, he

was afterward hungered *(Matthew 4:1 [KJV])*. There is nothing wrong with eating, but Jesus fasted and denied His body because God would have us understand that our higher purpose cannot be guided by our needs. **Man shall not live by bread alone, but by every word that proceedeth out of the mouth of God** *(Matthew 4:4 [KJV])*. Jesus overcame Nazareth; He was now overcoming the demands of His body, and soon He would overcome the world.

This world is full of problems, and people hunger for solutions. We all have a past, and many of us have suffered pain at the hands of someone else. Our past pain cries out, *"Feed me!"* It lives by haunting us, but it offers no fruit of joy. **I am come that they might have life, and that they might have it more abundantly** *(John 10:10 [KJV])*. Our past can make us stronger when we become unattached to living in it. Our future is filled with life when we are dead to that which offers only regret. We are to starve the past pain by not giving it attention with our thoughts. There is no life or joy in it, and God's will is that we enjoy His blessing of purpose.

That I may know him, and the fellowship of his sufferings, being made conformable unto his death *(Philippians 3:10 [KJV])*. Our Lord Jesus suffered, yet at no time did He whine like a victim, even though He made Himself a victim of our sin. We are not called to be victims, but to have victory through Him. **We are more than conquerors, through him that loved us** *(Romans 8:38 [KJV])*. The biggest mistake I have seen from believers is in not understanding this verse. Jesus overcame everything because His Spirit could never fail. We have that Spirit in us, too, and it will never fail because it's Him in us. Our carnal mind can never serve God and, therefore, will never be perfect. Jesus did not have a flesh (mind) that desired to sin (pride), so we are not to say that He was like us. Rather than beating ourselves or others for not measuring up, God would rather us understand that His Spirit is always available to all. We can be encouraged because, with His Spirit, we can have victory over (pride) the world that our minds alone could not achieve. However, pride would rather be miserable and accuse itself or others, or the world, for its continuous state of misery.

God's Blessings in Families versus Satan' Devices

Many that even achieve stardom and the glory of this world still hate themselves and end up abusing their health to the point of death. The core purpose of a human being is to love their families, and in doing so, they love themselves. There is no fulfilling purpose in vanity, for it always leads to misery because it destroys its purpose to love.

Satan attacks families because they are central to the purpose of human beings.

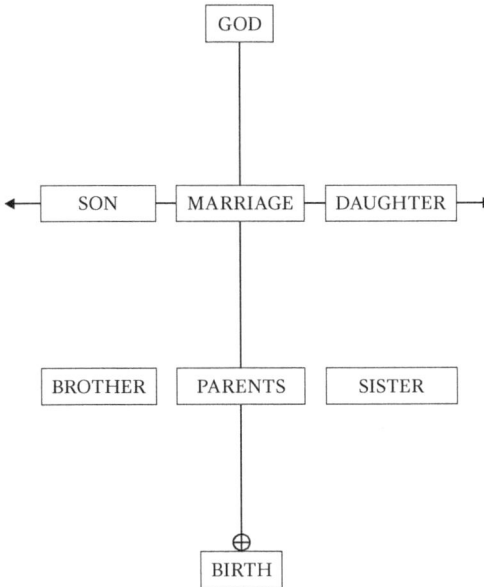

God's will is for us to sow seeds of love that extend life by creating blessings through our loved ones. Love continually creates purpose, even after death, as in the case of Jesus. We are not to be self-centered, but, rather, on a moving course of extending God's love through others.

Circles of Self-Importance
Anger-Resentment-Fear-Blame-Resistance

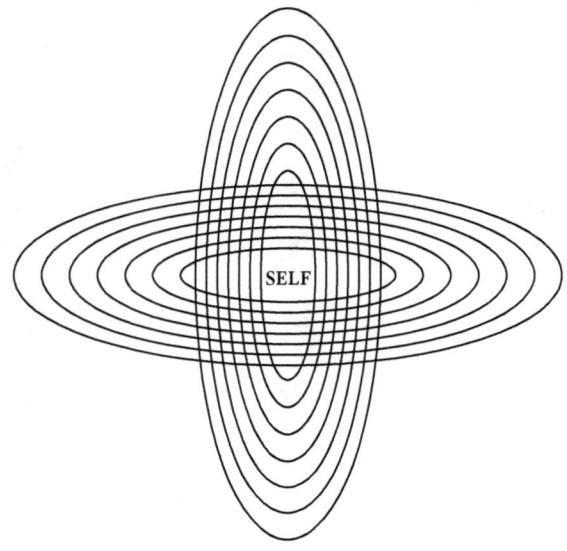

As the circles become larger, the emotional pain becomes greater.

Satan is a serpent and thrives on causing pain throughout the world. What better way than to have this world's inhabitants blame each other and perpetuate his devices. Satan's will is that the world rejects God's grace and the gift of life. He attacks the family unmercifully because its defeat leads to the downfall of humanity. He enslaves people to be centered on themselves by looking back into the past, focusing on circles that repeat themselves. These rings of dysfunction give the illusion of being different, but they are the same, and always miss God's purpose. In the book of *Numbers* (see chapters 13-14), some of the Israelites embraced fear and rejected their faith in God's promise of a fruitful life in His chosen land for them. The consequence was forty years wandering in the desert in a circle.

God offers everyone today the promise of grace, which embraces the forward purpose of God in a person's life. However, to move forward in grace, one must first let go of the circles of the past. In the book of Numbers, some of the Israelites refused to let go of their past life of slavery, and today the Earth is full of people who can't let go of their pasts (modern slavery). The past has no life in it because it can't change or grow, whereas each new day is a new creation of God. **Therefore, if any man be in Christ, he is a new creature: old things are passed away; behold all things are become new** *(I Corinthians 5:17 [KJV])*. God's will is to wipe away the past and give the blessing to our future. Satan's power is diverting attention to the past and thereby distracting us from our future. The way to give place to the devil is to live in the past (death), constantly blaming others for hurting us. **Neither give place to the devil** *(Ephesians 4:27 [KJV])*. God would want believers to understand in His word that, Satan himself, or his devices have no future. Satan offers this world death, and we see it play out every day as his pawns throw away their future by destroying themselves or others. **That old serpent, which is the Devil, and Satan** *(Revelation 20:2 [KJV])*. Snakes bite and the wound causes pain. The devil's intention is to inflict people with an addiction to pain so they—as this world—will never seek peace. In their addiction to pain, they feel justified to mirror the past and to take revenge, but they are only acting as pawns of the devil.

Satan is the god of the past and accused God Himself. God (Life) blesses us with families (purpose) and Satan (past) attacks (future-purpose) them. Most believers are unaware that Satan first divided Adam from Eve (see Genesis 3:1). Then he succeeds by bringing up what God did in the past and it never even came to Eve's mind the future God had for her. Satan attacked grace (future), which is what God is and wills, which has nothing to do with the past. The very instruments God created for our benefit, Satan uses for our destruction by dividing the bonds of family by looking backward instead of to the future a family creates.

Being judgmental of a parent leads to an attitude of superiority. A child could not exist without the parent, and therefore the resentment makes the child resent (past) their life (future). They are in fact, unconscious; they have divided themselves from desiring a future with purpose. This skewed, dysfunctional attitude, often leads to divorce and broken relationships. Consequently, some believers can have worse personal lives than atheists. All of us must overcome family dysfunction.

Verily, verily, I say unto thee, Except a man be born again, he cannot see the kingdom of God *(John 3:3 [KJV])*. When people give attention to the rearview mirror, their personal lives can crash. Even though we may call ourselves Christians, Satan diminishes our witness by blinding us to that which harms us. Unforgiveness! Which is saying to God in our hearts that His work on the cross wasn't good enough? So, we bring wrath on ourselves. When we do not extend the freedom of grace to others, we do not experience it ourselves. **For whatsoever a man soweth, that shall he also reap** *(Galatians 6:7 [KJV])*. Those who sow unforgiveness reap unforgiveness in their own conscience (**Which shew the work of the law written in their hearts, their conscience also bearing witness, and their thoughts the mean while accusing or else excusing one another** *(Romans 2:15 [KJV])*.

He that is without sin let him cast the first stone *(John 8:7 [KJV])*. The Lord allows us free will on whether we choose to accuse (guilt) to be our guide. Many are oblivious to the human element that there is the actual choice that has to be made to let go of the past (guilt). Many hear of its importance, but most continue a path they have known from childhood. Being miserable is not a good thing, yet many chose it regularly, using their past as a scapegoat of their misery. Case in point is today this world has so many luxuries (compared to a hundred or two thousand years ago), but because of its despondency, it has no gratitude for those who paved the way for its easier life. Can you imagine our ancestors (some had the shirt on their backs) being perplexed how we think we have problems? Exactly what was there health care system five hundred years ago? It doesn't matter how much money or glitz we have in today's society we think we have problems. In our heads, we do face many more dilemmas than our ancestors suffered for they didn't have time to consider issues besides family and survival.

Some believers mistakenly believe our faith implies automatic healing without dysfunction. Parents naturally judge their own parenting skills. I remember when I was a new parent, thinking: *How could my parents do that to me?* Later I became conscious of repeating some of the same mistakes. We truly reap what we sow. **Judge not, that ye be not judged** *(Matthew 7:1 [KJV])*. Family members irritate each other not because they are different as they believe, but because they are too much alike. Many are ignorant of this truth. Consequently, they unconsciously mirror family member's behaviors they disapprove and as a consequence are angry at themselves.

How precious also are thy thoughts unto me, O God! how great is the sum of them! If I should count them, they are more in number than the sand: *(Psalms 138:17-18 [KJV])*. God's thoughts are higher than the stars in heaven for all of us. They are for our future, not to condemn us with our past. God has so many good things he wishes to give all of us, but our tendency is to close the door on God's grand will and to remember our past. Our nature has small plans in comparison to Gods grand will for our lives. **Trust in the Lord with all thine heart; and lean not unto thine own understanding** *(Proverbs 3:5 [KJV])*. We comprehend by a perspective which comes from living in the past. God asks believers to let go of their understanding because it originates from what will always miss His best. **In all ways acknowledge him, and he shall direct thy paths** *(Proverbs 3:6[KJV])*.

Jesus Moves to Capernaum

Through the family of Mary, His needs are met. **Father knoweth what things ye have need of before you ask him** *(Matthew 6:8 [KJV])*. Jesus' needs in Capernaum were provided by an aunt named Salome who had a house in Capernaum.

That it might be fulfilled which was spoken by Esaias the prophet *(Matthew 4:14 [KJV])*. Isaiah wrote prophecies about Jesus 700 years before He was born. Sometimes when we reflect on our lives, we can connect the dots for why God allowed certain things to happen. I've heard stories from other believers who lost a job, only to be surprised by how well it worked out. Jesus' Aunt Salome probably didn't know the significance of God selecting her husband, or how God would use a fisherman named Zebedee. He had family on the Sea of Galilee, and God would use them to bring the Gospel.

Jesus would perform eighteen of thirty-six recorded miracles in the immediate neighborhood of the Sea of Galilee. In the city of Capernaum alone, He performed eleven of these miracles; more than anywhere else in Israel. The city was located twenty miles northeast of Nazareth.

And it came to pass, that, when Jesus was returned, the people gladly received him: for they were all waiting for him *(Luke 8:40 [KJV])*. The Sea of Galilee today is eight miles wide with a circumference of thirty-three miles. Since some of His disciples—many of them possibly family—were in the fishing industry, He easily visited many Galilean communities by boat. From any given port, He could travel to many surrounding communities. On this occasion, a crowd had gathered, knowing He would return to the town from one of His outings.

And, behold, there came a man named Jairus, and he was ruler of the synagogue: and he fell down at Jesus feet, and besought him that he would come into his house *(Luke 8:41 [KJV])*. Jesus was accepted and revered by the ruler of the synagogue. What a contrast to the treatment Jesus received in Nazareth and Jerusalem! It's significant that the Spirit of God has given the ruler's name. Years later, the early church knew who he was and what significance his family played in the ministry of Jesus. They understood the relationships that we seem to have no comprehension.

Jesus had family in that synagogue who believed in Him the day He was born, and that synagogue knew Him even before He moved there. We should understand that Mary was close to her sister and visited her regularly. Jesus, therefore, was already known and was warmly received by the synagogue. **From that time Jesus began to preach, and to say, Repent: for the kingdom of heaven is at hand** *(Matthew 4:17 [KJV])*. What I'm trying to convey is what should be obvious by looking through the lens of family relationships. Jesus' family story was known in Capernaum, but He didn't begin preaching the Kingdom of God until He moved away from Nazareth.

And when he came into the house, he suffered no man to go in, save Peter, and James, and John, and the father and the mother

(Luke 8:51 [KJV]). Jesus didn't start out with twelve apostles. His original disciples were probably cousins or friends of the family who lived near Capernaum, and they witnessed more events during His ministry.

Zebedee

What is greater honor there than having one's name recorded in the Gospels for serving Jesus? Trophies of this world—even the coveted Heisman and the various Halls of Fame—attract dust and are forgotten. **Lay not up for yourselves treasures upon earth** *(Matthew 5:19 [KJV])*. Yet, the heroes—and villains—recorded in the Bible will never be forgotten. Zebedee is mentioned thirteen times in the Gospels, and yet I wonder how many believers have heard a sermon on him.

And going on from thence, he saw other two brethren, James the son of Zebedee, and John his brother, in a ship with Zebedee, their father, mending their nets; and he called them *(Matthew 4:21 [KJV])*. Nothing Zebedee specifically did or said is recorded. Since he partnered with Simon Peter, I surmise that they may have been brothers. Zebedee lived in Capernaum, whereas Peter lived in the nearby suburb of Bethsaida. The Jordan River ran between them, emptying into the Sea of Galilee from the north.

While we don't hear of Zebedee's actions, we can read between the lines and see his contributions to Jesus' ministry. Andrew and John, who had already taken leave of the family fishing business to follow John the Baptist, began to follow Jesus in Judea after John baptized him. They asked Jesus to visit Capernaum where Zebedee lived with his wife, (Salome) Mary's sister.

Andrew and John were the younger brothers in their working families and would have been needed to work. Their parents made sacrifices, for if they weren't working, then someone else had to provide for them. Their families wholeheartedly believed in God's call to follow both John the Baptist and Jesus. This took faith because it made their burdens heavier. No doubt Zebedee is honored in scripture because he supported his family's contribution to Jesus.

And straightway he called them: and they left their father Zebedee in the ship with hired servants *(Mark 1:20 [KJV])*. Mark tells us that Zebedee also had hired men, besides family, to keep the business going. Jesus would not have accepted their service if Zebedee objected, and we know this for two reasons. First, Jesus wrote the commandment to honor our parents, as He honored His parents before He started His ministry. Second, the Word of God acknowledges Zebedee for letting his sons and partners follow Jesus with his blessing. He clearly supported John the Baptist and his cousin Jesus.

Andrew (Simon Peter's brother) was likely older than John and may have been given responsibility for looking after him as they traveled back and forth over eighty miles between Capernaum and the Baptist's ministry locations in Judea and along the nearby Jordan River.

James, John, and Peter became the closest disciples of Jesus, which would make sense, especially if Mary's sister was the mother of James and John and told them the story of His incarnation and birth. **And after six days Jesus taketh Peter, James, and John his brother, and bringeth them up into a high mountain apart** *(Matthew 17:1 [KJV])*. These three were privileged to witness the Transfiguration, among several other key events of Jesus' ministry years. They may have grown up together and traveled to Jerusalem every year to celebrate the Passover and the Feasts of Tabernacles.

But they, supposing him to have been in the company, went a day's journey; and they sought him among their kinsfolk and acquaintance *(Luke 2:44 [KJV])*. When Jesus was twelve and stayed behind in Jerusalem, Joseph and Mary sought Him among family and friends. They were apparently in the habit of entrusting Jesus to trusted family and friends, so they didn't immediately notice that He was missing. We can assume similar types of relationships and connections throughout the communities in which Jesus and His disciples grew up. Mary was probably from Cana, as I believe her sister, Salome. The town was six miles from Nazareth and sixteen from Capernaum. Cana may have been the rendezvous point for the group who traveled each year to Jerusalem, sixty-five miles to the south. Jesus would have been close to His cousins on His mother's side, as well as many friends of His family, some of whom became His first disciples.

And he saith unto them, Follow me, and I will make you fishers of men. And they immediately left the ship and their father; and followed him *(Matthew 4:19-20 [KJV])*. This was not the first time these men met Jesus, nor was it the last time they left their father, with his permission. We need to know why Jesus is talking to them to connect to the verse. The first question we ought to ask is why Jesus asks them to follow Him. Who do we immediately follow that we don't know? This is an initial call not what Bible expositors have interpreted it. He doesn't walk by strangers and instruct them to leave their living that supports their families. In today's real life relationships sometimes we ask people we know to have a cup of coffee or play a round of golf. This was Jesus' initial call, an invitation to spend time with Him as He would eventually build their faith to leave the fishing business. In other words, they knew Jesus, and He respected hard work, and as such, he was telling them He would eventually make them fishers of men if they followed His ways. This was accomplished after His resurrection. At the last supper, the apostle John was leaning against the Lord's chest, certainly not for the first time, demonstrating a closer intimacy with Jesus. **Now there was leaning on Jesus bosom one of his disciples, whom Jesus loved. Simon Peter therefore, beckoned to him, that he should ask who it should be of whom he spake** *(John 13:23-24 [KJV])*. To me, it helps to understand the verse better if we connect John and Simon were kin to Jesus and knew they would not betray Him.

CHAPTER 12

Calling of the Disciples

And Jesus went about all Galilee, teaching in their synagogues, and preaching the gospel of the kingdom, and healing all manner of sickness and all manner of disease among the people *(Matthew 4:23 [KJV])*. This is Matthew's summary of a period before Matthew himself came into the picture as one of Jesus' disciples. **And his fame went throughout all Syria: and they brought unto him all sick people that were taken with diverse diseases and torments** *(Matthew 4:24 [KJV])*. Jesus had already cured many people and was famous.

And Jesus returned in the power of Spirit into Galilee: and there went out a fame of him through all the region about *(Luke 4:14 [KJV])*. Luke, as did Matthew and Mark, began an account of Jesus' ministry after Jesus had already become famous through teaching and performing miracles. His early ministry is given to us only by what I call the "inside Gospel" of John, who was Jesus' first cousin. He knew of Jesus' movements at this time, whereas Mary was in Nazareth. Luke, along with other Gospel writers, relied on testimonies of others, of which I contend many were relatives, whereas John writes primarily from what he witnessed.

John, the son of Zebedee

The Gospel of John is, in my biased opinion, the most beautiful composition of words ever written. I believe the first chapter—in fact, the first sentence—gives the key to understanding the entire Bible: **In the beginning was the Word** *(John 1:1 [KJV])*. Cults disregard this most beautiful statement to humanity and make up ridiculous religions. John spelled it out as clear as it can be: *Jesus Christ is God*. He is also in us. **I in them, and thou in me that they may be made perfect in one** *(John 17:23 [KJV])*.

Walking in the fullness of our purpose is only possible when we understand God's will for us: **What shall we do, that we might work the works of God?** *(John 6:28 [KJV])*. Jesus answered: **This is the work of God, that ye believe on him whom he hath sent** *(John 6:29 [KJV])*. Serving God is not complicated. These types of profound, simple verses are uniquely found in the Gospel of John.

Little John could have been as young as eight when he started serving the Baptist. In the book of Samuel, his mother gave him to a prophet to be in the service of the Lord. Like John the Baptist, Samuel's birth was a miracle, and he would go on to be a great prophet. It's very probable that little John's family dedicated him to God's service at a very young age.

He most likely had grown up idolizing Jesus, having known Him from His birth. I picture Jesus picking him up as a toddler and sitting him on His lap. Then, it becomes very understandable that he refers to himself as the disciple whom Jesus loved. He adores Jesus and still cuddles with Him when he was twelve or in his early teens. **Now there was leaning on Jesus bosom one of his disciples, whom Jesus loved** *(John 13:23 [KJV])*.

While all the adult males fall asleep at Gethsemane, we should understand that John doesn't (or we do not find it in his Gospel). While other Gospels will say that all the disciples forsook Him and fled, we should understand that little John does not. Is there a contradiction in the Gospels? No, we are disconnected to the writer's intent and the context of story they are conveying to us. John was a child, but all the men forsook Jesus. As a child John wasn't afraid: he will go near the location where Jesus' trial was taking place, and he will witness some of Pilate's words. He will stand by Jesus' mother, and while the others doubt, he will believe: **he saw and believed** *(John 20:8 [KJV])*. John's purpose was not to testify about himself or how he had more faith than the other apostles, but we should clearly see that he did. He writes a Gospel, and later he will write a profound book in Revelation.

John is the last of the Gospels to be written and let's assume that he knows what is in the other Gospels. He gives us details that are not in the synoptic Gospels. In *"Thru the Bible:"* [*MATTHEW through ROMANS*] J. Vernon McGee wrote that the Gospel of John was chronological, which I believe assists us in understanding the sequence of events in Jesus' life.

John alone will give us an account of Jesus calling His first disciples. If we understand that he is family, we should also ascertain that is why he is the one telling us about family events such as weddings and Jesus' brothers' denial that He was divine. Our connection is stronger when we see that Jesus' movements were not always unpredictable. They had to do with the fact that His relatives had boats that took Him around Galilee, and then Jesus went with His family to the feasts twice a year. On the way there and back, they made stops in towns where John witnessed such events.

The Calling of Andrew and Peter

One of the two which heard John speak and followed him, was Andrew, Simon Peter's brother *(John 1:40 [KJV])*. Andrew and John followed Jesus after He was baptized in the Jordan, then came back home to Capernaum with Him. **He first findeth his own brother Simon, and saith unto him, We have found the Messias, which is, being interpreted, the Christ** *(John 1:41 [KJV])*. Why would Peter (Simon) care? Fishers have one primary concern—will they catch fish? Peter couldn't support his family while looking for the Christ.

Peter's little brother came up and said, "We found the Christ." Some might respond, "I didn't know he was lost" or "Good for you, Brother. Now help me fish tomorrow." Many wouldn't be impressed with a little brother who pops off about something unrelated to making a living. But Peter, like Andrew, James, and John, was waiting for Jesus to begin His mission. They already knew Jesus was the Messiah.

And he brought him to Jesus. And when Jesus beheld him, he said, Thou art Simon the son of Jona: thou shalt be called Cephas, which is by interpretation, A stone *(John 1:42 [KJV])*. Many Bible expositors believe this is the first time Jesus meets Simon. What we should note is that Jesus, upon seeing him, calls him Simon, son of Jona. Capernaum wasn't a city of a million people, and Jesus knew that Simon was the son of Jona, who named him originally.

And Jesus walking by the sea of Galilee, saw two brethren, Simon called Peter, and Andrew his brother, casting a net into the sea: for they were fishers *(Matthew 4:18 [KJV])*. Matthew's account reads as though Jesus was walking by the lake and stumbled upon two brothers, but John's Gospel clarifies that both brothers had already made Jesus' acquaintance. **And he saith unto them, Follow me, and I will make you fishers of men** *(Matthew 4:19 [KJV])*. This is the record of Jesus officially calling the brothers to join His public ministry. Mark introduces us to Peter in the same fashion. Luke tells us about two events not recorded in the other Gospels, including Jesus' healing Simon Peter's mother-in-law at his home.

And it came to pass, that, as the people pressed upon him to hear the Word of God, he stood by the lake of Gennesaret. And he saw two ships standing by the lake: but the fishermen were gone out of them, and were washing their nets. And he entered into one of the ships, which was Simon's, and prayed him that he would thrust out a little from the land. And he sat down, and taught the people out of the ship *(Luke 5:1-3 [KJV])*. This was not a ship, by our standard, but a small boat.

Now when he had left speaking, he said unto Simon, Launch out into the deep and let down your nets for a draught. And Simon

answering said unto him, Master, we have toiled all the night, and have taken nothing: nevertheless at thy word I will let down the net *(Luke 5:4-5 [KJV])*. The professionals had caught nothing by themselves, but now the carpenter gave them a suggestion that made no sense. Peter listened, but called him "Master." This title traditionally was used to show respect for a Jewish teacher. **And when they had done, they inclosed a great multitude of fishes: and their net brake. And they beckoned unto their partners, which were in the other ship, that they should come and help them. And they came, and filled both the ships, so that they began to sink** *(Luke 5:6-7 [KJV])*. The miracle was trifold: This was the wrong time of day for fishing, the net had gathered different species of fish than it was designed to hold, and two boats were not able to carry them all.

There are three types of fish in the Sea of Galilee today, and scholars believe it was the same in Jesus' time. There were sardines, tilapia (the size of small trout), and biny (a carp the size of a salmon). These men were likely fishing for sardines, which run at night in schools. Tons probably could be harvested at the height of fishing season, as they are today. Predatory fish, such as the biny, feed on the sardines, so the smaller fish move closer to the shore only under the protection of darkness. During the day, the schools of sardines avoid the shoreline. So, Jesus' advice would have seemed foolish to Peter, who was also in a bad mood after being skunked the previous night.

When Simon Peter saw it, he fell down to his knees, saying, Depart from me; for I am a sinful man, O Lord. For he was astonished, and all that were with him, at draught of the fishes which they had taken *(Luke 5:8-9 [KJV])*. Peter was cut to the heart and repented immediately. He had not trusted the carpenter's deity and now calls him Lord instead of Master. **There is therefore now no condemnation to them which are in Christ Jesus, who walk not after the flesh, but after the spirit** *(Romans 8:1 [KJV])*. Jesus encourages Peter, as His will is for all of us. But we need to see the resistance in our own understanding, and the fruit of fear, which always produces and stops us from following Him. Jesus demonstrates that God could easily take care of the family's needs. Peter was being called to something so much more important than toiling for fish during the night.

And Jesus said unto him Simon, Fear not; from henceforth thou shalt catch men *(Luke 5:10 [KJV])*. Peter isn't called to fear, but only sees his lack of faith that came from rejecting God's' call. Peter was out of the will of God, and the consequences for being outside of His will are that things don't work out, even when we are sure they should. I've been there several times: swimming against the current and not understanding the futility of swimming harder. Then there is the opposite when things strangely fall into place when they shouldn't because the Master Carpenter has brought it about, in my life.

The movies of Jesus' life portray Him as saying "Follow me," and they become instant apostles. They miss that God trained Jesus' disciples, much as He fashions His believers today. Discovering Jesus' deity is an awakening, but God prepared believers, and much more of God's training remains.

> *Jesus first calls to Simon in the Gospel of John was alerting him to the fact that he was welcome, as were James and John, to observe His movements as He went throughout Galilee. That Jesus was going to use them and their boats to deliver the Gospel instead of fish. Jesus was also alerting Simon that he would leave his old life and have a new life as Peter (Cephas).*

> *Jesus' second call in Matthew was telling them to let go of the fishing business and follow Him, that he would give them a new purpose (fishers of men).*

> *Luke's account is the third call from Jesus to Peter to follow Him wholeheartedly. No doubt Peter hadn't entirely left the Fishing business. Can we blame him? They needed to support themselves and their families, but they are hesitant to follow Jesus wholeheartedly.*

We can find encouragement in Simon Peter when we see that he was an everyday person just like us. What we should see is the Lord's continued work in Peter and the building of his faith; that even though Peter witnessed great miracles, he would continue to stumble. God knows our nature has no faith - "the spirit indeed is willing, but the flesh is weak" (*Matthew 26:41 [KJV]*). Thus, we might surrender and walk in moments of a different understanding, which is contrary to what we believe is in our best interests.

Peter tried hard, but fell short; and despite this, God uses him mightily. Many believers stumble like Peter, and hopefully, they will see God's encouragement to him and all of us: *"Fear not, you might have fallen, but I am going to do great things in your life."* It's one thing to come to know God's existence, and it's quite another to surrender to Him. I've heard a few believers insinuate they have accomplished this (complete surrender) but as I write this, I find that to be an impossible thing for me. **Being confident of this very thing, that he which hath begun a good work in you will perform it until the day of Jesus Christ** (*Philippians 1:6 [KJV]*). Peter's faith grows, and yet, he will have more failures. God's grace meets them, as does His will for each of us.

And so was also James, and John, the sons of Zebedee, which were partners with Simon (*Luke 5:10 [KJV]*). Jesus had carefully prepared Peter and, similarly, he had cultivated each of his disciples in the days—perhaps years—leading up to this official calling. God calls believers to move mountains, but they are not literal mountains - rather, they are mountains of unbelief. **Ye shall say unto this mountain, Remove hence to yonder place; and it shall remove; and nothing shall be impossible** (*Matthew [KJV] 17:20*). These mountains are found in our own unique perspectives. They are never God's understanding, which is why He calls us continuously to let go of them. **Trust in the LORD with all thine heart, and lean not unto thine own understanding** (*Proverbs 3:5 [KJV]*). And when we do, we get to see the power of His hand: Mountains disappear that were once seen by our little perspective. God doesn't call believers to be crushed by the rocks of perils that fall on them. On the contrary, His will is for us to walk over the tops of the mountains that cause them.

The Calling of Philip and Nathanael

The day following Jesus would go forth into Galilee, and findeth Philip and saith unto him, Follow me. Now Philip was of Bethsaida, the city of Andrew and Peter. Philip findeth Nathanael, and saith unto him, we have found him, of whom Moses in the law, and the prophets, did write, Jesus of Nazareth, the son of Joseph *(John 1:43-45 [KJV])*. Bethsaida was a suburb of Capernaum, separated by the Jordan River. Peter and Zebedee most likely sold fish to both towns. Philip had a relationship with Nathanael, who happened to be from Jesus' mother's hometown, Cana (see *John 21:2*). "*Findeth*" is a better translated "*searched out,*" used twice in this passage. Jesus went looking for Philip, specifically, who then went looking for Nathanael. They already knew each other, and didn't bump into each other by accident and say: "*Nice to meet you.*"

Matthew, Mark, and Luke list the twelve apostles, but the names do not match up. Nathanael isn't described as an apostle, and John never mentions a particular twelve. John has Nathanael in the inner circle, together with those identified as apostles in the other three Gospels. In the Synoptic Gospels, the first six names are the same—but not in the same order—and Bartholomew is one of them. Nathanael is mentioned at the beginning and end of John, leading many commentators to believe he was the same as Bartholomew. According to John, Jesus' first six disciples were called from Capernaum, or just across the river in Bethsaida. They were with Jesus in the beginning, and they were there at the end.

Can there any good thing come out of Nazareth? *(John 1:46 [KJV])*. Some commentators believe this was a derogatory remark about Nazareth, and some feel the city wasn't the focus of the conversation. Many Bible expositors believe Nathanael doesn't know Jesus and wonders if anyone born from Nazareth could be the Messiah. What if Philip was kin and Jesus asked him to tell Nathanael that He was beginning His ministry? What if Nathanael knew Jesus' history in Nazareth and was asking what any of us might: *"Can there any good thing come out of the disaster of Nazareth?"* After all, how could the King rise out of such rejection? Their hopes of what Messiah's actions would be and the future of Israel was quite different than what would actually occur. Some of them were hoping to be attached to the King who would bring glory to Israel and cast out the Romans.

Philip saith to him, Come and see *(John 1:46 [KJV])*. Philip's response was the same as Jesus' response to John's disciples when they asked Him where He was living. This is invitation to spend time with Jesus. Philip (and Nathanael, most likely) was a disciple of John the Baptist and, I suspect, kin to Jesus. They all already knew of Him and met Him several times.

Jesus saw Nathanael coming to him, and saith of him, Behold an Israelite indeed, in whom is no guile *(John 1:47 [KJV])*. Since the Old Testament Jacob (renamed Israel after he wrestled with God) was known as a trickster, many commentators suggest that Jesus was saying: "There is no Jacob in this one, for he walks in the godly way of Israel." What I believe Jesus was saying is this: *"This one has no secret agendas but desires in his heart to commune with God."*

Whence knowest thou me? Jesus answered and said unto him, Before that Philip called thee, when thou wast under the fig tree, I saw thee *(John 1:48 [KJV])*. The interpretation from this translation is they are just meeting for the first time and as such Jesus saw Nathanael for the first time. Nathanael was wondering how Jesus knew his thoughts. Jesus saw *(not with eyes)* Nathanael's heart and referred to the Scripture on which he had been meditating under the tree. This is an example of our disconnect with the context of what Jesus was talking about, yet Nathanael's response is one of understanding Jesus' words.

Nathanael answered and saith unto him, Rabbi, thou art the Son of God; thou art the King of Israel *(John 1:49 [KJV])*. Nathanael believed that Jesus had done something only God could do (not just saw him near a tree). We should notice that Nathanael exclaims: "**Thou art the Son of God.**" How would he know unless someone already told him? It's critical we notice this is the very beginning of Jesus' ministry. Nathanael was already aware of Jesus' reputation, and so this miracle solidified his conviction about Jesus' identity.

And he saith unto him, Verily, verily, I say unto you, Here after ye shall see heaven open, and the angels of God ascending and descending upon the son of man *(John 1:51 [KJV])*. In an article in the British Bible School, *[Nathanael: The Man Who Saw for Himself]* John Griffiths wrote that Nathanael had been meditating on Jacob when he'd been sitting under the tree. This last statement from Jesus clinched this interpretation for me. Jesus was referring to Genesis and Jacob's dream of a ladder, with angels ascending and descending (see *Genesis 28:10-22*) Jesus was telling Nathanael that he would actually see them doing the same on the Messiah, Who was standing before him.

The Calling of Matthew

And as Jesus passed forth from thence, he saw a man, named Matthew, sitting at the receipt of custom: and he saith unto him, Follow me. And he arose, and followed him *(Matthew 9:9 [KJV])*. There is no direct evidence that Matthew was related to Jesus, but considering the many links between them, it's very likely that he was. As we continue through the book, we will explore these connections that give additional purpose to Matthew's Gospel not commonly realized by believers today.

Matthew was a tax collector. He was also named Levi, after the patriarchal head of the priestly Levite tribe, and may have been related to John the Baptist (and, therefore, also to Mary and Jesus). His call followed the same pattern as the other disciples,' and some were related to or already knew Jesus.

The fact that he wrote about the wise men's' visit indicates that he may have been a relative of Jewish leaders who relayed the episode to Matthew.

However, rather than serving in the temple, he collected taxes for the Romans. He was excommunicated from the Jewish temple and most likely avoided by his family. Joseph's family shunned Jesus, so He understood what it was like. I picture Matthew not participating in any family events or going down to Jerusalem with the family every year. Then Jesus walks up to him with His first disciples and says, "Follow me." Matthew was most likely stunned at this expression of acceptance, especially if Jesus was a relative and family had returned to claim him. Matthew had lost hope. While John and Andrew prepared for Jesus' ministry by serving John the Baptist, Matthew became wealthy as a tax collector. Tax collectors were shunned by the Jewish leaders because they were competitors for what little money the working class had. The religious invented a system called money changing where they would convert Roman money into religious temple currency. It was a scam, and Jesus will overturn their (money conversion) tables and called them thieves for using God to rob people who sought the Lord (see *Matthew 21:12*). The Jewish leaders didn't like competitors, and as such they had them ostracized, and the people were told (such as relatives) to make a choice. God or the Tax collectors who betrayed Israel and God. Consequently, the family was expected to shun their Tax collector relative if they wanted to be able to participate in the Jewish Temple (see *Matthew 9:11*). Apparently, Jesus wasn't afraid of the Jewish leaders and came to get Matthew. Our God is not scared of this dark world; He comes for us all and says "Follow Me the Light of this World."

It's a much more compelling story when we see that Matthew was wealthy and estranged from his family and leaving that line of work implied a serious change of heart. When Jesus said, "Follow me," Matthew followed because he'd already heard from the family about the miraculous births of John the Baptist and Jesus. While we may judge the actions of others, God would rather that we show grace and understand that He can always do great things. Matthew was no doubt judged and ostracized, yet God used him and just one other apostle to write a Gospel. My subtitle of Matthew's Gospel would be: The Gospel of rejection and reconciliation. Bible expositors have missed the premise of his beautiful story, which we will explore later in the book. He lived it and felt its pain and looked for it throughout his Gospel. The Lord's grace does not value the judgment of the self-righteous, but rather, the heart that is open to doing His will.

Lay not up for yourselves treasures upon earth, where moth and rust doth corrupt, and where thieves break through and steal. But lay

up for yourselves treasures in heaven *(Matthew 6:19 [KJV])*. Appropriately, this instruction from Jesus is only found in Matthew.

He obeyed Jesus' challenge to the rich young ruler: **Sell all that thou hast** *(Matthew 20:21 [KJV])* because **with God all things are possible** *(Matthew 20:26 [KJV])*. It's my opinion that this happened a few years after Jesus was in Capernaum and his gift, along with others, helped support the apostles who left the fishing business entirely in Jesus last year of ministry.

God met his faith, and he would use his Gospel to bring many to Christ. Matthew was very meticulous about Jewish law. He knew of Jesus' Messianic qualifications, such as His birth in Bethlehem, and one of his purposes in writing was to show that Jesus fulfilled the Jewish law and the Messianic prophecies. For this reason, I believe his is the first Gospel written, a small debated issue that on the surface doesn't have great connotation. Seeing his purpose helped me unlock the resurrection events to where they are cohesive and are not contradictory as seminaries have taught.

Another key to connecting to this great Gospel is seeing that he saw the big picture. As such his Gospel gives us a general scope of the resurrection accounts which is by far the shortest of the climatic event even though his is the second longest Gospel in length. Furthermore, he gives us no details of Jesus' actual birth but again is general in scope. He gives us scrupulous details, such as Joseph's genealogy because they are needed to fulfill qualifications of the Messiah. He states plainly that he arrives later than Jesus' other disciples *(Matthew 4:23-24)* and then meticulously gives us things that he witnessed. Later in this book, I will show evidence regarding who Matthew's parents were and further linking the possibility that Matthew was a cousin to Jesus.

The Calling of James, Joses (Jude), their mother (Mary) and Cleopas (Alphaeus)

The Gospels did not record when Jesus called one other set of brothers, James and Joses (also known as Jude). They were very important, and we should note that their mother would stand by Jesus' mother: **Among which was Mary Magdalene, and Mary the mother of James and Joses, and the mother of Zebedee's children** *(Matthew 27:56 [KJV])*. The Gospel of Mark tells that she will go with Salome (sister of Jesus' mother, Mary) to the tomb and meet angels, who tell her that Jesus has risen. **Mary Magdalene, Mary mother of James, and Salome, had brought sweet spices, that they might come and anoint him** *(Mark 16:1 [KJV])*. These are the same women standing next to Jesus' mother at the cross. The mother of James and Joses was obviously in the inner circle, but her importance continues. The Gospel of John identifies her to be someone important. **Now there stood by the cross of Jesus his mother, and his mother's sister, Mary the wife of Cleopas** *(John: 3:19 [KJV])*. She is the wife of Cleopas, who, along with someone else, happens to be one of the first two men to witness Jesus' resurrection. We are so disconnected from the family story that Bible expositors don't know who that man is. The fact that Jesus chose him to appear to first should be a clue that he is paramount to the story in the Gospel.

These included Peter, and James and John, and Andrew, Philip, and Thomas, Bartholomew, and Matthew, James the son of Alphaeus, and Simon Zelotes, and James the brother of James *(Acts 1:13 [KJV])*. Cleopas is also referred to be Alphaeus, as in this verse. Knowing this fact helps us to enjoy the beautiful resurrection story.

Cleopas (Alphaeus) and his wife (Mary) are both witnesses to Jesus' resurrection. They have two sons who are apostles, giving us three sets of brothers. Three women are standing next to Mary, the mother of Jesus. Doesn't it stand to reason that we suspect they are related to Mary? Two of the ladies provide four sons to be apostles, and ultimately witness the resurrection of Jesus. One of their husbands is one of the first two men to see the resurrection. Let's take a look at the coincidence of how they named their children.

James and Joses

	Mary, Mother of Jesus	Mary, Wife of Cleopas	Salome (Mary's Sister)
First Born	James	James	James
Second Born	Joses	Joses	John

If we discount the fact that Jesus was born supernaturally and called by God, then James was Mary's natural firstborn; the child she named. We have examples of women naming sons in the Old Testament, beginning with Cain, whose mother was Eve (see *Genesis 4:1*), and Samuel, whose mother was Hannah (see *Samuel 1:20*). We should consider the mathematical probability of two ladies named Mary who were not related and yet gave their first two sons the same names. No doubt particular names were popular, but we shouldn't ignore a coincidence that may encourage our lives. We should ask ourselves: what did Jesus value? Faith in His deity is perhaps one answer, and those who had faith loved Him. Jesus honored that faith. In my opinion, these two women who raised four apostles have not been given their due. We have two sets of parents who led their sons to the Lord, which is why we don't hear of their personal conversion. Yes, Jesus called the apostles only because they were ready and prepared for the call because of their parents. God values parents who teach their children about the Lord. Our children are the greatest responsibility we have as believers, and God takes notice of it throughout the Bible. Ironically, Bible expositors don't see that the translations have led them to miss what is important. Families are important to God, which is why the Bible is full of Genealogies. Bible expositors and teachers need to rethink their teachings and see Jesus for the family man and the family-friendly God He is throughout the Gospels.

While we may become discouraged and have trials, we should find hope in the brokenness that Mary had with her children. God remembers her, and this book is about our first mission of family and surrendering to God's best, which is so far greater than our own.

Jesus' family story is twofold: On one hand, it's about one extended family and their mutual love for each other; and on the other, about division and how God uses it to bring us the greatest story of healing ever told.

The Calling of the Other Apostles

This leaves us with Judas Iscariot, Thomas, and the one identified by Luke as "Simon also called Zealot." All eleven apostles, except Judas Iscariot, were from Galilee, which was significant in Jesus' resurrection: **Ye men of Galilee, why stand ye gazing up into heaven? This same Jesus, which is taken up from you into heaven** *(Acts 1:11 [KJV])*. The Angels essentially told them, "Don't just stand there, knuckleheads. You've got work to do." There is some debate among Bible expositors of how many miracles Jesus performed and where they took place. I settle on thirty-six with eleven of them taking place in Capernaum, hence where I believe His eleven apostles had some connection.

Later in this book, we will discuss the fact that Judas Iscariot had come out of Jerusalem which contributed to the reasons he betrayed Jesus.

Mary Magdalene

Mary called Magdalene, out of whom went seven devils *(Luke 8:2 [KJV])*. The context of the healing that occurred here is debatable (will be explained later in resurrection chapter), but her importance isn't. She is the first person to witness His resurrection. Curiously, she is only mentioned in this verse and *Mark 16:9* before His resurrection, and then ten more times in the Gospels, for a total of twelve. However, little is known about her, and heretics have theorized that she was married to Jesus, thereby attacking the validity of His deity.

There will be four women at the cross, and three of them were named Mary. One was called Magdalene because of the extended family, for some reason, probably favored the name Mary, and for clarity, there were nicknames. It seems obvious that Mary, mother of the Lord, was held in very high esteem in her family: Blessed art thou among women *(Luke 1:42 [KJV])*. Because Elisabeth's (the wise mother of John the Baptist) testimony was believed among all the women of that family, some of them may have named their daughters after her. I suspect that Magdalene is the daughter of either Joanna, Susanna, Salome, or Mary the mother of James and Jose. I suspect the culture would accentuate first and have nicknames for the youngest. Interestingly, Jesus calls Mary, his mother, "Woman" in reference to Eve's original name by Adam. Then in the resurrection (see *John 20:15-16*), He first calls Magdalene "woman," then calls her "Mary."

She is with two other ladies standing by Jesus' mother, witnessing Jesus' last words. Very Holy moments witnessed by those who were an inner circle. It is without question that Magdalene loved Jesus, which is important, but she wasn't chosen because she had faith in Jesus' resurrection. She was distraught about Jesus' body being taken and not expecting to find a risen Lord. She was chosen because of the purity of her heart, and the enemies of the Gospel have portrayed her as Jesus' wife or a prostitute.

The fact is that seminaries down through the ages have missed the connections between Jesus' relatives because they never looked for them. For this very reason, I contend that believers have also missed connecting with the beautiful resurrection story.

And said, Verily I say unto you, Except ye be converted, and become as little children, ye shall not enter the kingdom of heaven *(Matthew 18:3 [KJV])*. I suspect that Magdalene was a contemporary of little John and stood next to her mom at the cross. She was tender and perhaps only twelve years old. John is the clue. I imagine that he is standing next to his mother, with Magdalene standing next to hers, also. They stand with that mother who has suffered the complete humiliation of a town and now the debauchery of the cross. To my way of thinking, Magdalene could not have been a contemporary of Jesus. The heretics say she was, and we should know that their aim is to pervert the truth: "**ungodly people who pervert the grace of God into sensuality and deny our Master and Lord Jesus Christ**" *(Jude 1:4 [ESV])*.

Magdalene, like others, arrives in Scripture, and yet we are not told of her conversion. As I mentioned previously, this is because they already believed in Jesus because of the witness of Mary's family. God would want us to see parents leading their children to the Lord, and see their example, to encourage us. Magdalene was healed because of faith, and Jesus clearly had mercy on Mary's family. I don't know when it happened, but I believe that Mary, Jesus' mother, knew He could do anything and witnessed many miracles before He turned the water into wine at the wedding of Cana. John says, in his Gospel, that Jesus did many more things (see *John 21:25*), and it's my contention He had done some of them before the Gospel writers witnessed them. Love in the family is our real treasure, and God will bless it. If we can't love our own family, how can we love the family of God?

Later in the resurrection story, in this book, I will reveal whose mother I believe her to be.

Joanna, Susanna, and Others

When we understand that Luke's Gospel is really, to some extent, Mary's (mother of Jesus) Gospel, it connects us to clues. Luke is telling us that certain women supplied all the needs of Jesus and his apostles, which meant that they traveled with them and cooked for them, etc. God no doubt believes they're important. **And Joanna the wife of Chuza Herod's steward, and Susanna, and many others ministered unto him of their substance** *(Luke 8:3 [KJV])*. Joanna plays a part in the resurrection story, and it's my belief the women who are named by Scripture because they witnessed much of what we have in the Gospels. Joanna's husband is a talented man, as Herod's steward. We should suspect that he probably gives us Jesus' encounter with Herod, coincidentally only found in Luke's Gospel. Before this, he may have known someone in the household who witnessed the wise men's visit with Herod.

CHAPTER **13**

A Divided Family

God is in union with Himself, and as such willed, the divided earthly families be reunited with His Heavenly family. He left His throne above the stars and restrained Himself in humanity. **And the Word was made flesh, and dwelt among us (and we beheld his glory, the glory as of the only-begotten of the Father), full of grace and truth** *(John 1:14 [KJV])*. God used His blood from the cross to redeem the families of this earth and to be whole (Holy) with His eternal family. Inexplicably, Christians don't know that Jesus chose His earthly blood-family to propagate the Gospel to all families of man.

Most believers are completely unaware that Jesus spent most of His time with a few exceptions in a small area because that's where His earthly family resided. When Jesus left Galilee, He always traveled with His relatives to attend the feasts in Jerusalem. This should give us further insight that Jesus' movements involved family.

Jesus didn't visit every town in Israel or even go, to all the twelve tribe's territorial borders. He didn't go knocking on stranger's doors demanding they listen to Him. He patiently built the faith of His family to trust in Him and leave their occupations. In the interim, He limited Himself to that which they (His human family) allowed Him to work His message to the local people. There is quite a book in just that but suffice to say, it's the same with us today. Our lack of faith limits Him and His power in our lives. He is not a control freak, and He will not push Himself on to us. We may invent a religion and pray how we want things to go in this life but what He wants is our trust in His purpose. None of us have faith that is worthy of Him, and as such His mercy will provide grace to be sufficient for our lack of trust. Out of the depth of His mercy, He alone creates a purpose for our lives. Every day violent acts or atrocities are committed by human beings that reject life. We may mourn these tragedies of hate and chaos, but believers should understand that if it were not for His omnipotent merciful hand, hate would overcome humanity in an instant on this planet.

God is patient, whereas we naturally would like to see quick resolution on many things in our own lives and this world. Jesus' life revolved around His family, and teachers of the Bible have ignored this. Consequently, Christians are unaware how meek and patient God was in Jesus. The next series of events are of great importance to understand the dynamics of Jesus' household. The wedding of Cana has been empathized as Jesus' first miracle and has been well studied over the centuries but the other events involving Jesus' household have been much less scrutinized. When we understand the home is essential to Jesus, we will come up with a much deeper connection to the events that have a great teaching to our family dynamics today.

Family Movements

I believe it's likely that Jesus and His first six disciples—family or close friends of family—worked in a type of rhythm. The disciples might fish at night and then take a day or two off and come with Jesus as He visited towns around the Sea of Galilee. I envision them leaving Friday morning and getting to some town where Jesus would preach on the Sabbath. When we comprehend that Jesus went to Jerusalem twice a year—for the Feast of Tabernacles which commemorated His birth, and Passover, which commemorated His death—we can understand that the Gospel writers are telling us about special trips. **And the Jews' Passover was at hand, and Jesus went up to Jerusalem** *(John 2:13 [KJV])*. John tells us that Jesus attended Passover before crossing paths with John the Baptist again. It's my view that John's Gospel describes two Jewish festivals before other Gospels begin to give us Jesus' ministry.

Cana

And the third day there was a marriage in Cana of Galilee, and the mother of Jesus was there. And both Jesus was called, and his disciples, to the marriage *(John 2:1-2 [KJV])*. Many commentators interpret the wedding background (please read *John 2:1-11*) of Jesus' first miracle, as underscoring the importance of marriage which He, the Creator, invented. Furthermore, marriage reveals much about the eternal relationship between Christ and His bride, the Church. While the importance of this marriage teaching is unquestionable, this interpretation, as many about Jesus, ignores the importance of the household dynamic between Jesus, Mary, His siblings, His disciples, and Cana. Many of our teachings such as this do indeed reflect upon the goodness God would have us consider, but they completely miss critical junctures of Jesus' life. Consequently, believers are disconnected to these events and how they relate to Jesus and His family.

Some things in this wedding account should get our attention, such as, why was Mary there? The same reason why Jesus and His disciples were there: because Mary and her sister were originally from Cana and had relatives there. Why were the disciples called (invited)? They are related to the either the bride or groom. This was a family wedding that all of them were expected to attend and, as such, the disciples were related to them, too.

And the third day there was a marriage *(John 2:1 [KJV])*. It's debated what John meant here, but it makes sense that it was the third day of the feast. And they ran out of wine. I bring this up because confusion with the syntax here has caused misunderstandings of Scripture for us that the contemporaries of this Jewish culture would have easily grasped. For one thing, they would have understood that this is a member of Jesus' family that got married.

And when they wanted wine, the mother of Jesus saith unto him, They have no wine. Jesus saith unto her, Woman, what have I to do with thee? Mine hour is not yet come (*John 2:3-4 [KJV]*). Two things should leap out at us on this verse. One is Mary has a need and two she expects Jesus to do something about it. The fact that Mary will ask Jesus to provide should give us pause to consider this is His younger sibling's wedding. Jesus replies that His "hour" or time for removing Mary's (family) disgrace in Nazareth had not yet come. Jesus didn't want to perform a miracle just to make His siblings accept Him and Mary when they should have done so without such a demonstration. Jesus was not a people pleaser, but a God pleaser. But Mary was not taking "no" for an answer and proceeded to act in faith. **His mother saith unto the servants, Whatsoever he saith unto you, do it** (*John 2:5 [KJV]*). This verse has some bombshells and reveals a great deal which I haven't heard commentators discuss. Evidently, Mary expected Jesus to obey His mother and perform a miracle, which begs the next question. If this is the first miracle done by Jesus and He never performed one before, why does Mary expect Him to oblige her? The next thing we should notice is Mary directing the servants. Why does she take upon herself to give orders to the servants of the wedding? We should strongly suspect she is the mother of a member of the bridal party. Believers have missed a great deal for not being taught this, and there is a book in it by itself. Mary's confidence demonstrates that Jesus had performed miracles before in her presence—maybe even to help His poor family at a previous wedding for one of His siblings. And now He did so again to honor His mother.

If believers want to know how Jesus conducted Himself at social functions, all they have to do is read *Luke 14:10*. Jesus took the lowest seat and with Joseph's family that was all right with them. Our God is humble, and one side of His family took full advantage of His graciousness in their treatment of Him. Our term would be that Jesus got pushed around, but unlike many of us, it didn't haunt Him. I believe it was His will to provide for His siblings until they came of age and were married. He was driven out of Nazareth earlier by His siblings, and He apparently accommodated them because James assumed the head of the family in the community. What is my basis for this reasoning? Several, but regarding this episode, if we understand Mary felt responsible for the family reputation at this wedding we should surmise this was her child. Next, we should notice that there is incompetence because they run out of wine which was a big deal to Mary. The incompetence was caused by His brothers, not by Jesus. Now Mary knows this, and she comes to Him and asks Him to bail them out. He is resistant but respects His mother through His entire life. If Jesus was treated with the respect that was due to His head of the family, then we should know He would have done a better job managing a wedding. He wasn't! His brothers took the head of the household away from Him and what does he do? I don't know about the readers but I have been stuck between a rock and a hard place many times. It's as if either choice is wrong and I find it fascinating that a few times scripture highlights Jesus was there too. He won't demonstrate to His siblings He is God and at the same time He respects His mother. He graciously supplies the need and let's look at what happens with the light of glorying His personhood.

When the ruler of the feast had tasted the water that was made of wine, and knew not whence it was: (but the servants which drew the water knew;)the governor of the feast called the bridegroom *(John 2:9 [KJV])*.The bridegroom is most like Jesus' youngest brother Simon, and he is honored publically. My suspicion is the Governor of the feast is Mary's relative who hosted the event. When John makes a point to communicate that the servants knew, He is telling us everyone else (besides His disciples and Mary) was unconscious to Jesus performing the miracle. Jesus doesn't humiliate His brothers and say: "*I did it*." He graciously lets them have their hour even though they despise Him. When John says: "*This is beginning of miracles did Jesus in Cana of Galilee,*" he is not telling us this is the miracle Jesus first performed. John in the conclusion of his Gospel makes a point that Jesus did many miracles, and he doesn't tell us about all of them. The Gospel of John is about connecting the dots to what story he is telling us.

When John further says "*Jesus manifested forth his glory*" he expects us to be clued in on the fact of the incredible grace Jesus shows His family. Not for us to wonder if Jesus made real wine but for us to consider the God of wonder is more humble than any of us. No matter how horrible the treatment He received, He could never change from being what He is, Goodness and Love. That even though he was the Creator, He was usually shown by His contemporaries the back of the room. He was maligned and blessed them anyway because the God of creation had but one purpose, He loved them until the end. Believers do not know His entire story, which is why they haven't connected the whole meaning of: *"Father, forgive them; for they know not what they do"* (Luke 23:34). This wasn't the first time He prayed that prayer, nor was it the last. He prays it every day for us all.

Continuing the Celebration

After this, he went down to Capernaum, he, and his mother, and his brethren, and his disciples: and they continued there not many days *(John 2:12 [KJV])*. The key words here are "his brethren." Jesus' brothers were at Cana and now will be traveling with Jesus and His mother to Capernaum. John is telling us that it didn't take long for them to go to Capernaum, which is in a different direction than Nazareth. It is where Zebedee lives, and Jesus' entire family is going to visit and needs a place to stay. We connect to this family story when we see that Salome is Zebedee's wife and Mary's sister.

Jesus was in Capernaum, had called six disciples, went to Cana, and is now returning. Before we continue the story, I'm going to make a forward detour to underscore how well received Jesus was in Capernaum. We're going to fast-forward perhaps a year.

So Jesus came again into Cana of Galilee, where he made the water wine. And there was a certain nobleman, whose son was sick at Capernaum *(John 4:46 [KJV])*. Jesus went through other towns, including Cana, on His way back to Capernaum. I suspect that it was a meeting place where Mary would bring her children from Nazareth and Salome, her younger sister, would bring hers from Capernaum. They would travel together to Jerusalem and pick up the family along the way. On the return route, they would stop at Cana. The nobleman referred to in *John 4:46* obviously knew of Jesus' ability to heal, but he also knew Jesus' customary movements, as he couldn't wait for Jesus to come all the way back home. We should understand that he knew of Jesus' relatives and that he would find Jesus at Cana, so he begged for Jesus' help. Jesus healed the man's son via long distance. **This is again the second miracle that Jesus did when he was come out of Judea into Galilee** *(John 4:54 [KJV])*. John wrote to primarily Jewish believers, and he and they both understood the culture of the time. They would have understood the importance of the feast. This is Jesus' return trip after attending this particular feast (Passover) the second time. He is with His disciples in Cana and is coming back from Jerusalem. This is not Jesus performing His second miracle, but the second time He performed a miracle in Cana. By this time, Jesus had performed many miracles, or in the first place, the nobleman wouldn't have been looking for Him to heal his son in Capernaum.

The Return to Nazareth

John doesn't tell us about Jesus' return to Nazareth because it can be found in the Gospel of Luke, whom we know relied on Mary's witness to Jesus' birth. **And he came to Nazareth, where he had been brought up: and, as his custom was, he went into the synagogue on the sabbath day, and stood up for to read** *(Luke 4:16 [KJV])*. After the wedding, we were told by John that Jesus' mother and brothers stayed with Him in Capernaum. Jesus' brothers witnessed how well received He was, and (my suspicion) invited Him to return Nazareth. We are given many examples in the Gospels where Jesus complies with requests. It is fundamental to understanding how he worked then and in our lives today. Through the graciousness of prayer, He moves instead of pushing Himself on others. When Jesus was asked to leave some towns, He left, and when He was requested to stay, He stayed. Thus, Jesus returned with His family to Nazareth because His family asked Him to.

And there was delivered unto him the book of the prophet Esaias *(Luke 4:17 [KJV])*. It's critical that we see Jesus was handed the scroll for the first time. He did not go and take the synagogue's copy of Isaiah by His own accord at any time in His life. This is His first teaching in Nazareth because after He read and shared His shocking interpretation (applying the prophecy to Himself), they tried to kill Him. If Jesus had taught before, we wouldn't have this reaction, and for the reasons stated earlier in the book, the scroll was never given to Him because He was considered illegitimate. I wish believers would pause and consider the greatness of His power and yet the grace of His humility and meekness. That for several years He sat patiently in that synagogue that looked down upon Him and never shared because they never asked. We should consider His meekness before we throw verses to convict others. We should consider if that judgment weren't strange work (*Isaiah 28:21*) to Him we wouldn't exist. That He is The God of mercy, not condemnation and the truth that only He can pay the price for our eternal perfection.

Let's not forget that the townsfolk of the synagogue would likely have included many members from Joseph's side of Jesus' family.

And all bare witness, and wondered at the gracious words which proceedeth out of his mouth. And they said, Is not this Joseph's son? *(Luke 4:22 [KJV])*. I picture Mary hoping that finally her disgrace will be removed, now that Nazareth can hear Jesus' authoritative teaching and see His miracles. But the declaration "Joseph's son" would have stirred up the old rumor that Jesus was born of fornication, which would, in part, explain the hostile reaction.

And he said unto them; Ye will surely say unto me this proverb, Physician heal thyself: whatsoever we have heard done in Capernaum, do also here in thy country *(Luke 4:23 [KJV])*. Jesus knew that Nazareth had heard about the miracles He'd performed elsewhere, but their insulting response prompted Him to say, in effect, "You're demanding I prove to you that I am not illegitimate, but the Son of God." **Verily I say unto you, No prophet is accepted in thy country** *(Luke 4:24 [KJV])*. Jesus reminds them of the whole sequence of prophets who had been rejected through the centuries. As such, Jesus didn't take rejection or anything personally, and we should note He speaks mostly of His deity in the third person.

And rose up, and thrust him out of the city, and led him unto the brow of the hill whereon their city was built, that they might cast down headlong *(Luke 4:29 [KJV]).* They were going to prove once and for all that Jesus wasn't the Son of God. **But he passing through the midst of them went his way** *(Luke 4:30 [KJV]).* Jesus could have escaped at the beginning, but He stayed long enough—enduring humiliation and rejection—to let these people show what was always in their heart towards Him. The event is recorded, for our benefit, as a warning. God exposes that which is in the deepness of our hearts. We can profess words, but our heart shows us for what we truly are.

Jesus' brothers did nothing. Instead of rising and defending their mother and brother, they chose to be invisible. This was a test of His brothers, not just of Nazareth. His brothers heard of His miracles and saw how well He was received in Capernaum. They even invited Him to Nazareth in hopes that He might win back their family's dignity.

Siblings may fight among themselves, but they also are naturally protective of each other. Jesus had four brothers, and they did nothing because of fear of being associated with Jesus. They resisted God's call and wanted their lives to be expedient. Jesus wanted His brothers to follow Him because of His deity, not because they could ride His coattails and make life easier for Him.

The moment of truth had come. Do they stand with their mother and believe her story and the miracles Jesus had performed, or do they try not to inflame a bad situation and stay invisible? God will wipe out their illusion of His will, as He does for many believers who trust in their perceptions. For love is in unity with the eternal truth but our opinions, like this divided world, will end in a blink of an eye.

They hoped that Jesus would be accepted and their family honor would finally be realized in Nazareth.

A nightmare occurred, and their personal hopes were dashed. They wanted nothing to do with the losing side. This event caused an irrevocable break within Jesus' family. We don't need a Scripture to know how Mary felt. Her sons' inaction was a decision showing disbelief and disrespect for her integrity.

What we should see is the graciousness of God. That He knew what was going to happen and went anyway. God has all power, and He can do what the least in our societies of this world cannot do. Walk in humility and have no will (desire for power) to use power over another creation. God is a creator because love creates but this world thirsts for power over His creations.

I really wish Christians would get this lesson and know who He is and who we are suppose to be. Little lambs who hear His voice and have no fear of the world of wolves that desire to bite. His lambs hear His voice and know there is nothing to dread from being bitten because the bite of the wolves has no power over them.

Mary Leaves Nazareth

Previously, Jesus' family had always traveled to Jerusalem together. After this, Jesus didn't go with His brothers, but with His disciples, to Jerusalem (see *John 7:3-8*). Their last family reunion occurs (see *Matthew 12:47-50*) when Jesus is in Jerusalem, and He is contending with the Pharisees. Jesus is told that His mother and brethren wish to speak to Him. Connecting the event to Nazareth, it's not hard to imagine why. Mary held Jesus to be the head of the family, and Joseph's sons held James to be the chairman of the household.

Jesus will turn and point to His disciples and say, **Behold my mother and my brethren!** *(Matthew 12:49 [KJV]).* We have no visual aids in these verses, and as such, it is believed the family is standing away in the distance from Jesus and His disciples near Him. **For whosoever shall do the will of my Father which is in heaven, the same is my brother, and sister, and mother** *(Matthew 12:50 [KJV]).* Understandably most Bible expositors seize upon the truth that Jesus is teaching that whoever does the will of His Father is actually family to Him. This view is true indeed, but I also understand every day I am never in His perfect will yet I am still in the family of God through Jesus. There is a missing element that has always grieved me because it gives a mental impression that there is a break with Jesus and His mother, Mary and that His household was not important. It creates the impression one can abandon blood relatives that are not believers in the service of doing God's will. It also is ignorant of the fact that at least two of His disciples came from His mother's sister.

My view of the event, like many of my interpretations in this book, is quite different. It's based on many things which I will list only a few.

1) Mary never doubted Jesus as we will later see that she is in front of him at the cross.

2) Luke makes it clear there isn't one lady whom Jesus held more dearly than her. When God says "Blessed art thou among women," He means just that.

3) God had a high opinion of motherhood in general throughout the Bible.

4) That God is not the author of confusion and speaks straight manner without innuendos (Shaming).

Given that, my visualization is quite different from what is customarily believed. I see Mary in the middle, on Jesus' left His siblings (Judah), on His right His disciples who are mostly family (Levite). Mary, as well as Jesus, came from two tribes (Judah and Levite). When Jesus says "Behold my mother," He means just that. He is looking right at her, and when He says, "my brethren," He is looking at His siblings who come from the tribe of Judah. Then He turns and points to His disciples who are standing to His right and who come from the tribe of Levi.

What we need to keep in mind is what the family story in the Bible is from the beginning. Cain murders the first brother born, and his seed rejected God's forgiveness, which was then destroyed by God. Later Joseph, the son of Jacob, was sold into slavery to Egypt by his brothers. Ten of Joseph's siblings were half brothers that hated him (some wanted to kill him) and one full brother who didn't. The story isn't about Joseph; it's about what God does (salvation), and He redeems a godless divided family using one family member (Joseph). Highlighting for us to consider that Cain's family had no Godly member for God to use to save them. Then God raised up a king named David and after two generations the twelve tribes again split against themselves with ten against two. For one brother tribe remained loyal to a sibling tribe. From the seeds of two tribes (Judah and Levi) comes Mary, her son Jesus and at least six siblings (I settle on six plus Jesus is seven which becomes significant later). Her (divided) family is godless (the siblings of Jesus), and they oppose another brother (Jesus) and Joseph (by not honoring Mary), who coincidently had a father named Jacob (please see *Matthew 1:16*). They are rebelling against God by not honoring their mother. Jesus will save them with His grace as He saved the other Joseph's family in Genesis. They will come face to face with royalty (see *Genesis 45:4-5*) and see they hated Him, but He has mercy and saves them regardless.

All flesh come from two tribes (Adam and Eve). God chose the tribe of Eve to be born in order to reconcile all tribes of the flesh (Adam and Eve). Israel has twelve tribes which signify six tribes for Adam and Eve. God gave them an extra tribe as He gave the week an extra day (Sabbath). God commanded that the tribe of Levi not be counted and God who is infinite can't be counted. Christians all come from the flesh but through faith (Jesus Christ) are reconciled to tribe of God (Levites who are a symbol of all believers in Christ). The Apostle Paul spoke (see *Romans 7:4-25*) of the two warring parts that all believers are divided within themselves. Jesus' purpose is that we all become one in Him and one family of God (*John 17:21*).

His early disciples came from His mother's family (Levites), and they thought He was the Messiah. They envisioned a different outcome than Jesus going to the cross. When Jesus taught, His teachings were always towards awakening His disciples, so it is here, like other times before He is pointing out that doing the will of God had nothing to do with them being blood-related to Him. That the left and the right side of Mary were both related, but only one side was open to serving God (Levites). What God would want us to know, is He loved both sides as He does with all families today. He wants His believers to be as He is and love His and their family to the end. Jesus illustrates the example of detachment believers can learn from. Jesus didn't beg His brothers to love Him; they didn't and instead cast Him out. He accepted that and moved on with His purpose without bitterness towards them.

We will later see in the writings of James (His sibling), Peter (possibly brother to His uncle) and John (His cousin). None of them spoke (familiar tone) of Jesus being blood-related because He had become their savior and God.

This confrontation leads to the final break in the family, and it's my assumption that after this conversation, Jesus instructed Mary to live with her sister, Salome. This assumption is based on the fact that Mary was with Jesus' brothers, attending the feast, but after the discord in the family, she attends the feasts with Jesus and her family, who supports Him.

Jesus' Brothers Reject Him

We should understand that Jesus' brothers felt they had good reasons to be afraid of His enemies. **After these things Jesus walked in Galilee: for he would not walk in Jewry, because the Jews sought to kill him** *(John 7:1 [KJV])*. John tells us point blank that the Jews want Jesus dead before he relates this meeting with Jesus and his brothers. I assume John tells us things for a reason and, uniquely, from other Gospels, tells us about this family confrontation. The brothers were acutely aware that Nazareth and Jerusalem wanted Jesus dead. **For there is no man that doeth anything in secret, and he himself seeketh to be known openly. If thou do these things, shew thyself to the world** *(John 7:4 [KJV])*. We should note that Jesus was first born and, as such, His brothers should have been subject to Him. Nazareth was a horrible environment, and Jesus' brothers felt that their problems would go away with His death. Jesus' brothers accused Him of hiding when He should have been going to Jerusalem for the feast. In a sense they accused Him of being afraid and yet it was they who were afraid of His enemies. They knew the Jews sought to kill Jesus, but they appeared to show no concern for His safety. They apparently attempted to use some of Jesus' words against

Him. Their challenge was an insult, especially since Joseph was dead and Jesus was head of the family. In their eyes, a bastard should not have the rights of the firstborn son. As far as the brothers were concerned, James was the firstborn of Joseph, and Jesus had no part in their inheritance or privileges. Thus, we can infer that they were all against Him, and spoke against Him to each other. **For neither did his brethren believe in him** *(John 7:5 [KJV])*. John can't be any more point blank that His brothers don't believe in Him. Despite their attitudes, however, Jesus loved them.

Then Jesus said unto them, My time is not yet come: but your time is always ready. The world cannot hate you; but me it hateth, because I testify of it, that the works thereof are evil *(John 7:6 [KJV])*. Jesus meant that it was not yet His time to die. **Now the Jews' feast of tabernacles was at hand** *(John 7:2 [KJV])*. This conversation most likely occurred six months before the Cross because the Feast of Tabernacles (Jesus' Birth) occurred in September or October. Jesus' brothers suffered a horrible burden: The world hated them. Jesus' grace pointed out that the hatred was aimed at Him alone. The world hates us because of Jesus and His truth (for He is the Truth). He tells us not to take it personally because whatever anyone does to us they do to him (see *Matthew 25:40)*.

Jesus knew better than to trust His brothers at this time (see *John 7:8-11*). We should note that the Jews ask where Jesus is. *We should understand they are asking His brothers.* Jesus traveled with His family and the Jews knew that. When He eventually did go to Jerusalem and started preaching openly, we can imagine that His brothers were at a loss for words. If Jesus told them anything, they might have informed His enemies in His town, who were in communication with His enemies in Jerusalem.

The Family Who Came to Jesus

At the cross Jesus charges little John, who is standing right beside his mother (Salome), with taking care of Mary (the mother of Jesus). After the break in the family, Mary is already living in the home of her sister, the mother of John, and he will take charge of her in place of Jesus. It should be clear to us that Jesus wouldn't have done this unless His brothers completely disrespected His mother. It was their responsibility, but Jesus mercifully doesn't send Mary back to Nazareth, where she was despised.

Seeing the blessing of the story requires us to see the reality of Jesus' rejection by His brothers, and then we can enjoy the thrill of their redemption. Mary gave us her witness at the beginning of the Gospel of Luke, but she is not with Jesus at the beginning of His ministry in Capernaum. John provides us with this detail, and it's my assumption that Mary is with the other women who support Jesus in His last year of ministry. She, along with Salome, her sister, and others, help support the apostles after they leave their vocations and dedicate themselves full time to Jesus. How do I know? If Mary wasn't with Jesus and His apostles, then why would He give John charge over her after His death? If James, Jesus' half-brother, had already stepped up and taken charge of her, Jesus wouldn't be asking John to be responsible for her.

CHAPTER 14

Judas' Father

Certain events occur in all four Gospels, for which God provides different witnesses for our better understanding. We should look at these developments with the mindset of how they complement each other to give us a clearer picture, not as some seminaries have done, looking for contradictions.

The betrayal of Jesus is a more dastardly event than what believers have been told. Judas' betrayal and Mary's (Lazarus' sister) anointing of Jesus before His burial are linked, in the four Gospels. This Mary knew Jesus was going to die, and it should be noted that she performs this loving act right in front of those who hate Him and plan to betray Him.

> Verily I say unto you, Wheresoever this gospel shall be preached in the whole world, there shall also this, that this woman hath done, be told for a memorial of her *(Matthew 26:13 [KJV])*.

Jesus is rather point blank that her action would be mentioned in every Gospel to honor what she did, for it shows the contrast of one who loved Him and those who hated Him. I noted in my studies that Jesus often uttered the word "verily," which means, "You can count on it." Consequently, it makes sense for us to assume that it is indeed, and look for it in all four Gospels. Bible expositors are rather dogmatic in an opposite opinion, based on the fact that they believe Luke's account occurred in Capernaum. Matthew, Mark, and John tell us point blank that it's in Bethany, just before Jesus' crucifixion. Adding to the confusion is the disagreement about who the woman is and how many women did the same thing. There are four Gospels for a reason, and we need to put them together to see who Judas' father is; and when we do, we see the motivation for why he betrays Jesus.

Then assembled together the chief priests, and the scribes, and the elders of the people, unto the palace of the high priest *(Matthew 26:3 [KJV])*. Everyone—every religious person in the know—met together about the problem of Jesus. This was not the first time. Jesus had been a thorn in their side for a few years. The Gospel stories in the movies neglect to show that He had many enemies who wanted Him dead for some time but feared the people. The Jewish leaders will hypocritically declare to Pilate that they were under the Roman law, and, hence, needed them to execute Jesus. Interestingly, even today, Bible expositors have accepted their lies. Clearly, in the book of Acts with the stoning of Stephen and their plans to kill Paul, they demonstrate that they didn't need the Romans to kill anyone. The Jewish leaders used the Romans for cover from the possible blow-back from the people.

And consulted that they might take Jesus by subtly, and kill him *(Matthew 26:4 [KJV])*. Matthew can't be any clearer: They want Jesus dead, and with their (perceived) clever minds, plan in the shadows to fool Jesus and the people. **But they said, Not on the feast day; lest there be an uproar among the people** *(Matthew 26:4-5 [KJV])*. They have their timetable and apparently came up with a plan to fulfill it without fear of reprisal from the people. Their plans were all frustrated, though, as God chose His own method for Jesus' death which, ironically, was much worse than what His enemies would have chosen.

Now when Jesus was in Bethany, in the house of Simon the leper *(Matthew 26:6 [KJV])*. We should note that Jesus is in Simon's house and a very important detail has been overlooked by Bible expositors and the movies of this event. Simon was a leper, but, of course, he wasn't when he was having dinner with people before Passover. There is only one person born who could have healed him. We would naturally think he loves Jesus and is grateful to Him.

One line from the movie *The Godfather* goes, "Keep your friends close and your enemies closer." Matthew's previous context may be alerting us that Simon is one of the conspirators. **Then Jesus six days before the Passover came to Bethany** *(John 12:1 [KJV])*. The Jewish Passover celebration continues for seven days. This incident occurred six days before Jesus was betrayed and seven days before he was crucified.

There they made him a supper; and Martha served: but Lazarus was one of them that sat at the table *(John 12:2 [KJV])*. Bible expositors assume that the event happens in Lazarus' house because of this verse in John. However, Matthew tells us point blank that it's in Simon the Leper's house. John even tells us why he is telling us that Lazarus is in attendance: **Much people of the Jews therefore knew that he was there: and they came not for Jesus' sake only, but that they might see Lazarus also, whom he raised from the dead** *(John 12:9 [KJV])*. What if the betrayal of Jesus was an important event to John, and he gives us more information to understand the conspiracy? What if John expects us to figure out that Simon isn't a good guy? Maybe he was in on the plot to kill both Jesus and Lazarus. Clinching this view is John's next verse: **But the chief priests consulted that they might put Lazarus also to death** *(John 12:10 [KJV])*. They want them both dead, and John couldn't make it clearer that Simon's intentions are not devout. He expects us to know this from the previous accounts in the Gospels already.

And being in Bethany in the house of Simon the leper, as he sat at meat, there came a woman having an alabaster box of ointment of spikenard very precious; and she brake the box, and poured it on his head *(Mark 14:3 [KJV])*. Mark's version of the event has the woman breaking the box and pouring its contents on his head. John's account has Mary anointing Jesus' feet. This discrepancy makes Bible expositors believe that these are different women. What if John knew Mark's account and is giving us more information; that Mary (Lazarus' sister) is anointing Jesus' feet in addition to His head?

She hath done what she could: she is come beforehand to anoint my body to the burying *(Mark 14:8 [KJV])*. She is clearly the same woman as in Matthew's account. Jesus told His apostles on the second day of the feast that He was going to die. Now He told them that Mary (Lazarus' sister) had anointed His body for death. Jesus' body would not be anointed immediately after His crucifixion because there isn't time before the Sabbath begins. That's why the women came to the grave on Sunday.

John tells us an important connection to the story. **Then saith one of his disciples, Judas Iscariot, Simon's son, which should betray him** *(John 12:4 [KJV])*. Simon the leper was Judas' father and that both father and son were insulted because of the grace shown to Jesus and the grace Jesus showed to this woman in their home. John will even say it again, so we can't miss the fact that Simon is Judas' father. **And when he had dipped the sop, he gave it to Judas Iscariot, the son of Simon** *(John 13:26 [KJV])*. We should understand that the story of Jesus' betrayal was important to John and he communicates it as simply as he can, which would have been understood by the early believers. **Why was not this ointment sold for three hundred pence, and given to the poor** *(John 12:5 [KJV])*? John tells us that Judas was good with numbers and knew the value of Mary's sacrifice. **This he said, not that he cared for the poor; but because he was a thief, and had the bag, and bare what was put therein** *(John 12:6 [KJV])*. John informs us that Judas' motives were to steal the money, as treasurer.

And Judas Iscariot, one of the twelve, went unto the chief priests, to betray him unto them *(Mark 14:10 [KJV])*. After this event, Judas will visit the chief priests.

The betrayal is even much worse when we consider the fact that Simon was a leper healed by Jesus. In the continuum of the story, sins against Jesus will escalate. Luke's version is deemed to be a separate event but, as stated before, let's assume that it's not. There is only one woman who anoints Jesus before His death, and He said she is in every Gospel. Luke gives us some information that puts the whole betrayal story together for us and explains that John is giving us certain information, including the identity of Judas' father.

Behold, a woman in the city, which was a sinner, when she knew that Jesus sat at meat in the Pharisee's house, brought an alabaster

box of ointment *(Luke 7:37 [KJV])*. This means that Judas' father was a Pharisee. As we go through the narrative, we come to understand why betraying Jesus was paramount to him. His house is located in Bethany, just two miles from Jerusalem. Jesus' apostles were from Galilee, except Judas, who betrayed Him. Judas was from this Jerusalem suburb.

And stood at his feet behind him weeping and began to wash his feet with tears, and did wipe them with the hairs of her head, and kissed his feet, and anointed them with the ointment *(Luke 7:38 [KJV])*. Mary knew that Jesus was going to be martyred, and she loved him. Jesus comforted and defended her: **Now when the Pharisee which had bidden him saw it, he spake within himself, saying, This man, if he were a prophet, would have known who and what manner of woman this is that touched him: for she is a sinner** *(Luke 7:39 [KJV])*. It is my guess that Mary was the woman taken in the act of adultery to trap Jesus. In any event, Simon knows who the woman is. What should be evident to us is that Jesus knows the woman, and it's not an acquaintance doing this so that he will forgive her. Simon judges Jesus, and for what purpose? To justify betraying him. In his conscience, he is questioning if Jesus was a prophet because He healed him when he was a leper. He is rationalizing the healing to come from some other reason than Jesus being God's Son.

And Jesus answering said unto him, Simon, I have somewhat to say unto thee. And he saith Master say on *(Luke 7:40 [KJV])*. "Master" was a term of respect, but Simon didn't call Jesus "Lord." The Pharisee was blind to the grace of God. Even though Jesus healed him, Simon has no gratitude, **And he turned to the woman and said unto Simon, Seest thou gavest me no water for my feet: but she hath washed my feet with tears, and wiped them with the hairs of her head** *(Luke 7:44 [KJV])*. In *"Through the Bible" [MATTHEW Through ROMANS]* J. Vernon McGee stated in his commentary on the Gospel of Luke that Simon didn't offer Jesus the common courtesy of the day, a clue that not only did Simon not respect Jesus but also that he was a spy. However, McGee did not equate this event in Luke with the same occurrence that occurred in Matthew, Mark, and John.

Thou gavest me no kiss: but this woman since the time I came in hath not ceased to kiss my feet. My head with oil thou didst not anoint: but this woman hath anointed my feet with ointment (*Luke 7:45-46 [KJV]*). She anointed the lowest of his personhood. That's when Jesus told Simon a parable about forgiveness and love. What escaped Simon in all of this was that he needed to be forgiven by the one who could forgive and could pay the debt for his sins. **Wherefore I say unto thee, Her sins, which are many, are forgiven; for she loved much: but to whom little is forgiven, the same loveth little** (*Luke 7:47 [KJV]*).

Jesus is the truth, so He doesn't deny Mary's sins were many, but religious hypocrites are ignorant that this speaks of them too. Judging hates grace because it's the enemy of its arrogance, which justifies its own self-importance. God is perfect; consequently He doesn't get all that excited that He can spot an imperfection. Imperfections desire to be perfect in their imaginations and therefore get really excited (glory in themselves) when they spot the imperfections of others. Bible expositors disagree that this story is the same occurrence because of the woman's reputation. They believe this occurred in Capernaum, and there could be many Pharisees named Simon. We should note that Luke omits her name (Mary) for this very reason, in this account. It shows Jesus' grace to her by not making her sins public, which were forgiven by the Lord. Luke's Gospel is not chronological and does not primarily tell us where the event took place.

What should stand out to us is Judas' first action upon meeting Jesus face to face when he betrays Him. *Luke 22:48 [KJV]*: **But Jesus said unto him, Judas betrayest thou the son of man with a kiss.** Remember what John has told us about how indignant Judas was at the action of Mary. He witnessed this entire exchange between his father and Jesus. John gives us Judas' words, whereas Luke gives us Simon's. Judas is angry and rationalizes that anger towards betraying Jesus. He remembers the conversation between Jesus and his father, who will take Him to the Pharisees, who are Jesus' enemies. Judas leads the soldiers to where Jesus is. In his head, before he comes up to Jesus, he remembers Jesus' words to his father: **"Thou gavest me no kiss."** Judas likely thinks to himself, "*You want a kiss? I will give you your kiss*!" It was out of spite and anger that Judas kisses Jesus. Judas wasn't naive. He knew very well what they would do to Jesus.

I believe the Gospel writers' intentions were to be transparent, and we must remember that they didn't write to doctors of law. They wrote to people who understood the importance of family and lived a simple life. The Jewish leaders made knowing God complicated in Jesus' lifetime and I believe that we have made it complicated in our time. We will continue the story and see why Simon was so desperate to have his son betray Jesus.

Simon the Leper's Story

And as he entered into a certain village, there met him ten men that were lepers, which stood afar off: And they lifted their voices, and said, Jesus, Master, have mercy on us. . . . And one of them, when he saw that he was healed, turned back, and with a loud voice glorified God, And he fell down at his face at his feet, giving him thanks: and he was a Samaritan *(Luke 17:12,15 [KJV]).* We know this wasn't Simon. Evidently, all the Jewish men were ungrateful. But perhaps Simon was one of the other nine: **And Jesus answering said, Were there not ten cleansed? but where are the nine?** *(Luke 17:17 [KJV]).*

Nine lepers got completely healed and were not grateful. We know Simon was never grateful and was resentful toward Jesus for healing him. Why? Jesus stood in the way of his agenda. When he became a leper, he was cast out, and therefore, no longer could he be in the Jewish temple wearing his Pharisee robes or attending the Sanhedrin meetings. He wanted back in. Jesus healed him, but Simon didn't want to be associated with Jesus because he was on the side of Jesus' enemies. And Judas, his son, was his pawn.

At the Last Supper, the apostle John asked Jesus who would betray him: **Lord, who is it?** *(John 13:25 [KJV]).* Then Jesus showed him the answer: **He gave it to Judas Iscariot, the son of Simon** *(John 13:26 [KJV]).*

Judas didn't approach the Jewish leaders alone, but his proud father brought him to prove his loyalty to them. **Then one of the twelve, called**

Judas Iscariot, went unto the chief priests *(Matthew 26:14 [KJV])*. The Gospel writers have already given us the backdrop to the story. The Jewish leaders have a plan to kill Jesus after the feast. Simon knows this plan. No doubt, he has already been working on Judas to betray Jesus. Judas has been profiting as a thief by stealing money from the treasury. He is furious because a potential windfall was wasted, in his view, on Jesus. Now his income was surely going to end, and if he wanted severance pay, he needed to act before the Jewish leaders activated their own plans on killing Jesus.

Timing is everything. No doubt, Simon understood this, and tells Judas, "*Jesus is as good as dead after the feast.*" The Gospel writers have made it clear that the Jewish leaders have decided not to kill Jesus during the feast. **But they said, Not on the feast day; lest there be an uproar among the people** *(Matthew 26:4-5 [KJV])*. The question is: what motivated them to change their minds? One of their own is solving the problem of the Jewish leaders. Judas presented the opportunity of the moment. They had a competition between sects. They wanted credit for saving Israel from the issue of Jesus; and besides, their leaders —former and current high priests—wanted Jesus dead.

Then Judas, which had betrayed him, when he saw that he was condemned, repented himself, and brought again the thirty pieces of silver to the chief priests and elders *(Matthew 27:3 [KJV])*.

> *Failure is always an opportunity for blessings when we realize our purpose in life is not to be great, but to be only forgiven.*

While we may never measure up to Jesus, we can appreciate His grace to love us anyway, that we might have peace and forgive ourselves, that we might let go of guilt and let God go with our lives.

And he cast down the pieces of silver in the temple, and departed, and went and hanged himself *(Matthew 27:6 [KJV])*. Judas gets the rap for Jesus' betrayal, but let's not leave out his father. We should see the contrast: Whereas Mary's family brought their children to Jesus; Simon brought his son to betray Him.

Where are the parents of this country leading their children, in the ways of Simon, or the ways of Zebedee (little John's father)? While the politicians fruitlessly debate this country's problems, most of them are caused by the breakdown of families. Parents teach manners and respectful behavior, and families give purpose other than: *life is all about "me."* Simon led Judas in his way, but it failed him. Judas had to come to grips with the fact that his father got what he wanted, which was to belong to a group; but Judas apparently had no one. The people he had known, who trusted him, were not going to be his companions any longer.

Simon taught Judas that there was no such thing as forgiveness. Judas chose to believe that lie and killed himself. Judas' thoughts may have come to terms with the fact that his father was healed of leprosy and he'd reciprocated by betraying the very person who had healed him. In his deepest heart of hearts, Judas did not want Jesus dead. He'd just wanted his agenda accomplished. Judas may have initially thought that Jesus was the Messiah and hoped he would do well to be attached to Him. Jesus healed his father, and this attracted Judas to Jesus' power but not to His heart of mercy. Then, when he found out from his father that Jesus was going to be killed anyway, the expedient path was to profit from His death. *What did Judas gain?* And *what did he lose?* Judas wasn't related to the other apostles and hence didn't have to face them. Simon wasn't capable of loving Judas, or being kind, as Jesus' family had been to him. Once Simon got what he wanted, Judas was likely disposable to him.

I imagine Judas as being very temperamental. He could have been a spoiled brat used to getting his way when daddy was isolated from his family and society. He may have gone back to the elders with the delusional hope of being a hero so he could rejoin Jesus' followers. His throwing down the money may have been the reaction of a temper tantrum. Then, when he left, he may have even regretted having no money. We were told that's what he cared about, and the dysfunctional cycle that led him made things worse. Now Judas' actions had left him no options. He was used by his own father and there was no part of society that would accept him, give him dignity he longed for.

At any rate, we should see that Jesus would have forgiven him and loved him; that whatever Judas did, he did for the wrong reasons. Judas was incapable of doing right because he rejected the grace of God and the light of wisdom that comes with it.

CHAPTER 15

The Blessing of Simon Peter

The end of the Gospels presents us with three Simons: Judas' father (whom I believe was Simon, the leper), Simon Peter, and a third. **And as they led him away, they laid hold upon one Simon, a Cyrenian, coming out of the country, and on him they laid the cross, that he might bear it after Jesus** *(Luke 23:26 [KJV])*. Possibly we should look for a connection in the story regarding Simon Peter. God is omniscient, so I believe that He knew what name was going to be selected to carry that cross.

Catholics hold the traditional belief Simon Peter was crucified upside down. I believe *Luke 23:26* as well as *John 21:18-21* are both connections to his future martyrdom. We should recognize that the Lord built his faith to be used for spiritual greatness, climaxing in Simon Peter offering himself up on the altar for the cause of Christ.

Simon Peter is a principal player in the Gospels. His contributions are for believers' edification. As stated in Chapter twelve, I believe he had connections to Jesus' family but was not blood-related. It is possible that he was just friends with Zebedee, but the culture of the times should at least make us suspect them to be brothers. My suspicion is that he was married to another cousin of Mary cementing his bond towards the Baptist and Jesus. I believe Peter watched Jesus grow up, and later the Lord healed his mother's wife because she had faith in Him *(Matthew 8:14)*.

There is a consensus among many expositors that Peter looks at himself as a leader and confidant to Jesus, which leads him to the point of giving Jesus advice and experiencing some stumbles. Catholics, especially, see him as being vital throughout the Gospels and in the book of Acts. Curiously, they, along with many Bible expositors, have missed the importance that he plays in the resurrection story. Before we go to a happy ending, we need to take a step back.

Peter's Declaration

Whom do men say that I the Son of man am? *(Matthew 16:13 [KJV])* Jesus asked His disciples this question. Then he asked them, **But whom say ye that I am? And Simon Peter answered and said, Thou art the Christ the son of the living God** *(Matthew 16:15-16 [KJV])*. The conventional wisdom is that Jesus was asking the disciples who they believed He was, and that Jesus was overjoyed when, by some miracle, Peter got the answer. Yet, in the first chapter of John, we find that from the beginning, Andrew, Philip, and Nathanael knew that Jesus was the Messiah. John the Baptist had been announcing Jesus' identity publicly for several years—my guess twelve years.

Ironically, it has been taught that the apostles just thought He was a great teacher, and only Peter knew Who He was. This type of disconnection has run its course to where religion doesn't believe that Jesus was the Son of God, contrary to the purpose of the Gospel.

Jesus asked them to follow Him because he was the Christ. John the Baptist told them who He was. Jesus had fulfilled His earthly duty in Nazareth, and His call to John's disciples was alerting them to His divine purpose.

And Jesus answered and said unto him, Blessed art thou, Simon Barjona: for flesh and blood hath not revealed it unto thee, but my Father which is in heaven *(Matthew 16:17 [KJV])*. God did not build our salvation on Peter. Consequently, the rock he is talking about is Himself. Barjona means "son of Jona." Jesus is saying that you can't get this from flesh and blood. Simon is a relative by marriage and, as such, had heard the stories from Jesus' family. Perhaps Jona or some other blood relative told Peter that Jesus was the Messiah. The word "flesh" is best translated by human means—in other words, what was passed to Simon.

When Jesus says, "but by my Father in Heaven," He is talking about spiritual faith, not only to Simon but also to all of us. There are many religious perspectives on Earth, but eternal attachment to Christ comes only by spiritual means, not through temporal means. While we may think we do good things because of our understanding, God only accepts what is eternal: His Spirit and work in Christ (*I Corinthians 3:11-15*).

Jesus is telling Simon that he can't discover the secrets of God by human means. He can only have the spiritual understanding by the Spirit of the Father. What we should understand is that He is talking to all the apostles who were there, and is teaching them a great spiritual truth, for disciples were prepared by John the Baptist and knew of Jesus by family bonds.

And I say also unto thee, Thou art Peter and upon this rock I will build my church; and the gates of hell shall not prevail against *(Matthew 16:18 [KJV])*. Jesus first used the birth name of "Simon," but followed in this pronouncement, using the new name of "Peter" (Cephas). In English Peter means rock or stone but Jesus spoke to him in Aramaic and called him Cephas which means little stone. The word Jesus used for Himself describes bedrock or a large-enough boulder to be utilized in a building's foundation. After Christ's resurrection, Peter will write letters to the churches and use words like, **"Ye also, as lively stones"** *(I Peter 2:5 [KJV])*. A living stone is one found **"acceptable to God by Jesus Christ"** *(I Peter 2:5 [KJV])*. Peter was no longer the clueless fisherman, Simon, but a new man filled with the Holy Spirit, proclaiming **"Christ as a rock of offense"** *(I Peter 2:8 [KJV])* **"and an immovable boulder: Behold, I lay in Sion a chief cornerstone"** *(I Peter 2:6 [KJV])*.

Those "called out" (the meaning of the Greek word commonly translated "church") would prevail—even over the doorway to death. When Jesus used the word *church*, He was talking about those who are called out of this world of flesh to be born of the Spirit. He was not talking about a physical building, which would have been the opposite of

His point. The early church in Jerusalem, Rome, and hundreds of other cities and villages met in homes and synagogues (like Jewish schools), not a cathedral. Our Lord Jesus built physical homes as a carpenter, but He built the heavenly church by His blood. This episode, when interpreted to mean that Jesus is telling us that Peter is special, misses a great truth: We are all equally unique to Him in the Father, being called out of death. For those who believe in Christ are in Christ.

Simon was given a new name—Peter—because he has another Father, who is eternal. In the book of Revelation (see *Revelation 2:17*), He gives all believers a new name. God would want us to know that He has a purpose now and eternal purposes for all of us, as His children. God will use Peter mightily, and He still does to this day, in Scripture, for our edification.

Simon's Boldness Leads to His Denial of Christ

Most believers know the general context of Simon Peter's denial of Christ, but the connection to the resurrection appearances has not been realized. Just as the personal relationships involved in the resurrection accounts have largely been ignored. We will explore this in the concluding chapters of this book in the hope that believers will see a complete picture of the love Jesus had for them.

My intention is not to make things up, but to help believers connect the reality of who these people were and the glorious grace Jesus rains on them. I have come to understand that my words are worthless unless they have some attachment to what matters, which is why it's important that we get closer to what actually happened in the resurrection so that it will empower our lives with His grace. Peter will become a spiritual giant and will offer himself on the altar, but let's look at how far Christ's work took him. Let's see his fall, how he was judged, and how Jesus responded to him

I say unto you, that one of you shall betray me *(John 13:21 [KJV])*. In the last supper, Jesus will tell His apostles which of them will betray him. Peter beckons little John, who is cuddling with Jesus, to find out who.

Simon Peter is rather indignant that someone is going to betray Jesus. It surely wouldn't be him. **All ye shall be offended because of me this night** *(Matthew 26:31 [KJV])*. Simon doesn't like this statement because it puts him in the same class as the other apostles. He hadn't learned from the stern rebuke from Jesus (see *Matthew 16:23*) when he attempted to give Him advice. He will show less concern for what is going to happen to Jesus and be more concerned about his (ego) image. So, he makes a bold statement for comforting himself, not Jesus. **Though all men shall be offended because of thee, yet I never be offended** *(Matthew 26:33 [KJV])*. Simon Peter is ignorant of the carnal nature which is always obsessed with its pride. Love speaketh the truth and is not self-promoting. Peter is talking to "The Truth" in Jesus Christ, but he spends energy trying to frame it his way, which brings judgment on himself, instead of grace. God would want us to understand that this isn't just Peter; it's all of us, so we might learn our tendencies to lie to ourselves. Pride always lies and can never choose the purpose of God, but, rather, the purpose of refusing grace. **Jesus said unto him, Verily I say unto thee, That this night, before the cock crow, thou shalt deny me thrice** *(Matthew 26:34 [KJV])*. The Lord-Word doesn't quiet Simon. **Though I should die with thee, yet will I not deny thee** *(Matthew 26:35 [KJV])*. What we should learn about Jesus' betrayal is that Judas, Simon Peter, and the entire world would rather choose pride and die than accept the grace of Jesus Christ. **Simon, Simon, behold Satan hath desired to have you, that he may sift you as wheat** *(Luke 22:31 [KJV])*. This should humble Simon. For one thing, Jesus is calling him by his old name. Simon will proceed to act like a fool, as will everyone who refuses His grace. Pride hates humility. **But I have prayed for thee, that thy faith fail not: and when thou art converted, strengthen thy brethren** *(Luke 22:32 [KJV])*. Note His enduring love that never wavers, despite any of our actions. His way is always grace and prays not just for Simon, but for us all.

On 9/11, Muslim extremists committed a cowardly murder, to their own detriment. Pride is not brave; it is a coward; for it fears the light of truth that reveals its darkness. Committing suicide is not a heroic act, but that of a coward, it's afraid for it can't build a future. Pride wants to be a god and control its hour and does what comes to mind. For its jealous of the giver of eternal life that will eventually end its illusion. Pride hates the truth and would rather be dead than acknowledge its need for the grace of God.

Then Simon Peter having a sword drew it, and smote the high priest's servant, and cut off his right ear *(John 18:10 [KJV])*. Simon would rather die than accept that Jesus' words were true. In the firefight, he can show the relatives that Simon will not deny Jesus, but die for Him. Simon is unconscious that he is acting out against the truth and, therefore, the will of God. **Thinkest thou that I cannot pray to my Father, and he shall presently give me more than twelve thousand legions of angels** *(Matthew 26:53 [KJV])*? God's omnipotence keeps Simon alive despite his death wish. Some Bible expositors believe Simon is acting bravely. **A man's pride shall bring him low** *(Proverbs 29:23 [KJV])*. Then why does he keep digging a bigger pit of sin? He just got rebuked by the Son of God and yet he will not yield. Pride hates the humility of God, which is why when Lazarus was raised from the dead, the Jewish leaders just wanted to kill Lazarus and Jesus. They had their own agenda and had no interest in finding grace in the blessing of life.

Simon's Denial

Simon denied The Truth, right to His face and chose instead to believe his own opinion (illusion) of himself. Is it surprising that God knows what happens next? Simon will deny Jesus. **But Peter followed him afar off unto the high priest's palace, and went in, and sat with the servants, to see the end** *(Matthew 26:58 [KJV])*. Simon will follow the soldiers to find where they take Jesus. The words "to see the end" in the King James Version (KJV) Bible has been better translated to "see the outcome" in the New International Version (NIV) Bible. I mention this because, at times, the NIV and other translations help us; but at other times they are not helpful, for reasons which I believe are obvious:

A few Hebrew or Aramaic words created problems when translating them into Greek, and then into English.

Simon will go with John into the temple area. John tells us something significant (see *John 18:15*): He is known personally by the high priest. We are aware John the Baptist was Levite and little John faithfully served him (more evidence indicating that little John was Levite, as was his mother, Salome). Peter, however, is not known, and, therefore, has no connection to the High Priest.

There is parallel to the words "Peter followed him afar off." It's not a good way to follow Jesus, and Peter will deny Jesus three times. **Then Saith the damsel that kept the door unto Peter, Art not thou also one of this man's disciples? He saith, I am not** *(John 18:17 [KJV])*. Little John went into the temple area and found a girl who would let Peter in. As Simon Peter walks in, he denies knowing Jesus to the little girl. He will be recognized, and continues to deny, and escalates with his words: «I know not the man» (see *Matthew 26:69-74*). **And Peter remembered the word of Jesus, which said unto him, Before the cock crow, thou shalt deny me thrice. And he went out, and wept bitterly** *(Matthew 26:75 [KJV])*.

We should understand that little John probably witnesses the entire episode. We know from his account that he walked in with Peter, as the little girl asked if he was "also of this man's disciples," because little John told her he was. In other words, little John not only did not deny Jesus, but he also affirmed that he was one of His disciples. It's a great teaching for us to ponder that, on the one hand, Peter grabs a sword; and on the other, he is afraid of a little girl. Everyone makes mistakes, and the best thing we can do is recognize them so we don't keep digging in the wrong direction.

> Lord, I am ready to go with thee, both into prison, and to death.
> *(Luke 22:33 [KJV])*

> Though I should die with thee, yet will I not deny thee.
> *(Matthew 26:35 [KJV])*

Though all men shall be offended because of thee, yet will I never be offended *(Matthew 26:33 [KJV])*.

For a just man falleth seven times, and riseth up again *(Proverbs 26:47 [KJV])*. My translation: No one is perfect, but the people who recognize that God is, rise to live a life of purpose anyway. **But without faith it is impossible to please him** *(Hebrews 11:6 [KJV])*. Little John didn't deny Jesus because he had faith, being led by love in his heart. Today, believers follow Jesus, but what leads them to follow Him on a day-to-day basis? Jesus tells us to follow Him with a childlike faith but many of us, at some point in our lives, follow Him as Simon: very bold and full confidence in our motives but shocked when we fall into a pit. His grace stands ready to lift us out of any trap. We need to believe in His omnipotence and understand He doesn't want us to be surprised by our shortcomings. He can use them for good, so we learn to surrender, to the reality of being powerless over them.

For ye have not received the spirit of bondage again to fear *(Romans 8:15 [KJV])*. We should recognize that, as believers, we can be easily troubled on a day-to-day basis. Acknowledging, that we might have faith, but we have prideful nature that has but one goal: to reject humility. At times it has all the answers and sometimes it has none. It wants to be in control of all things yet it can't master its own tongue, which James 3:6 says is on fire and defileth our walk with God. **Pride goeth before destruction, and a haughty spirit before a fall** *(Proverbs 6:18 [KJV])*.

One of the most important things that I have learned is that pride falls because it always sees the inadequacies of others, including itself; therefore, it condemns itself. **And he went out, and wept bitterly** *(Matthew 26:75 [KJV])*. Many believers are convinced that weeping is the same as repentance and that it's good to hate whatever they have done wrong. This has led to some very dysfunctional teachings which erect walls, thereby hindering believers from living an empowering life. This has led to many walking in a guilt complex that loath themselves. True understanding is accepting of God's grace to the humble and shows it by letting go of one's dysfunctional nature that excels in drama. Pride weeps because it's surprised by its failures and will never accept that it lies to itself, telling itself that it could do the contrary. God has something much more empowering for those believers who walk in humility and are not shocked at their shortcomings. They are grateful that they can see the grace of God, which uses all things for His purpose in them. **And we know that all things work together for good to them that love God, to them who are the called according to his purpose** *(Romans 8:28 [KJV]).*

CHAPTER 16

There is Something about Mary

God ordained four Gospels to complement and complete a story that couldn't be told by one Gospel and yet emphasizes one woman's name.

> Then took **Mary** a pound of ointment of spikenard, very costly, and anointed the feet of Jesus, and wiped his feet with her hair (John 12:3 [KJV]).

> Now there stood by the cross of Jesus, his mother, and his mother's sister, **Mary** the wife of Cleopas, and **Mary** Magdalene (John 19:25 [KJV]).

> And many women were there beholding afar off, which followed Jesus from Galilee, ministering unto him: Among which was **Mary** Magdalene, and **Mary** the mother of James and Joses, and the mother of Zebedee's children (Matthew 27:55-56 [KJV]).

> **Mary** Magdalene and **Mary** Mother of Joses beheld where he lay (Mark 15:47 [KJV]).

> In the end of the sabbath, as it began to dawn toward the first day of the week, came **Mary** Magdalene, and the other **Mary**, to see the sepulchre (Matthew 28:11 [KJV]).

> The first day of the week cometh **Mary** Magdalene early, when it was yet dark, unto the sepulchre, and seeth the stone taken away from the sepulchre (John 20:11 [KJV]).

It should be apparent that other women's names are omitted for one reason: Their names aren't Mary. The Scriptures are like sounding a horn with Mary's name, who, ironically, isn't named and is given the title "mother of Jesus."

Matthew 28:11 references *"the other Mary"* giving us three Mary's who comforted Mary the mother of Jesus and became witnesses of the Resurrection events.

And when he had considered the thing, he came to the house of Mary the mother of John, whose surname was Mark; where many were gathered together praying *(Acts 12:12 [KJV])*. This particular Mary played a predominant part in the first Christian Church by hosting it in the book of Acts. She had a house in Jerusalem, and it was where the first church was praying for Peter's release (who was held in prison in the book of Acts 12:3-18). It's my contention it's the same house were the Apostles met and witnessed the resurrection of Christ Jesus and perhaps the numbering of the verse (*Acts 12:12*) should get our attention. This verse is evidence to suspect Mary the mother of Jesus, as well as her sister, were staying with this other Mary (the mother of John Mark). We connect to the story when we see that there were three Mary's comforting the Mother of Jesus and it's my contention they were all named after her. This Mary had a son, and his name surname was Mark, and his original name coincidently was John. Apparently there were many John's in the family, and consequently, he was given a surname to differentiate. He was a companion, as was Luke, to the Apostle Paul and would go on to provide us with a Gospel. I suspect he was Levite and named after John the Baptist. I will build upon my theory later, but it is my contention that two of the Gospels come from sons whose mother's name was Mary, which is a great lesson of godly motherhood. This world we live in today does not value godly motherhood. It's my hope that churches will study the significant influence of the mothers in the Gospels.

There were four ladies at the cross, and three of their names were Mary. There are four Gospels that have four "Mary's" playing instrumental parts within the Gospels.

Three of the Gospels are called synoptic for the reason they resemble each other but are different. Those three Gospels were greatly influenced by the four Mary's witness of certain events. Luke was heavily influenced by all the Mary's in his Gospel, for we see he references this other Mary in the book of Acts.

God highlighted John the Baptist's importance throughout the Gospels and ironically his, and the mothers' of the Apostles, contribution has been ignored.

The Resurrection story opens up when we see that this (other) Mary's house was the meeting place of the first church because (pointedly) that's where Jesus appeared to all of them. This other Mary hosted Salome, Mary the wife of Cleopas, and Mary Magdalene, who were comforting and loving Jesus' mother. The men connected to them were either staying with them or near them. All of the women in the house went to the grave site except the mother of Jesus.

Even though the Gospel of John tells us Mary's sister is right beside her at the cross, it is not obvious to many Bible expositors that some of the women visiting the tomb are relatives of Mary per the custom of any time period. When I attend a funeral, I don't have to ask who is burying the deceased it's quite apparent the family almost always makes the arrangements.

Christians, of course, understand Jesus rose from the dead which is a critical fact of their faith but beyond that, there is little to no comprehension of His personal encounters with the people involved in the Gospels. The main reason is the unfamiliarity of Jesus relationships which centered around His family.

Which leads me to wonder: "Where is Mary, the mother of Jesus, in the story of Jesus' resurrection?" Perhaps she was devastated beyond comprehension or perhaps Mary knew what no one else knew that Jesus wouldn't be in the tomb. Mary got a full measure of suffering because she was the mother of the greatest blessing to this world. God took notice of it, and He didn't forget about her.

Before we look at this beautiful conclusion of the story, we should acknowledge someone else. God took notice of Joseph, and he will make an exclamation mark that he was dead but, yet, is remembered and honored by God. He honors both names at the cross.

Honor Thy Father and Mother

And after this Joseph of Arimathea, being a disciple of Jesus, but secretly for fear of Jews, besought of Jesus: and Pilate gave him leave. He came therefore, and took the body of Jesus (*John 19:38 [KJV]*). When the Gospels were written, the contemporaries knew the story and the custom. The writers sometimes give us information because it was contrary to custom. Fortunately, John identifies him clearly, so there is no controversy that this could be Joseph, His mother's husband. John gives details that show us what a remarkable act he did.

Joseph of Arimathea was afraid, and if there was ever a time to be afraid, it was when the Jews used Romans to get their enemy killed on the cross. This Joseph had good reason to fear, but now he is led by love and mercy. True love does not fear because it's not from this world. **For ye have not received the spirit of bondage again to fear; but ye have received the Spirit of adoption, whereby we cry, Abba, Father** (*Romans 8:15 [KJV]*). We should see that our savior feared nothing in this world, and when we do, we deny Him; that when we overcome fear and chose faith, He can do great things in us.

We should also see the obvious fact that His brothers and apostles are nowhere to be found, except John. They were kin to Him, and at least they should have been there to claim his body. We are clearly told that they are hiding. Ironically, James, brother of John, and James, half-brother to Jesus, are both not mentioned in the Gospel's concluding chapters. It was the time of the feast, so we know they were customarily all there.

Jesus was given many gifts and support from His followers, but we should note that He received three gifts generally reserved only for the richest: The gifts from the wise men, the anointing from Mary, and now a tomb from Joseph of Arimathea. Evidently, it was his own tomb, and now he generously uses it for Jesus. Two of the gifts were given to him by people who had the same name as his parents in this world. **Honor**

thy father and mother: that thy days be long upon the land which the LORD thy God giveth thee *(Exodus 20:12 [KJV])*. And God does so throughout Jesus' life, including after He died.

Ironically, after Jesus' death, Joseph of Arimathea gives something precious to Him. He will, of course, receive it back, empty, to be used for his own burial at a later time. He would also be filled with the knowledge that he, too, will be alive, though he be dead.

Some people really have pride in titles, yet Nicodemus will choose something of far greater value than his title in the Sanhedrin by choosing to help Joseph bury Jesus. I believe the story is relevant to help us to reflect on what is important, rather than fear the loss of our status in this world. By grace, I believe that He gives us help to do the right thing (letting go of self-expediency), and we should see His blessings in this matter. The fact is this world is corrupt, and God is glorified when we pay the personal cost of an ethical walk. We are told Nicodemus was a secret disciple and he comes out in the open. I suspect he was from the tribe of the Levi and had connections to the family of John the Baptist.

God the Father ordained the resurrection and a tomb; otherwise, a criminal would have been thrown in a garbage dump by the Romans. We should see that His enemies took pleasure in mutilating Jesus' body and wanted to get control over it after His death. We should see God's omnipotence and triumph over evil at the cross, and that Jesus was honored and provided for by His real Father in anointing His body.

I find it interesting that, in the absence of Mary's husband, Joseph, God provided a different Joseph to tend to Jesus' body; perhaps in part as a comfort to Mary and a gesture of honor toward her deceased and honorable husband for the role he played in Jesus' life. That one Joseph may have carried Him when He was born, and another took Him when He died.

It is my suspicion that Joseph was one of the first Martyrs for the Gospel. The Gospel begins with the immaculate conception, and Joseph participated in giving out this good news. Rather than being accepted gleefully by Nazareth, it was rejected, and Joseph was despised for his testimony of the birth of Christ. We should observe how Nazareth attempted to murder Jesus and understand that many in the town thought Joseph was actually Jesus' father. Then it's not too big of a stretch to suspect the town of Nazareth may have had something to do with Joseph's death. Joseph completed his mission bravely, and now Jesus' real Father saw to the burial of His Son.

CHAPTER 17

The Preordained Resurrection

It's my assumption that from God's perspective, the resurrection appearances are a big deal to Him (see *Ephesians 1:4, I Peter 1:20*); that he planned them before He created the world and for this very purpose we were born to enter His salvation, and that the Gospel didn't begin in Matthew but in Genesis 1:3 where God says: "Let there be light (The Light of the World is Jesus Christ)." When God said: "Let us make man in our image" it is critical we understand whose image that is. How many Gods do we know that make footsteps? It appears many seminaries don't seem to understand whose footsteps were walking in the Garden in Genesis 1:8. Those footsteps were not walking in anger to judge man; they were steps of grace towards the first divided family, saving them (with the gift of salvation) from the serpent.

We should know who the author of confusion is and who likes to twist God's word so it loses its power to believers. Many Christians have been told this world was perfect before Eve ate of the fruit and few see how destructive that lie is. This world had a serpent, and it could never be perfect with Satan. The serpent would have us believe it was perfect and perfectly alright for him to call God a liar (*Genesis 3:4-5*). Satan's version of perfection is calling God names, and the Lord has told us point blank this world naturally believes his lies. Consequently, many in this world curse His name: He who extends them grace to their existence by creating a day just for them. Therefore many think this world was quite perfect with Satan in it and they haven't been told otherwise. Furthermore, Christians through the ages have been taught Eve sinned first and accepted this lie without question. Satan sinned before Eve and yet how many sermons have been given about how Eve sinned first? Some may say I am splitting hairs here; "after all: everyone knows the serpent is evil and there were consequences from Eve's sin." I'm not arguing the consequence of Eve's sin; on the contrary, I'm stating the importance of not accepting the Serpent's perspective on things. I see the harm in believing Satan's half-truths as the first mother equated to the Truth. The subtle lie is everything was good, but God didn't know what was going to happen with the serpent in the garden. God made a mistake, and the serpent points that out by him being in the garden in the first place. Therefore, it was God's fault for having the serpent in the Garden, and Jesus takes responsibility (implies God has a guilt trip) for His mistake by dying on the cross. The fact is that the seminaries do not see that the subtle lie they have swallowed blinds them from seeing many things. Consequently, Jesus' birth story has been told wrong and His resurrection appearances have been skewed into ambiguity as well. For they do not observe God has preordained His grace and therefore use that basis for interpreting scripture. This world was in darkness (*Genesis 1:2*), and we should ponder how that could be with the eternal light of God (*Revelation 21:23*). Anything God does is good, but that didn't make this dark world perfect. What was good is that He brought His salvation by His Word.

God is not a part-time God; He didn't just get started 10,000 or six billion years ago. He is eternal which means He has been creating for eternity. This dimension may have come into existence a few billion years ago but the universe is infinite, and as far as we know, God may have many of them in different dimensions. God is fully capable of creating the few days of this tiny world, which is why He sees the future. Whereas this world can't create one day and therefore has no clue what the future holds and consequently is continuously gripped in fear. For this world is in darkness (fear) and its god is Satan but his days are numbered (see *Isaiah 14:12-16*). This is the reason this world is at war (sin) with God. This world wants to fight with God, but I wonder if many Christians realize God has no desire to fight with it. This world loves to hate and have wars and disagreements. God is the God of peace and sees no benefit of strife or the destruction of any of His creations. Satan rebelled against God and another term for it would be that Satan wanted to steal everything, including God's throne. Unlike us who would lash out and defend what was taken, God chose not to fight Satan for this dimension; God said: "you can have it"(see *II Corinthians 4:4*). In a blink of an eye, God could have vanquished this world, but His heart is merciful. What shall it profit a man, if he shall gain the whole world, and lose his own soul *(Mark 8:36 [KJV])*? Satan got the world of darkness but he lost his soul. God let the world go but not our souls (see *Ezekiel 18:4*). He wouldn't fight for this world, but he chose to fight for us. In popular culture our movies have the good guy who defeats the enemy with his strength. Yet, God's ways are not our ways, and He came to battle as a lamb to be slain that He might bring us with Him into a new day, eternity.

The Bible is a dead book without the Light of Omnipotent God, Jesus Christ. Then said I, Lo, I come in the volume of the book it is written of me *(Psalms 40:7 [KJV])*. Our God is too wonderful to be described by one name. He is the Ancient of Days (see *Daniel 7:9-10*), and if we seek Him, we will find Him throughout the Old Testament. I wonder how many believers see Jesus talking to Abraham in *Genesis 18:1-33*. Many teachers do recognize and call His appearance "the pre-incarnate Christ" but miss the fact that His steps are the same from beginning to end in His Word. Jesus tells us that whoever sees Him has seen the Father and in fact, it's the Father speaking all the words of Jesus *(John 14:8-11)*.

God left His throne, and He took a new name for our benefit, but He has always been God. God allowed himself to be a man, but He was still God as He has always been God. The form of Jesus is finite, but the spirit of God is infinite *(Psalm 139:7)*. Everything exists within God whether we are conscious of it or not *(John 17:21)*. God is going to create a new world where Satan and his followers won't be in it, and of course, it's important we understand that. Furthermore, we need to comprehend God that never had a beginning. We may change from our beginning, but we must understand He never had one. He has always been omnipotent and knows all before anything comes about because they can't exist without Him.

God does everything for a reason. When He added a day to a week in Genesis, it wasn't because He thought the number seven was cool but the fact He saw we needed Him to save us. The Gospel of John makes it clear which God spoke the world into existence. He created this world in six days (six divisions, not literal days, because the sun didn't exist until it was created to have a solar day) and added a day to complete not only His work of creation but our salvation. The six divisions become unified in One (one day is Jesus' birth) for God foresaw He would join Himself to this creation with His birth.

God is infinite and unfathomable *(Romans 11:33)* even for the angels *(I Peter 1:12)*. Great as He is, yet He is meek and is willing to constrain Himself in One dimension. That One has always been God and is the face of God to finite creations. For God saw that He would come (added a day) to bring salvation to a world of darkness (the world with lies from a false god, Satan) and He would come into it with His Birth.

There will be no more six days in eternity because eternity has only One day, but that One day will never end (it began with His resurrection). Jesus was begotten of the dead (see *Revelation 1:5, Psalms 2:7-12*). If you read the Psalm, you will notice a voice proclaiming Jesus His Son after His resurrection. Why? The feast of Tabernacles was eight days, and on the eighth day of His Birth, He was named Jesus. God had ordained this before it happened and consequently, Orthodox Jews celebrate Passover over eight days. The eighth day is another One day being added to start a new week. This One day is Jesus' resurrection, being the first begotten of the dead, and a new week is a new creation *(Revelation 21:1)*. Jesus' appearance to The Apostle Paul is the last resurrection appearance given to us. What Paul says about it is interesting: And last of all he was last seen of me also, as one born out of due time *(I Corinthians 15:8)*.

The Resurrection Song

I have attended many worship services over the years; it appears to me as though the music has never been better. It seems to improve year after year. When I was a teen, the musical instruments were usually confined to one person who played the piano in the worship service. Many churches today have a band that plays together, very in sync, and they appear professional to my untrained ear. Today's music and worship of Him is beautiful because it appears to recognize it's all about Him. Our songs may have evolved to highlight His omnipotence, but many of our passed-down Biblical interpretations don't give Him the glory he is worthy of.

God has given believers a resurrection song to answer the skeptics of the Gospels. I call it a song because of its beauty and it's empowering to believe we have a great Orchestrator over all things. His notes are not random noise, as is this world's chaos; on the contrary, we're to see His purpose completed in His wonderful redemption song written before the world was even formed.

The resurrection should be the revival song to our souls, but errors in our translations have blocked our ears from enjoying the full beauty of it. Christians have had this song stolen from them, and they don't even know a theft has occurred. I want believers to have this song that is uplifting and gives them joy every Easter for days to come.

It's my opinion many seminaries through the ages looked for discrepancies in the Gospels and then spent time trying to explain them. Apparently, some of them didn't believe the Gospels are the infallible Word of God. Many skeptics who study in the realm of religious studies do not think the Gospels were originally written by Jesus' disciples but were in fact written hundreds of years later. There will always be a great debate about many things about the Gospels, but God would have us look for simplicity of His grace.

One particular Easter, the sermon at the service I attended didn't even mention His resurrection. I was astonished, for it appeared to me I was the only one that noticed there was something horribly wrong with that. In *The Passion of Christ*, we saw Him be mutilated, and it showed perhaps for the first time an accurate portrayal of what was done to Him. I ask the reader to ponder: Have you noticed the pinnacle of our faith (His Resurrection) in our movies of Him only shows seconds to a few minutes of the best part of the story? Shouldn't we have a movie that highlighted His resurrection? I believe His suffering was even worse than portrayed in the Passion of Christ, but fundamentally there is a darkened reason that's why the movies highlight His misery. This was Satan's swan song, his time, and he wants to glory in it. I want believers to know God's hour, which is our eternity and that was His resurrection.

Since God seems to be partial to seven or eight, we should then look for those numbers in His resurrection appearances? As we go through Jesus' resurrection appearances we will see that the witnesses have given us Jesus in eight separate accounts before His meeting with the Apostle Paul. Incredibly, they are given to us in two sets of sevens in seven books. They are witnessed in the Psalms, Gospels, the book of Acts and I Corinthians. This is God's exclamation mark to the believer that He has preserved His word; that nothing is missing from the Gospels, that He has preserved Jesus' Words for us today.

Heaven and Earth shall pass away, but my words shall not pass away *(Matthew 24:35 [KJV])*. I believe God preserved His word but as human beings, we need to acknowledge we are not infallible. We make mistakes, and there are errors in translations, otherwise why do we have so many of them? It would be impossible not to have mistakes over two thousand years. This is the context I use and why I believe the resurrection appearances are fathomable and comprehensible; that God wants us to know them, and the original writers did the best job they could to make it easily understood by us. God gives us a context (Jesus' Deity) to guide us that we might comprehend His Word. He gives us genealogies so that we understand that he calls all of them to be reconciled (In Jesus) to the One family of God.

God's will is that all choose Him, but He knows that will not be the case. He chose twelve, and one betrayed him. It wasn't God who had

Judas betray Him. He is merciful and lets things play out in the few days of the world, and so all the ones who stand before Him will know God let them make their choice (*II Peter 2:9*).

Four Gospels

J. Vernon McGee held the belief that the Four Gospels were preordained by God and wrote about that in his commentaries on the book of Ezekiel "Thru the Bible" [Proverbs Through Malachi]. Some people get hung up on predetermination and fate, but to me, it's very simple. God sees the future and adds grace so it may play out for our benefit. This time we live in is an afterthought with God. He has a whole eternity that awaits Him and His followers.

God's word is a woven glove; it completely fits to together from Genesis to Revelation. It's our interpretations that do not fit together, and as a consequence, many believe the Bible is contradictory. We have the time lines and the sequence of the Lord's resurrection appearances from the Apostle Paul but believers have never heard this powerful unified storyline. The movies that have been made mostly take small snapshots from Mark and Luke's account, but not all four gospels.

The different accounts of the Gospels of the resurrection of the Lord can be very confusing by themselves. Yet we can decipher some of the events when we understand the perspectives are from different people at different intervals of time. What is critical to understand to decipher the Gospels is that different verses are not to be taken as a complete perspective of an entire event or story. On the contrary, each Gospel can only give us one account in a particular time, such as Jesus' meeting with Pilate. Jesus' meeting with Pilate can be put into a cohesive sequential storyline that can be understood by us. We should notice that each Gospel presents distinct perspectives with Pilate, as they do with the resurrection; that each Gospel is true but tells a part of the story—not the entire story, because a witness' perspective is limited to the event the witness sees. Taking the same process to the resurrection events as we do the meeting of Pilate, we can come up with a story that is more comprehensive, unified and tells the story of Jesus' family in the resurrection.

Jesus' meeting with Pilate was actually over a period of two separate days. We know this because we already know Jesus met with him on Thursday and then it was ordered he be crucified on a Friday. Because we are aware of the timeline, we can make sense of the four different accounts that would seem contradictory.

And he answered him never a word; insomuch that the governor marveled greatly (*Matthew 27:14 [KJV]*). If we solely interpret Matthew's perspective on the conversation with Jesus and Pilate, then we would be led to believe that Jesus never spoke to Pilate. Matthew tells us Jesus talked to the Roman Governor in the early verse. **And Jesus said unto him, Thou sayest** (*Matthew 27:11 [KJV]*). Is Matthew contradicting himself since Jesus did speak to Pilate? No: Matthew's later verse needs to be understood in the context of the conversation with Pilate. The entire Gospels need to be understood in the framework of the story. Many false doctrines are built by religions that take one verse and make a religious belief without any understanding of the context of the verse as it relates to the story the writers of the Gospels are telling us.

Jesus' encounters with Pilate are a subplot to the entire Gospel. All four Gospels record the story of Pontius Pilate's encounter with Jesus (*Matthew 27:11-26, Mark 15:1-15, Luke 23:1-24, John 19:1-22*). Mark will tell us mostly what Matthew tells us: that Jesus didn't answer Pilate on any charges but did answer that he was king of the Jews. Matthew is the only Gospel that tells us information about Pilate's wife having a dream and warning him. Luke is the only Gospel that tells us that Pilate actually sent Jesus to Herod to be judged and then Herod sent Jesus back to the Roman Governor. John is the only Gospel tells us what was exchanged between Pilate and Jesus when he came back from Herod's.

The point is that they are all true, but it takes all four Gospels to get the complete story. Jesus never answered the charges brought against him by the Pharisees. Pilate is mystified, so he sends Jesus to Herod. Herod is no help to Pilate, so when Jesus comes back from seeing him, Pilate will be exasperated and says *"knowest thou not that I have power to crucify thee" (John 19:10 [KJV])*. Only the Gospel of John gives us this account of this conversation between Pilate and the Lord. Jesus answered, **Thou couldest no power at all against me, except it were given thee from above** *(John 19:11 [KJV])*. So Matthew's statement that Jesus never answered Pilate with a word was from the context of his conversation with him at that time. The Gospel of John completes the entire story for us, for without it we would not know Jesus does talk to Pilate. Without Luke's Gospel, we wouldn't know the timeline of the context of the story. Luke tells us Pilate sent Jesus to Herod and then apparently this conversation happened after that. I say apparently because the conversation is just before Pilate gives Jesus to be crucified. There's some deduction involved with the Gospels, but when the timelines are put together cohesively into a story, that makes sense. The Gospels are accurate, but a single Gospel or verse does not fully explain the entire story. There are many different characters that consequently experience an event at a certain time at certain place. Jesus' resurrection appearances were over forty days, making it much more difficult to ascertain than Jesus' meeting with Pilate. Of course, God knows this, and He gave us seven books in the Bible to comprehend His resurrection appearances.

CHAPTER 18

Called Out of Egypt

The first day of the week cometh Mary Magdalene early, when it was yet dark, unto the sepulchre, and seeth the stone taken away from the sepulchre *(John 20:1 [KJV])*. Mary Magdalene was the first person to visit the sepulcher before sunrise Sunday morning. John gives us details that were not in the other Gospels, which was one of his purposes in writing it. He uniquely tells us that Magdalene was first to arrive at the tomb while it was dark.

Jesus is the light of the world and didn't use the sun to lighten the darkness of death. There is a parallel between Jesus rising while it was still dark and Joseph rising before dawn to carry him off to Egypt. Joseph took Jesus into Egypt to be called out. So, here, Jesus went into death to be called out by His Heavenly Father. Jesus is God, yet He left Heaven to come to this world and had a stepfather (Joseph) who guided Him in this world. Most of us also have or had fathers; yet God would have us understand that He is our eternal Father. His will is that earthly fathers should be like Joseph, guides in this world, so they lead their sons toward the purpose of heavenly Father. Our Heavenly Father will then call all believers out of the death of this world, as He did with Jesus.

It's my position that John wants us to know, clearly, that Magdalene arrives at the tomb first. **And when the sabbath was past, Mary Magdalene, and Mary the mother of James, and Salome, had bought sweet spices, that they might come and anoint him.** *(Mark 16:1 [KJV])*

This verse has led to interpretations being debated, to this day, and to allegations that there are contradictions in the Gospels. John states that Magdalene is alone, whereas Matthew and Mark give a different impression. The Gospels are correct; it is the seminaries that have been in error. An explanation, which will be shared a little later in the story, is quite simple.

And very early in the morning the first day of the week, they came unto the sepulchre at the rising of the sun. And they said among themselves, Who shall roll us away from the stone from the door of the sepulcher? *(Mark 16:1-3 [KJV])*. But God had already answered their prayer: As they arrived, the large stone was already moved for them. We should note that there are no men in their company, and they arrived as the sun was coming up, while Magdalene was already there in the darkness.

God tells us how the stone was moved. **And behold, there was a great earthquake: for the angel of the Lord descended from heaven, and came and rolled back the stone from the door, and sat upon it** *(Matthew 28:2 [KJV])*. This had happened before any of them arrived. As J. Vernon McGee said, paraphrasing: "Not to let Jesus out, but to let the woman see the tomb was empty."

Out of the Mouths of Babes

At that time Jesus answered and said, I thank thee, O Father, Lord of heaven and earth, because thou hast hid these things from the wise and prudent, and hast revealed them unto babes *(Matthew 11:25 [NIV])*. Tradition believes Magdalene was a single woman who was caught in adultery and heretics have hinted that she was Jesus' wife. There is no debate today that the Gospels and Epistles credit her as the first person to see the resurrected Christ. The other women saw angels, which has not been discussed as a central issue of debate. Putting the entire resurrection story into a single comprehensive story has failed for one important reason: Seminaries have been unable to see the simplicity of the story. They don't assume the writers were simple folk telling us a clear story of relationships between family members that would have been easily comprehended by the audience at the time. For example, why would Magdalene know where Peter and John were located, as the apostles had scattered and were hiding? Why, particularly, would she get to the tomb first, when several women were heading there, and why would the apostles, with the exception of John, not believe her? We should naturally suspect Magdalene was a contemporary (the same age) of Peter or John. At Jesus' trial in the temple area, John got a young girl (see *John 18:15-17*) to let Peter in. We should expect that John knew the girl because she was a distant relative and around his age.

When we compare Magdalene's experience to the other women's encounters with the angels, it appears that she is very childlike, which is why she is not afraid, even though she is alone. John tells us that Magdalene runs, and it may be a clue that she is not a contemporary of the other women. We should note that several women arrive at the tomb, but she alone runs to get John and Peter. I don't believe the other, older women ran; and if they did, they were not nearly as fast as Magdalene. She is mentioned as being with the other women in Mark, and yet, he makes it clear that the Lord appeared to only Magdalene while she was alone. Thus, somehow, she separates herself from the other women, an event to which John points by telling us that he, too, runs to the tomb and separates himself from Peter.

I believe that Magdalene was with her mother, Salome, and ran a little ahead of her and got to the tomb while it was still dark, before the other ladies arrived at sunrise. She and the other ladies are in shock when they believe the body of Jesus has been taken away. Magdalene runs to get her brothers (probably at the direction of her mother). Little John comes, but we should assume he is with other family members. We will see later in the story that the other apostles are very troubled by Simon Peter's denial of Jesus, and have distanced themselves from him. Peter is John's uncle, and that's why they are together. James would also have been with his brother John, so it makes sense to assume he is bewildered by what happened to Jesus. We should put ourselves in their position: they thought he was going to be King, not be abused and mutilated on the cross. Andrew, Simon's brother, also doesn't come to the tomb, and I believe it's for the same reason. Some Bible expositors don't seem to grasp that they are visiting Jerusalem for the feast, as they have always done. They do not live in Jerusalem; they are all from Galilee, some ninety miles away, and stay with friends or relatives of Mary's, about whom Luke told us at the beginning of his Gospel. Apparently, James, Simon and other apostles disregard Mary's plea to all of them for the reasons I'm going to share. John doesn't tell us every detail of the personal dramas that happened between them, but as we continue the story, logic dictates that they are all in close proximity to each other.

Then she runneth and cometh to Simon Peter and to the other disciple whom Jesus loved *(John 20:2 [KJV])*. Magdalene arrived first, and the other women came later. She will leave, and while she is en route, the other women will see angels (see *Mark 16:5-8, Luke 24:3-9*), as recorded in other Gospels. John is telling us what happened to Magdalene. The seminaries became preoccupied with the syntax of the words and missed what is important: the context of the story and how it relates to the relationships of the characters. Hollywood has relied on these interpretations which is why the movies produced detached storylines.

Mary ran as fast as she could, probably only a few miles, to get Peter and John, assuming they were with relatives or near the other Mary's house *(Acts 12:12)*. Luke told us that Elisabeth was in Juda (which, today, is called Ein Karim), which was, perhaps, four to seven miles away. There were many relatives throughout the area, and as Levites, some served in the Temple. **And, behold, the veil of the temple was rent in twain from the top to the bottom**. We are given this verse in Matthew 27:51 because of the fact he had relatives who served in the temple. As stated in the previous chapter, the women are naturally staying together and comforting the devastated mother of Jesus. We only connect to the story when we see the family loves Mary, the mother of Jesus. Magdalene didn't have to ponder where the others were located as she ran to the family meeting place. Mary Magdalene ran the entire way, whether it was two blocks or five miles, but it becomes more significant when we consider that it was some distance. Then John, much younger than Peter, was first to the tomb.

He saw and believed. For as yet they knew not the Scripture, that he must rise again from the dead *(John 20:8-9 [KJV])*. Jesus had told them repeatedly, but they were not yet able to comprehend. **Then the disciples went again unto their own home** *(John 20:10 [KJV])*. John very clearly tells us that they saw nothing, whereas the other women saw angels, as presented in other Gospels. This should clue us in that Peter and John are not with these other women; nor is Magdalene. John tells us point blank that they return home (they were visiting) and Magdalene stays. However, we are not told how far out of sight they are before Jesus appears. I suspect it was for a short time period. However, we should suspect that, after Magdalene's encounter with Jesus, she will run after them. It's rather obvious that they either would have returned immediately or dismissed her account entirely.

But Mary stood without at the sepulchre weeping: and as she wept, she stooped down, and looked into the sepulchre *(John 20:11 [KJV])*. She is in deep anguish over Jesus' missing body and refuses to leave, which is an entirely different reaction than that of the women in Luke and Mark: **and seeth two angels in white** *(John 20:12 [KJV])*. She apparently didn't know they were angels. They asked, **Woman, why weepest thou?** *(John 20:13 [KJV])*. Mary Magdalene does not fear the angels, as do the other older women, who came upon the scene after her initial visit to the tomb and before this encounter. She converses with the angels while others are speechless and this, again, should clue us into the fact that she neither has the same reaction to the supernatural as the other women nor is she with them. **Jesus saith unto her, Mary. She turned herself, and saith unto him, Rabboni; which is to say Master** *(John 20:14-15 [KJV])*. Jesus was affectionate with children and, as such, Magdalene's first instinct is to run into His arms, as she had done so many times before, and, yet, Jesus will tell her: **Touch me not** *(John 20:17 [KJV])*. She was his little cousin, who knew him from her birth. I imagine Magdalene and John, her brother, had always run into His arms, only to be picked up and kissed. They adored him and would sometimes both sit on each of His knees.

I suspect Mary Magdalene was named after Jesus' mother. Perhaps she was the only daughter of Salome, who named Magdalene (Mary) after her sister. We should note that a Mary was chosen by God first to witness (see *Luke 1:28-38*) His birth and another Mary was the first witness to His resurrection. Mary Magdalene's reaction to the living Christ is quite distinctive from the other resurrection encounters that show fear and apprehension over conversing with the supernatural, let alone the risen Lord. In my opinion, an exclamation point by the Spirit of God that Mary Magdalene's heart mirrored that of a child.

Now he tells her to **go to my brethren** *(John 20:17 [KJV])*. She knows his family well, as they are hers, also. And then he tells her, **I ascend unto my Father, and your Father, and to my God, and your God** *(John 20:17 [KJV])*. Magdalene understands that Jesus was her cousin, but also that His Father was God. She will run to the family. **And she went and told them that had been with him, as they mourned and wept** *(Mark 16:10 [KJV])*. His family is broken and His apostles, who were mostly cousins, had abandoned Him and were now together. **And they, when they had heard that he was alive, and had been seen of her, believed not** *(Mark 16:11 [KJV])*. Simon Peter had returned and told them that he went to the tomb and saw nothing. Why should they believe Magdalene? After all, she was a little girl, like other children who worshiped him in the temple. **Hosanna to the Son of David,** *(Matthew 21:15 [KJV])*. Apparently, they forgot Jesus' response to the Pharisees, who wanted to muzzle her and the children. **Out of the mouth of babes and sucklings thou hast perfected praise** *(Matthew 21:16 [KJV])*. The wisdom of this world is foolishness to God. Two thousand years ago they didn't have quite the medical knowledge we have today. We should suspect their terminology was entirely different such as describing Magdalene's disability as being possessed by seven demons. My strong suspicion is it would be called something quite different today. Consequently, I believe Mary Magdalene suffered from what we today call severe learning disabilities. From time to time at the store, I see parents with adult children who were born with this disability. I also had the blessing of volunteering as a helper during my youth in junior high and worked with these beautiful people. There is no doubt in my mind that to God they are very special; in fact, so special that He chose to appear to one of them first. Initially, the apostles didn't give her any credit, but we are wise to be mindful that God's heart is so much more enduring to what this world doesn't see (*I Samuel 16:7*), the innocence of a pure heart. This world rejected the ONE who was precious and hence is obsessed with the outward appearances that are unconscious of true beauty. While many covet things in this world, they walk in the opposite direction of a true compass. They are unconscious to the steering that purposely avoids the healing of wholeness (found only in Jesus). I believe Jesus healed Magdalene of the physical manifestations of her disability. My opinion is that she remained childlike, much as those born with the disability often remain throughout adulthood. These special people have insights that those born without the condition will never have because they are very much relationship oriented. I used to affectionately refer to them as "love bugs" (no disrespect intended). Furthermore, God is quite aware of the hardship of parents of these special people and blessed the parents of Magdalene abundantly with the knowledge of His grace as he does to some to this day. Jesus makes it clear that to enter the Kingdom of God one has to have the heart of a child (see *Matthew 18:3*). In the fifth century, a Pope suspected Mary Magdalene was a repentant sinner, which led to a belief that she was an adulteress or prostitute. This type of warped interpretational analysis has skewed our understanding of scriptures to this day. We have the first person whom the God of Glory chooses to appear to, and a Pope tarnishes her reputation. In two Gospels we are told, point blank, that she suffered from seven demons, and the seminaries don't suspect that she suffered some form of disability visible to the natural eye. This fact would most likely preclude her from being promiscuous as a prostitute.

At the cross, Jesus was likely crucified naked between two thieves, culminating in the humiliation of the Son of God. His mother, Mary, had a family ancestor named Eve, who was married to Adam. They both ate of the fruit, but the problem was that they had stolen it from God. They, too, were naked, and Jesus, their son, died for them, so that they might be clothed with His righteousness (see *II Corinthians 5:21*), that they might be with Him, also, with His Father and their Father.

The scene at the cross was a Holy preordained moment of God, and not just any woman was allowed to look upon the nakedness of His Son. The women who were at the cross had changed Jesus' diapers, but the one who didn't, who was named after his mother, was an innocent child.

Mary Magdalene's Healing

Before I formed you in the womb I knew you, before you were born I set you apart; I appointed you as a prophet to the nations (*Jeremiah 1:5 [NIV]*). God selected Mary Magdalene to be the first witness of Jesus' resurrection. Magdalene was healed so that she could speak of His glory. There is a huge lesson in this. We all need to be healed before we can be a true witness of His deity.

Salome and others loved Jesus from His Birth, and inexplicably their compelling story has been neglected. Jesus most likely healed Mary Magdalene before this fictional account that I'm going to share, but I want readers to ponder the family that suffered from loving Jesus. He took note of it and poured out many blessings upon them.

It was the First day of the week, and Mary's mother was going to take Magdalene into Capernaum where the daily market conducted trade. She eagerly anticipated the sweetness of figs, her favorite treat and reward for participation in the weekly walk into town. Mary wasn't apprehensive about what awaited her every time she went into town. Some children would hurl insults towards her, but it never crossed her mind that their taunts should bother her, i.e., last week: *"Lookout here comes the demon girl"* or *"there is the ugly fish face,"* in reference to her father Zebedee's occupation.

John, Mary's brother, walked in the front door and said, *"Hello."*

Salome asked her son: *"Well, how did it go?"*

"*They tried to kill Him,*" said John to his mother.

"*What!*" exclaimed Salome, and the conversation went on.

Magdalene listened intently and saw tears streaming down her mother's cheeks. She didn't understand most of the words between her mother and brother, but she inherently knew what Nazareth was incapable of discerning.

After Salome had stopped crying for a moment, she managed to get the words out, "*What about His brothers?*"

John sighed and then replied to his mother, "*They don't believe in Him either.*"

Mary seized upon her brother's last words and squeezed her mother's hand and received a responding hug in return.

Suddenly Mary bolted through the front door, but Salome wasn't surprised. She had seen this reaction before. She was running to Jesus. Magdalene saw Jesus smile as she ran as fast as she could into his arms. She spoke with the clarity that few but Jesus would understand. Yet, Jesus heard every word before she even spoke a sound. They were the words He yearned to hear His disciples say, that could come only from their hearts, "I *believe in you, Jesus.*"

Jesus looked into her eyes and spoke: "*Mary, you were beautiful from the day you were formed in the womb, and after today some in this town will believe it too.*"

He touched her grinning cheek with His right forefinger and with His thumb gently grazed her tongue, which partially protruded from her mouth, as was customary. Suddenly Magdalene felt a tingle in her tongue that went through both cheeks.

Salome thought to herself: "*How could the town that witnessed His goodness from the beginning try to kill Him? How could Mary's children refuse to believe her, the most blessed mother?*" Then a sound, as beautiful as it was, caught her completely off guard, "*Mother.*" In a blink of an eye, Salome's tears reappeared. They weren't from anguish as before, but from the well of pure joy that filled her from her head to her toes.

CHAPTER 19

Jesus Appears to Simon Peter

They Don't Believe Us

And it came to pass, as they were much perplexed thereabout, behold, two men stood by them in shining garments. And as they were afraid, and bowed down their faces to the earth, they said unto them, Why ye seek the living among the dead? *(Luke 24:4-5 [KJV])*. The Jesus Who walked the Earth has died, and yet His Glory was restored as in the book of Revelation, which is far different than his form than here on Earth. We should know Who He was, but worship Him for Who He is now.

He is not here, but is risen: remember how he spake unto you when he was yet in Galilee, saying, The Son of man must be delivered into the hands of sinful men, and be crucified, and the third day rise again *(Luke 24:6-7 [KJV])*. Jesus' followers, like all of us at times, had been unable to comprehend or were unwilling to accept His Word.

And they remembered His Words, and returned from the sepulchre, and told all these things unto eleven, and to all the rest. It was Mary Magdalene, and Joanna, and Mary the mother of James, and other women that were with them, which told these things unto the apostles. And their words seemed to them as idle tales, and they believed them not *(Luke 24:8-11 [KJV])*. Eleven apostles had scattered, but apparently, somehow they all get together in a short time on a

Sunday. They didn't have cell phones. How do you get the news out and get everyone together who had scattered? It was easily accomplished because as relatives they were staying together or knew where others were located. As stated in the previous chapter, I believe they met at Mary's (mother of John Mark) home that is, interestingly, given to us in a verse numbered *12:12* in *Acts*.

I contend that three sets of brothers account for seven apostles, of which all were cousins. Some of the women who are talking idle (fairy) tales are the apostle's mothers or aunts, and in some essence, their sons had no choice but to listen to them. The apostles don't believe them. Why? These are the same women who told them that Jesus was the Messiah and they had previously believed their mothers. Where did their faith get them? The apostles are devastated because their version of Jesus coming to the throne of David was quite different than what had transpired. Consequently, they don't believe their mothers who led them to the Lord. We should pause and consider this great lesson. These women beheld the face of Jesus when He told them: "Ye are the light of the world." There wouldn't be any Apostles without them, and because they didn't forsake Him, God honors them as the first witnesses of His Resurrection.

After that he appeared in another form unto two of them, as they walked, and went into the country *(Mark 16:12 [KJV])*. Mark tells us the story of Jesus' second appearance to two men. Ironically, they will not be believed, either; and to this day, they are not credited for being the first to see Him. Since this is Jesus' first resurrection appearance, we should attempt to determine who they are and why He chose to appear to them first.

This should stand out to us as believers, and be taught every Easter Sunday. This pinnacle meeting is part of the resurrection story and is given in two Gospels. Yet, it isn't explained or shown in any Gospel movie.

Traditional interpretations have gotten hung up on the words that translate as "in another form." The Gospel writers' intentions were not to suggest that Jesus appeared in some mystic form or in disguise. The various translations do not help us because they translate *Mark 16:12* as "another form," instead of "another time," which would be so much clearer and in context with the story; for it is His second appearance, which occurs after Magdalene's account.

Now You See Me and Now You Don't

Mark writes of Jesus' second resurrection appearance, but Luke gives us many more details in his Gospel. Luke wrote his Gospel after Mark, and he actually gives us the identity of the two men, which is ignored by Bible expositors to this day.

Then arose Peter, and ran unto the sepulchre: and stooping down, he beheld the linen clothes laid by themselves, and departed, wondering in himself at that which was come to pass *(Luke 24:12 [KJV])*. We should note that the previous and the following verses are connected to this event. Simon Peter had been sulking and miserable after first denying Jesus and then losing Him to death. At this point, after seeing the empty tomb and hearing the women's testimonies, Simon Peter was apparently hopeful, but not entirely convinced that such an amazing thing could be. He had not yet seen Jesus for himself, so he returns yet again and finds nothing.

And behold, two of them went that same day to a village called Emmaus, which was from Jerusalem about threescore furlongs *(Luke 24:13 [KJV])*. Emmaus may have been six miles south of Jerusalem and probably very close to John the Baptist's parents' home. One of the two men was Cleopas (see *Luke 24:18*), who was married to Mary, the mother of James and Joses. He is significant because his wife stood at the cross and his two sons are Jesus' apostles. He is also known as Alphaeus and is referred to as the father of James and his brother, who is known by the various names of Judas, Jude, or Joses (see *Matthew 10:3*, *Luke 6:15*, and *Acts 1:13*). There is a consensus by the Catholic Church and protestant expositors that Alphaeus and Cleopas must be the same person because the other Mary is the mother of these apostles and Cleopas is married to her. We have been told by the writers of the Gospels that the people commonly had two names. Complicating this issue is the fact that there must have been some difficulty translating some names from Aramaic (or Hebrew) to Greek. Alphaeus (Cleopas) is indeed important because he is, perhaps, the father of three of the apostles.

And as he passed by, he saw Levi, the son of Alphaeus sitting at the receipt of custom, and said unto him, Follow me. And he rose and followed him *(Mark 2:14 [KJV]).* The Gospel of Christ is about grace, mercy, and reconciliation. It's my belief that religious precepts will never get that and, therefore, will never see how beautiful the story is. All believers should know that it's God's will that all souls would be reconciled to Him by His Son. His purpose is that we all be reunited with the family of God. Thus, the Prince of Peace reunited families to one another when He walked the Earth. Let us look at Jesus' calling to Matthew (Levi) from that perspective. He walks up to him with his brothers and his parents and his cousins and says, "Follow Me." Matthew was ostracized as a tax collector, but Jesus calls him back to reconcile with his own family and the family of God. There are many believers with broken families today. God would have us examine ourselves to avoid sowing seeds of division by judging with the lenses of the past, which is the opposite of God's purpose for us.

Simon Peter denied Jesus and perhaps everyone knew this and was distant from him. He was reeling and went back to the tomb at least twice. Cleopas (Alphaeus), who had his own son restored to him by Jesus, knew in his heart that showing mercy was a much better choice than that of judging Simon. He had heard his wife talk about seeing angels and he accompanied Simon Peter, to also see for himself. They are gabbing away when a stranger joins them. Cleopas will do all the talking with the stranger, whom we know is Jesus.

And they talked together of all these things which happened. And it came to pass, that, while they communed together and reasoned, Jesus himself drew near, and went with them. But their eyes were holden that they should not know him *(Luke 24:14-16 [KJV]).* It's my contention they both knew Jesus from the time He was a little boy. The incident then becomes rather humorous. The lesson may be, **though we have known Christ after the flesh, yet now henceforth know we**

him no more *(II Corinthians 5:16 [KJV])*. We also no longer know Him in the flesh and only by His Spirit do we connect to Him.

And he said unto them, What manner of communications are these that ye have one to another, as ye walk, and are sad *(Luke 14:17 [KJV])*? From Jesus' perspective, why should they be sad after hearing that He was alive? Perhaps their egos lead them to feel jilted. **And the one of them, whose name was Cleopas, answering said unto him, Art thou only a stranger in Jerusalem, and hast not known the things which are to come to pass there in these days** *(Luke 24:14-18 [KJV])*.

We should understand that Cleopas, whom Jesus sought to appear to first, loved Jesus very much. He was a human being and reacted emotionally to Jesus' question, without any spiritual discernment. **But we trusted that it had been he which should redeem Israel: and besides all this, today is the third day since things were done** *(Luke 24:24 [KJV])*. There is a book in this verse. They, being the family, and others, thought things were going to pan out a little differently than Messiah Resurrection. They had known Him since His birth, and instead of Jesus being King over Israel and leading the people to freedom from the Romans, He was dead. They like the part about Jesus being King, and being closely related and attached to Him. They had mixed motives for serving Jesus, as we all do, including wanting God to do things that make life easier for us. They naturally had pride, which God doesn't accept. God sees through this, which is why He accepts our conversion through His Spirit. Our mind, as theirs, doesn't know the will of God. It doesn't even recognize when Jesus intervenes and meets us at critical points. **Yea, certain women also of our company made us astonished, which were early at the sepulchre** *(Luke 24:22 [KJV])*. Cleopas uses the term "company" in our translation, and we should know that to be his wife. **And when they found not his body, they came, saying, that they had also seen a vision of angels, which said he was alive** *(Luke 24:33 [KJV])*. I feel it's rather obvious that Cleopas doesn't believe his own wife. We should note that he will not mention what was important: Magdalene said Jesus was alive. He doesn't utter the words, discounting Magdalene as a child. **And certain of them which were with us went to the sepulchre, and found it** even so as the women said; but him they saw not *(Luke 24:24 [KJV])*. Most likely, all the apostles, at different times, went to the sepulchre to see for themselves. Cleopas is making the point that the scene was as the women said it was, but Jesus was nowhere to be found.

Then he said unto them, O fools, and slow of heart to believe all that the prophets have spoken *(Luke 24:25 [KJV])*. Anyone who doubts God is acting foolishly. He will then present the Word of God, where Christ was prophesied to suffer before returning as King. They will ask the unrecognized Jesus to stay and eat something with them.

We should remember that Simon Peter made three affirmations to Jesus, only to deny Him three times. We know he went to the tomb twice, and it's just my opinion that this is the third time.

Jesus began His conversation by asking them three questions (doubts):

1) *What is your conversation?*

2) *Why are you sad?*

3) *What things have happened today?*

After this, Jesus gives them and us three Scriptures (affirmations):

1) *He calls them fools for not believing God.*

2) *He tells them Christ suffered before Glory.*

3) *He gives them Scriptures concerning Himself.*

Jesus then does three things: He takes the bread, blesses it, and breaks it.

And it came to pass, as he sat at meat with them, he took bread, and blessed it, and brake and gave to them *(Luke 24:30 [KJV])*. Jesus was broken on the cross so that we might be reunited with the Father and the apostles were ignorant of this purpose (see *John 14:8-9*). **And their eyes were opened, and they knew him; and he vanished out of their sight** *(Luke 24:31 [KJV])*. There is a great deal in this verse.

Ironically, they see Him as the risen Christ, and then He vanishes. This signifies that we must have our spiritual eyes opened by Him to know the hidden truths. His apostles believed in Him with a human perspective but didn't understand the will of God.

And they said one to another, Did not our heart burn within us, while he talked with us by the way, and how he was known of them in breaking of bread *(Luke 24:32 [KJV])*. Jesus had communion with His apostles before He was arrested and taken from them. They marvel at the fact that they didn't recognize Him. It is a warning to believers today to not be so distracted that we can't recognize His face in our lives. **And they rose up the same hour and returned to Jerusalem, and found the eleven gathered together, and them that were with them** *(Luke 24:33 [KJV])*.

CHAPTER 20

Ye of Little Faith

Magdalene and the women report to the apostles. They are not believed. Peter is ostracized by some of the apostles and, troubled, goes back to the tomb with Cleopas. They meet the Lord and rush to where the disciples are gathered. Cleopas exclaims that the *"Lord is risen, indeed, and hath appeared to Simon."* Then he goes on to give details about the meeting.

In no other place in Scripture but Luke is Cleopas referenced as having had the Lord appear to him. Cleopas wasn't a main character in the Gospel, and evidently, he knew what many Bible expositors don't. Simon Peter is one of the main characters in all four Gospels. Cleopas is humble; he knew the Lord sought out Simon, who had denied Him and was devastated. Cleopas loves Simon Peter, because he doesn't disown him, and he is honored by Christ. If we understand that the story (Christ-like) was written to make sense, then we see the flow of what Luke has conveyed to us.

And they told what things were done in the way, and how he was known of them in breaking the bread *(Luke 24:35 [KJV])*. We should note the key words, "breaking the bread." Needless to say, the two men are giving their testimony of what happened when Jesus appeared to them. What two men? Cleopas told them Jesus appeared to Simon and recounts the event with Peter being mostly, and uncharacteristically, silent, because he is still embarrassed. We might surmise that Peter had been ashamed and wasn't talking to anyone, even Jesus.

Tradition has a different view which they have passed down through the ages. Why? One word: "Found." The seminaries are rather dogmatic about these two men are finding the eleven apostles already together. As Cleopas (and whoever) walks in, they are told by the apostles that the Lord hath appeared to Simon. Many Bible expositors believe that Jesus' appearance to Simon Peter was a private meeting that God purposely omitted from scripture. And the other apostles tell these two witnesses that the Lord appeared to Simon Peter. The interpretation makes absolutely no sense, especially when we look at the verse *(Luke 24:32-35)* with both of them recanting the story.

Apparently many interpretations just ignore the scriptures of *Mark (14:12-13)*. The Gospel of Mark is considered, by some, to have had additional details added to it after it was first written, whereby it doesn't bear the same credence. The consequence is that Christians are taught that the Gospels of Jesus' resurrection are irreconcilable with each other, about which Atheists exhort that there are contradictions presented about Jesus. This belief, passed down through the ages, throws the conclusion of the story into confusion. It robs believers of connecting to the pinnacle of our faith, Jesus' resurrection, and His mercy.

Luke gives believers a great gift in Acts 12:12, but do we receive it? We should suspect that Mark (known also as John Mark) witnessed the entire exchange between his cousins in his mother's house. When we know the background of the writer, our confidence and connection to the story intensifies. Mark was most likely a teenager and wasn't directly involved with exchanges. Perhaps this is the reason why his Gospel is much more condensed.

God would want us to see His grace, that we might exhibit it to ourselves and each other. He is fully aware that our carnal nature doubts His omnipotence, and as a consequence, we stumble often. That is why He has good news (Gospels): that although it's impossible for us to be perfect during our time on earth, His grace is sufficient for all of us.

God's Word is the Light of this world but errors in syntax are a problem for our translations. One word is misinterpreted, and the story is skewed. Simon is one of the eleven. **And they rose up the same hour and returned to Jerusalem, and found the eleven gathered together, and them that were with them** *(Luke 24:33 [KJV])*. Other translations don't help us either; let's look at the new living translation: "And within the hour they were on their way back to Jerusalem. There they found the eleven disciples and the others who had gathered with them. This illustrates a theme in my book that context is more important than particular words.

Mark 16:12's account of this event includes the word "residue", which I translate as "rest of." The translators have ignored this keyword, which makes it much clearer that the two witnesses returned to the rest of the disciples. Bible expositors seem to ignore that Simon got up and left the apostles earlier so obviously he had to return. Then there are some who do notice and think that when Simon left Jesus appeared to him, even when Luke makes it clear that he saw nothing upon returning to the tomb.

Movies diminish the best part of the story (His resurrection) because they don't know how to tell the audience what transpired. Typically, the movies that have been made show Jesus appearing to eleven apostles. They miss the best part of the story and what comes later. We should notice that in almost all translations there is written: "who had gathered with them." This means that there are other people with the apostles. Shouldn't we at least suspect those gathered together are the family of the apostles? In other words, Jesus appeared to the family of those who were with the apostles. There is a great lesson in that, but it's also ignored.

My translation of *Luke 24:33*: "They immediately returned to Jerusalem and reunited with the rest of the eleven who gathered together." When we change a couple of words, such as "found," and we use in its place "reunited," the verse is better translated. "Found" is an English word that implies they searched for them, and yet previously we were told they knew the gathering place. This again is a case where the translators were preoccupied with words and not the context. At the time of first translations, this is understandable. Today, it's not. We should see this story in the clear context with the additional evidence found in other Scriptures.

And as they thus spake, Jesus himself stood in the midst of them, and saith unto them, Peace be unto you (*Luke 24:36 [KJV]*). This verse comes after they (Cleopas and Simon Peter) told what things they saw. *Luke 24:36* gives the impression to Bible expositors that it happened instantly after unknown men were speaking. Actually, Cleopas and Simon Peter gave their accounts and were not believed, so a period of time occurred before Jesus appears to all of them (except Thomas, explained later). These are human beings, and as such, there was quite a bit of discussion with two men claiming they just saw Jesus, whom they'd all thought was dead.

Unfortunately, believers are so disconnected to the story that they don't see the beauty of His grace in appearing at such a time. His command was that they love one another, and there is great discord between them. He appeared to restore the unity of His family and disciples. His second coming has some of the same purposes as for His first. He will end the division between the earthly and the Heavenly family. As He says in the Lord's prayer: "*Thy Kingdom come, Thy will be done on Earth as is it is in Heaven.*"

When Jesus said, "Peace be unto you," He meant it. Bible expositors believe Jesus was calming the disciples down so they wouldn't be afraid of His appearance. There is some truth to that, but tragically, believers don't understand that the Prince of Peace wanted peace among His believers, as He does to this day.

As a believer, I've lost my way many times, but it's encouraging to see the apostles were not supermen. They were ordinary people who believed in Jesus but had their own perceptions of what that meant for their lives. Does it make sense that God would want us to be able to use His resurrection appearances to bless our lives by connecting to His apostles? It's critical that we see the reason for such appearances was not because the apostles had faith, but because of His incredible grace and mercy. Otherwise, we inherit the super apostle syndrome while interpreting the Gospels. We judge and compare, which is the opposite of what Jesus' life represents to us. We diminish the fact that God always wants to pour out His grace, but our own self-judgment blocks it. We have missed the great teaching that Jesus first appeared to Simon Peter and then the apostles to reconcile them amongst themselves.

Today many religions feel it's quite all right to fight amongst themselves and judge others. Many Christians don't reflect on what happened in this resurrection account of the apostles, that they might not do the same. Consequently, many believers don't even know what judging is. God calls us to have our eyes opened by the Word of God so that we can see ourselves in His grace, so as not to judge other people. Judging is not seeing; it's punishing people for not measuring up to higher, arbitrary standards. It looks in the past and justifies its actions by labeling people's behavior. For instance, a person gets their feelings hurt: *"Lisa did this to me and so I'm not going to talk to her."* Judging destroys relationships and creates division throughout the world. Jesus is God, and He did things for many reasons, but one of them was so that angels would look at us, in Him. They saw Him receive and still see His wounds, and no one is going to accuse (or look into the pasts of) the brethren in God's or their sight. The one that insisted on judging has a place where he can judge throughout eternity, but it's not heaven *(Revelation 12:10)*.

Mark's version is in just two verses, which apparently is why Luke elaborates more on the event in his Gospel. **After that he appeared in another form unto two of them, as they walked, and went into the country. And they, when they told it unto the residue: neither believed they them** *(Mark 16:13 [KJV])*. Mark tells us that these two witnesses were not believed. The apostles—except for John, who ran with him to the tomb—rejected Simon Peter, and we should understand that they felt they had plenty reasons to judge him. The truth is that he made a knucklehead of himself, and the Gospels don't diminish it. He boldly insinuated himself to be the greatest of the apostles by declaring, **"Though all men shall be offended because of thee, yet I never be offended"** *(Matthew 26:33[KJV])*. Not to mention in *Luke 9:46* and

22:46 where we find that the apostles were previously accustomed to disagreements between them about who was the greatest.

Why were their hearts hard? They judged, rather than showed grace, as Cleopas demonstrated. Most likely they assumed that Simon Peter was trying to gain back his self-respect and came up with this story. Perhaps they thought that Cleopas wanted to help him get restored. This would make sense if Cleopas were either a relative or married to a relative of Peter, perhaps his sister. The Gospel of John will corroborate Mark and Luke, not contradict them. It will give us more details, including the fact that the conversation with Simon Peter, Cleopas, and the rest went on for some time before Jesus appeared.

Many believers, like Peter, have been broken by failures. We would be well-advised to be compassionate, rather than judging them. We should be like Cleopas, who isn't ashamed to be with someone who has stumbled, and who wants his brother restored to the community, rather than ostracized. God chastises those He loves, and we would be wise not to judge His work on all of us. I have had many failures in this life which are nothing to take pride in. Yet I am willing to let go of them because I believe God can use imperfections and my weaknesses. His grace is always willing to meet them and take what was vain and use it to reflect His mercy.

Most of the apostles were cousins and may have wondered why Joseph's children rejected Mary and Jesus. It's my opinion that they had judged from their high horses, and consequently, did the same as they measured what they did. The apostles witnessed many miracles, but they too rejected the Lord's witnesses. Their mothers told them that angels proclaimed Jesus had risen, and Magdalene and Simon Peter did, too, but the apostles didn't believe them. The world today rejects His three witnesses: The Father, The Son, and The Holy Spirit.

The Apostle Paul's Affirmation

Do we think God would want us to know the resurrection accounts and connect to this glorious day? If Simon wasn't one of the two men, then would God want us to know and be certain? If He did, would He put it someplace else? Yes, he does: I Corinthians gives us three accounts of Simon Peter's encounter with the risen Lord.

The apostle Paul wrote a narrative of Jesus' resurrection in I Corinthians. Here are a couple of highlights: **For I delivered unto you first of all that which I also received, how that Christ died for our sins according to the Scriptures. And that he was buried, and that he rose again the third day according to the Scriptures** (*I Corinthians 15:3-4 [KJV]*). Paul then didn't need to repeat what Matthew, Mark, and Luke had already written.

And that he was seen of Cephas, then of the twelve (*I Corinthians 15:5 [KJV]*). Paul used the name Cephas—the Aramaic name for Simon Peter. Paul states explicitly that Jesus appeared to Simon Peter and then the disciples. The Spirit has placed the resurrection appearance to Simon Peter in two Gospels and the book of Corinthians, yet believers still are not taught it. The Apostle Paul will also tell us something very paramount to the family story which we will explore in the final chapter.

CHAPTER 21

Encore

Our society will change, but the primary context of human relationships won't change. We all are divided from each other. The Lord's purpose, which is to reunite and heal what was lost in division, doesn't change.

John's Gospel provides more emphasis than the Synoptic Gospels of Jesus' deity, which is boldly underscored in this resurrection appearance that only John recorded. In Luke (24:36), **Thomas, one of the twelve, called Didymus, was not with them when Jesus came. The other disciples, therefore, said unto him, We have seen the Lord. But he said unto them, Except I shall see in his hands the print of the nails, and put my finger into the print of the nails, and thrust my hand into his side, I will not believe** (John 20:24-25 [KJV]).

Now, it appears that Thomas, one of the eleven who were together in Luke 24:33, was absent from Jesus' appearance. Is this a contradiction? It's explainable. Somehow, he absenced himself before the moment when the Lord appeared on that occasion. Maybe he had to go to the bathroom or run an errand or tend to family. More likely, being true to his form, Thomas had heard enough from Simon Peter and stomped out in disgust. He was told something wonderful, and he had a horrible response because I believe he was very angry at someone (Simon Peter). He made a conscious decision not to believe, and Thomas would reap the consequences of that unbelief, coming face to face with the One who had received nail imprints for him and will keep them throughout eternity. God uses Thomas' unbelief to give us the Gospel. God is not deterred He uses everything, and He can turn our failures into great successes. **And we know that all things work together for good to them that love God, to them who are called accordingly to his purpose** *(Romans 8:28 [KJV]).*

And after eight days again his disciples were within, and Thomas with them: then came Jesus, the doors being shut, and stood in the midst, and said, Peace be unto you *(John 20:26 [KJV]).* Jesus appeared the following Sunday evening. Since the Jews started and ended each twenty-four-hour day at sunset, and since they counted part of a day as a whole day, the "eight days" probably included the end of their Sunday (a few hours before sunset).

Then saith he to Thomas, reach thy finger hither, and behold my hands; and reach thy hand hither, and thrust it into my side: and be not faithless, but believing *(John 20:27 [KJV]).* Jesus had heard Thomas's ultimatum (his prayer) and answered it with His appearance. He graciously indulged Thomas's implied request and invited him to see, touch, and believe. **And Thomas answered and said unto him, My Lord and my God** *(John 20:28 [KJV]).* Thomas's confession confirmed the truth that is evident throughout the Bible: Jesus has always been God. **I am the Alpha and Omega, the beginning and the ending, saith the Lord, which is, and which was, and which is to come, the Almighty** *(Revelation 1:8 [KJV]).*

Jesus saith unto him, Thomas, because thou hast seen me, thou hast believed; blessed are they that have not seen, and yet have believed *(John 20:29 [KJV]).* He speaks of us because He knew us before we were born and so we are all, in a sense, in scripture. When we slip into anger, we tend to judge ourselves, as did Thomas, for he missed a tremendous blessing. Sometimes we get what we ask for, but by His grace, many times we don't. Sequentially, this was actually Jesus' sixth resurrection appearance and it cements the union between the apostles, as Thomas wasn't there when He appeared previously. Jesus wanted His apostles to love one another as he wants us to love each other. He wanted no discord and John, as well as Mark, made it clear there was trouble between them. This is Satan's will for the world, believers, and families: to be divided in bitter discord.

Jesus' next appearance, and it is to me the most beautiful of them all, is one that few, if any, believers are aware of. My hope is that Christians see the Unity of the resurrection story, that shows His Love and how the Gospels beautifully complement each other.

Return to Galilee

The people of Nazareth may have hated Jesus, but He loved them. His brothers and their kin may never have wanted to see Him, but He wanted to bless them. **Then said Jesus, Be not afraid: go tell my brethren that they go into Galilee, and there shall they see me** *(Matthew 28:10 [KJV])*. I'm convinced that He was telling His disciples to gather His half-siblings—the sons and daughters of Joseph and Mary—in Galilee to witness Him, risen from the dead. Jesus' siblings had wanted nothing to do with Him. Jesus' instructions of "Be not afraid" clinch the view: "Don't be apprehensive. Tell them that they will see me in Galilee."

Matthew is, in my mind, the Gospel of rejection and reconciliation. He knew what it was like to feel the sting of its hate and the grace of its healing. That is the theme from the very beginning, starting with Joseph's plan to reject Mary. Matthew, like the other original writers, wrote to people who understood their time, and as such, they expected them to connect to their words. The writers didn't have computers with word processors to aid them; they wrote details that could be surmised easily, at the time, by the audience.

Matthew's Gospel of Rejection and Reconciliation

Event	Rejection	Reconciliation
Mary is Pregnant	Joseph considers rejecting (1:19)	Joseph marries Mary (1:24)
Infant Jesus is persecuted	Joseph is warned in dream (1:13)	Joseph is told he is safe (2:20)
Matthew is ostracized as Tax Collector	Hostility towards Matthew (9:11)	Jesus says, "Follow me" with his family (9:9)
The soldiers' treatment of Jesus	Soldiers mock Him (27:28-31)	Centurion confesses He is Son of God (27:54)
The Disciples	Disciples forsook Him (26:56)	Disciples follow Him (28:16)

Matthew begins his story by telling us about by Herod, and later the Jewish leader's rejection of Jesus. He doesn't give us every detail in his Gospel, but what was paramount to him. Jesus rose from the dead and reconciled his Earthly household with His heavenly Father's family. Let's not take my word for it, but rather, someone with a higher authority.

Let's look again at Paul's summary of Jesus' post-resurrection appearances: **And that he was buried, and that he rose again the third day according to the Scriptures: And that he was seen of Cephas, then of the twelve: After that, he was seen of above five hundred brethren at once; of whom the greater part remain unto this present, but some are fallen asleep. After that, he was seen of James, then of all the apostles. And last of all he was seen of me also, as of one born out of due time** *(I Corinthians 15:4-8 [KJV])*. When Paul writes: "then of the twelve," it's not a contradiction of Luke's Gospel stating: "found the eleven." When Christ appeared to the apostles, His mother's family was with them, as were other followers. Later in Acts (see *Acts 1:26*), the apostles started a tradition of replacing Judas and numbering others with the twelve. Matthias was elected and was apparently one of those who witnessed the Lord's resurrection with the other eleven apostles. The Apostle Paul is giving us a summary of appearances when he makes statements according to the scriptures (Jesus' appearance to

Magdalene), and then Cephas (Simon Peter) and "then of twelve" (who are all apostles, except Thomas). The translation apparently throws off Bible expositors; but the Apostle Paul, who is a higher authority, gives today's church the correct order of the appearances of Jesus Christ, and we should listen to him.

We have already been through the four appearances, but we missed something in the sequence. Paul tells us that before Jesus' appearance as given to us in the Gospel of John, Jesus appeared in Galilee to five hundred people at once.

Paul lets us know that over five hundred people came to witness the resurrection. No doubt news came to Capernaum and his half-brothers who were on the way back to Nazareth. How? **Then said Jesus, Be not afraid: tell my brethren that they go into Galilee, and there shall they see me** (Matthew 28:10 [KJV]). I'm convinced that He was telling His disciples (His family, His Mother, Aunts, and cousins who are all with them) to gather His half-siblings—the sons (and daughters) of Joseph and Mary—in Galilee to witness Him, risen from the dead. Jesus' siblings had wanted nothing to do with Him. Jesus' instructions of "Be not afraid" clinch the view. "Don't be afraid to tell them that they will see me in Galilee."

What a beautiful story! I visualize Jesus' cousins running towards Galilee in a hurried effort to overtake His siblings, who are on their way from Jerusalem to Nazareth. They would stop in Cana before going to Nazareth, and I visualize Jesus' cousins finding them and making a vain attempt to divert them to Capernaum. I suspect they rejected Mary's family's witness and were harsh with them.

The Apostle Paul tells us something not found anywhere else: that Jesus appeared to His half-brother, James. This resurrection appearance is the exclamation mark by God that Jesus appeared to His siblings. It grieves my heart that believers haven't been told this beautiful story through the ages. We are not given the conversation between them because our God is wonderful, full of grace, and wishes to spare all of us the shame we have chosen when we reject Him. We have the results of Jesus' meeting with James: **James answered, saying, Men and**

brethren, hearken unto me *(Acts 15:13 [KJV])*. And they will hearken unto Him as He will rise to be the leader of the Church. We know this is the brother of the Lord because James, the brother of John, was killed by the sword *(Acts 12:2)*. **But other of the apostles saw I none, save James the Lord's brother** *(Galatians 1:19 [KJV])*. James will later be considered an Apostle as head of the church and will meet with Paul, which is probably why we have this information in Corinthians. James will go on to write an epistle that is today a canon of Scripture.

My suspicion is that Jesus' siblings rejected the news of His resurrection and refused to go to Capernaum. I suspect that James was rather gruff about his disbelief, as Thomas had been, and he got an unconscious prayer answered that he didn't even know he'd prayed. Then Jesus appeared to James, the head of the household, as He'd appeared to Thomas, who didn't believe in Him.

Jesus' Eight Resurrection Appearances

	Apostle Paul's Summary	Gospels
First	1) *He rose again the third day according to the Scriptures*	1) Magdalene John 20:16-17
Second	2) *And that he was seen of Cephas*	2) Simon Peter Mark 16:12-13 Luke 24:13-34
Third	3) *Then of the twelve*	3) Luke 24:36-46, John 20:19-24 Mark 16:14
Fourth	4) *He was seen of above five hundred brethren*	4) Matthew 28:16-17
Fifth	5) *He was seen of James*	
Sixth	6) *Then of all the apostles*	5) John 20:26-27
Seventh		6) Apostles on Sea of Galilee John 21:13
Eighth		7) Christ's Ascension Acts 1:2-9, Luke 25:49-53, Matthew 28:18
	7) *Last of all he was seen of me*	

Jesus' appearance to the Apostle Paul occurred after His ascension into Heaven. We are given this by the Holy Spirit to complete a series of sevens, but it is not a resurrection appearance that occurred to Jesus' disciples or His family.

Is it important for Christians to observe Jesus' resurrection appearances? Now I ask the reader to please look at numbers three and six of Apostle Paul's summary. Please look up *I Corinthians 15:4-6* in any version you want, and what you will find is ambiguity on one of the most important scriptures in the New Testament. Number three on Paul's list: "then of the twelve" wasn't all the twelve, for the Apostle Paul is emphasizing that the Lord appeared to all the apostles in the sixth appearance.

Remember, John explicitly told us Thomas wasn't there for the first appearance to the apostles and then Jesus appeared eight days later to all the apostles. Apparently, "then of twelve" is the best translation some of our translations can come up with. But there is one problem: it's not correct, and it's confusing to all Christians that read the Bible across the world. Most heartbreaking of all, it robs Christians from knowing the Lord's resurrection appearances.

Let us look at some different translations of *I Corinthians 15:5*

> Living Bible—*"He was seen by Peter and later by the rest of "the Twelve."*
>
> English Standard—*"and that he appeared to Cephas, then to the twelve."*
>
> Amplified Bible—*"and that He appeared to Cephas (Peter), then to the Twelve."*
>
> New International Version—*"and that he appeared to Cephas, and then to the Twelve."*

Here is the crux of the problem with all the translations: they have microscopic thinking with no logical deductive reasoning to balance them. The Apostle John is a great witness, so we know the Lord didn't appear to all of them. All that is needed is the addition of one word that will connect the Apostle Paul's summary in I Corinthians to the Gospels. We add the word "some " to "then of the twelve." The translation then reads; "then to some of the twelve." Now we have cohesion and can appreciate Jesus' eight Resurrection appearances.

The problem with all our translations is that they are unable to balance the preoccupation with Greek syntax with other chapters of the Bible. As consequence, many Christians have been denied empowerment by Jesus' resurrection appearances in an order that is comprehensible and confirmed by the Apostle Paul.

Christians deserve a new translation that takes into account God's omnipotence, Jesus' deity, and how the particular verse relates to the entire Bible's composition. They need a translation that spells a person's name the same way (like "Cleopas"), instead of three different ways, so readers can connect to the story.

The Apostle Paul's Meeting With the Lord

And last of all he was seen of me also, as of one born out of due time *(I Corinthians 15:8 [KJV])*. I do not include the Apostle Paul's encounter with the Lord as a Resurrection appearance because the Lord had already ascended to Heaven. Jesus appeared to His disciples as they knew Him on the Earth so they could recognize Him. If you turn to *Revelation 1:12-18,* you will notice the Apostle John, who cuddled with Jesus, had a different reaction to the Lord with this encounter. This is the God that the Apostle Paul became aware of and it didn't occur within the forty days Jesus appeared to His disciples.

And now, O Father, glorify thou me with thine own self with the glory which I had with thee before the world was *(John 17:5 [KJV])*. There isn't one word that could describe either the wonder of His Humility or His Meekness. So God has graciously offered us an eternal life to attempt to speak what cannot be spoken even with eternity. How Good and Wonderful He is. He is the Great I Am, the High and Lofty One. For His great Love, He came be to a son of man. That in itself was humiliation, but He saw only His Love, and because He did, He suffered the greatest humiliation ever experienced by any man. We cannot do what He did; we didn't come from High Thrones, we came from the depths of sin. Yet what is the great ONE's response? **To him that overcometh will I grant to sit with me in my throne, even as I also overcame, and am set down with my Father in his throne** *(Revelation 3:21)*. The Highness desires to extend unspeakable grace on us all.

In conclusion, it's my contention that His resurrection appearances are straightforward, and they should be remembered every Easter. He preordained eight of them that we would connect to the Feast of Tabernacles and the Passover, that we would be grateful for One number beyond seven representing our eternity and victory in the One day of the Lord.

Family Farewell

To whom also he shewed himself alive after his passion by many infallible proofs, being seen of them forty days *(Acts 1:3 [KJV])*. Jesus finally ascended into Heaven forty days after His resurrection. Jesus spent time with them in Galilee, and then they all went to Jerusalem for His departure: **And he led them out as far as to Bethany, and he lifted up his hands, and blessed them** *(Luke 24:50 [KJV])*. Many of His kin walked with Him as He went to the Mount of Olives to say goodbye for the final time. Some of His apostles had questions that He refused to answer: **It is not for you to know the times or the seasons, which the Father hath put in his own power** *(Acts 1:7 [KJV])*. Many still hoped that Jesus would establish His Kingdom overtly—maybe militarily—and end the occupation of Rome. This is what they were expecting of Him from the beginning and as such their agendas blocked their ears from hearing Him. He told them many times He would die and rise again. They, as well as all of us, have our own perspectives on what God should do in our lives.

Then Jesus ascended out of their sight, and so, they were launched into the book of Acts with the hope of His similar return one day. **And when they were come in, they went up into an upper room. Mary mother of Jesus, and with his brethren** *(Acts 1:13-14 [KJV])*. Luke tells us that they were all in one accord, men and women, including, at last, Mary and Jesus' siblings. Jesus' every promise and assurance to His mother was being fulfilled. He is a man and a God of His word.

Mother's Day

I've heard preachers say that church pews are fuller on Mother's Day than on any other Sunday, including Easter. There was only one mother to the Son of God. Her name was Mary, and one Sunday, she received the greatest Mother's Day present ever.

But before that wonderful day, she suffered like few women have ever suffered. **Blessed art thou among women** *(Luke 1:42 [KJV])*. We must put the pieces together in Scripture, but that's only possible if we know the story. Mary's family was mentioned in Luke before Jesus was born. Nazareth hated her and took their sufferings out on her. Joseph's family blamed her for the shame they felt she caused. Her own children despised her and blamed their sufferings on her. She had to endure this life of torment and rejection throughout Jesus' earthly life—and then witness the debauchery of the cross without any support from her children. Among Jesus' many believers, she believed in him before he was born. There is no substitute for a mother's love and she loved Him more of His days than anyone on this earth.

Then we are told by Paul that James was visited by Jesus, Who was the leader of the family in Nazareth. We know that he once rejected Jesus, but he would rise to be leader of the church. Unfortunately, there hasn't been a movie dramatizing this encounter between James and the resurrected Christ, but all believers should know that it indeed occurred. We are told this beautiful end story in Acts, which has never been shown in movies about Him: His loving goodbye to His siblings and His mother, who happened to all be in Jerusalem. They finally left Nazareth. I wonder how emotional that reunion was between Mary and her children, so I thought I would attempt to write part of it, to end this book.

I imagine Mary at the cross, falling down in anguish.

Salome, her sister, John, and the other Mary help her up. Salome tells her daughter, *"Magdalene, watch where they take Him."*

Mary finds miraculous strength and tries to speak: *"I'm okay. Don't let her go alone."*

Salome looks at Cleopas' wife and says, *"Would you?"*

"I will go with Magdalene," says the other Mary.

Cleopas walks to Peter, who is pale from sobbing. Peter asks, *"What happened?"*

"They crucified Him. He is dead," says Cleopas.

Peter screams and runs to grab a sword, but is met by Cleopas. *"Remember, Peter: those who live by the sword, die by the sword. There is nothing gained by your death, now."*

The next evening, James, Salome's son, looks at his mother and tells her, *"I'm leaving at the appointed time, and it's only right now that I help my father."*

Salome looks at him and says, *"Ok, son, but despite what anyone believes now, I know my sister told the truth. Besides, we saw His miracles and remember; even your sister."*

Before the day dawns, Cleopas' wife says, *"Why don't you have Magdalene help us? She is of age."*

"She is the only one who has any life in her to smile. We will be fine. Joanna and others are also bringing spices," replies Salome.

Magdalene skips ahead and suddenly starts running. *"Magdalene!"* yells Salome, to no avail.

Salome sees Magdalene running toward her. *"What is it, child?"* asks her mother.

"The Romans have moved the stone." The sun comes out, and they can see the tomb is empty.

"Go tell your brothers!" exclaims Salome.

Magdalene runs into the house. *"They have taken Him out of the tomb, and we don't know where He is."*

After James asks her some questions, John and Peter get up and run toward the tomb, but James stays where he is.

It's been three weeks since that horrible day, and Mary retires to go to bed. Her sister, Salome, checks on her and kisses her on the forehead. During the third watch of the night, which is midnight, the room is suddenly bright. Mary is somewhat disoriented when a hand gently touches hers. A voice says, *"Woman, mine hour has come."*

Salome hears Mary's footsteps and sighs within herself. She gets up and notices Mary looking at the sea, as the sun has yet to come up. *"Are you ok, blessed sister?"* asks Salome.

"Today is a beautiful day," says Mary.

"The day hasn't begun yet, my sister," says Salome.

"Oh, but it has," replies Mary.

It's the third watch of the day when Salome notices a small company coming toward the house. She looks over at Mary and sees her face gleaming: *"What is it, sister? Why are you so happy?"*

Mary replies, *"You shall see."*

Salome looks on as the company draws near and recognizes James, who leads them. Magdalene grabs Salome's hand. *"What's wrong, Mommy?"*

They are wailing and Salome's heart sinks, and she sees tears flowing down Mary's face. *"Oh, God, please, no more! My blessed sister can take no more."*

Which child has died? She ponders. Salome scans them and sees that none are missing. Peter and Zebedee's sons, James and John, also see them from the shoreline and run toward the house.

The children of Joseph approach and suddenly James gets on his knees and his siblings join him, surrounding Mary, as they grab both her hands and her ankles.

James tries to speak and his words make no sense between his sobs. He tries again and is joined by all the siblings: *"Blessed art thou among women, Mother. Please forgive us."*

EPILOGUE

This World of Zeros

This world likes to count, but there is just one number that matters. Out of grace, it was given numbers so some in it might understand; they begin and end with ONE. Yet, out of greed, this world strives with ONE number, but its days are numbered.

To say that we are like Christ is akin to a zero saying it is like infinity. Our lives are a zero in comparison to what is infinite and eternal. There are 100 billion stars in one galaxy, and not until 1927 was man aware that there was more than one galaxy. Now astronomers are aware that the visible universe contains 100 billion galaxies, each with over 100 billion stars. The One who created it all, whose throne is above all creation, came to be one of His own creations, to save all creation that He might redeem us and we might be like Him, Who is perfect and eternal. By His mercy, He will end what is not perfect to restore final perfection. **I in them, and thou in me, that they may be made perfect in one** *(John 18:23 [KJV])*.

It doesn't matter how big the zero is: it's still a zero. Yet, this world is full of zeros that constantly compare themselves to each other. They expect other zeros to be better than a zero, and they're constantly disappointed that a zero is just a zero. Many zeros try to be great zeros, but in the end, each is just a zero.

You can put as many zeros together as you want, and you still have nothing:

00000000000000000000000000000000000000000

But just place a ONE in front of a zero, and you have a number with substance:

10

Now, the entire world is filled with zeros. Our society is full of dysfunction, disasters, and pain. The reason is because it rejects the only thing that matters: the only God, the only Lamb, the only Savior, the only way to God. Sadly, we know the world will always reject Him, even when He comes back. But when He puts the ONE in front of all of us, the world will have meaning.

100000000000000000000000000000000000000000

The number will go on forever, for He is forever, and He goes on forever, creating kindness and goodness for us throughout eternity. For He is the only I AM; the only purpose that matters. How I wish believers understood that He is the only ONE Who matters. **The Lord our God is one LORD** *(Deuteronomy 6:4 [KJV])*. We will never be the ONE. We can only put the ONE in front of our zero and see Him multiply the fruit of goodness in our lives.

Creation comes from His Word, and the Word is Jesus Christ. Zeros need to know they will never be the ONE; nor will anyone other than the ONE, be the ONE. They can have peace in the world of zeros when they see the zero in them has an eternal destiny to be attached to the ONE.

The Word of God is about the ONE, Who transforms zeros into tens and hundreds and thousands and tens of millions. It's never about the zeros. **Herein is my Father glorified, that ye bear much fruit** (*John 15:8 KJV*).

The ONE God loves and gives life to the dead. Every moment is an opportunity to die being a zero and let the ONE transform our zero into something alive. We can insist on staying a zero. We can choose to be dead or alive in Christ.

The world is full of zeros who want to be the ONE, but vainly fall so short. Zeros are empty, with nothing inside, so it's in vain that they look to fill themselves apart from the ONE. Pain and dysfunction and lack of purpose are guaranteed without connection to the ONE. A zero cannot create or restore life.

But whosoever drinketh of the water that I shall give him shall never thirst (*John 4:14 [KJV]*). The only thing that can fill a zero is the ONE. **For as the heavens are higher than the earth, so are my ways higher than your ways, and my thoughts than your thoughts** (*Isaiah 55:9 [KJV]*). There was only one ONE Who walked this earth, and His ways were high.

A zero is a circle that constantly goes someplace and nowhere at the same time. The ONE wants to turn every zero into something so much better than a zero. In fact, that's the purpose for which the ONE made every zero. All zeros die. But the zeros with the ONE go on throughout eternity, not just for 10 years or 100 or 10,000,000,000, but forever and ever. No book can contain the story that each of these zeros will live.

When God looks at us, He doesn't see a zero but His infinity expanding the circle thru eternity. What zero can comprehend infinity, living inside it? **Eye hath not seen, nor ear heard, neither have entered into the heart of man, the things which God hath prepared for them that love them** (*I Corinthians 2:9 [KJV]*). Abraham, Moses, David, Paul, and Peter are great heroes of the Bible. And yet, the Word of God says all of them failed when they gave in to fear. Fear guarantees that a zero will act like a zero. **For whatsoever is not of faith is sin** (*Romans 14:23 [KJV]*). Whatever is not done in faith in the ONE is a zero.

The Word of God is not about zeros being greater than other zeros. Believers need to stop judging other zeros and start glorifying the only

ONE Who matters, by letting Him add to their nothing and make it something.

The Bible is easy to interpret if we know the code is about the ONE. The subject is Jesus Christ, the action is God's mercy, and the purpose is salvation accomplished by God's work. Some think that serving God is complicated. **What shall we do, that we might work the works of God?** *(John 6:28 [KJV])*. But Jesus answered, **This is the work of God, that ye believe on him whom he hath sent** *(John 6:29 [KJV])*. Religion is complicated—so complicated, in fact, that Christ cannot be found in the center of it. Even though we have this simple Gospel, we have over forty thousand different Christian divisions.

Believe in ONE Jesus. He is the ONE way, the ONE truth, the ONE life, the ONE righteousness, the ONE bread that fills the soul, the ONE worthy Judge, the ONE Creator, the ONE Deliverer, the ONE blameless Who ever walked the Earth, our ONE strength, our ONE hope, our ONE love, our ONE peace, the only ONE in Whom we can find forgiveness for ourselves or anyone, the ONE omnipotent God.

All zeros frequently stumble or fall short of the ONE, even while seeking Him. But any zero can be reconnected to the ONE at any time. Zeros are not to judge, but to understand the ONE's willingness to extend infinite grace to be attached to his ONE. **For without me ye can do nothing** *(John 15:5 [KJV])*.

And when the ONE is attached to a zero, nothing can separate them. **For I am persuaded, that neither death, nor life, nor angels, nor principalities, nor powers, nor things present, nor things to come, nor height, nor depth, nor any other creature, shall be able to separate us from the love of God, which is in Christ Jesus our Lord** *(Romans 8:38-39 [KJV])*.

APPENDIX

Mary and the Apostle Family Genealogy

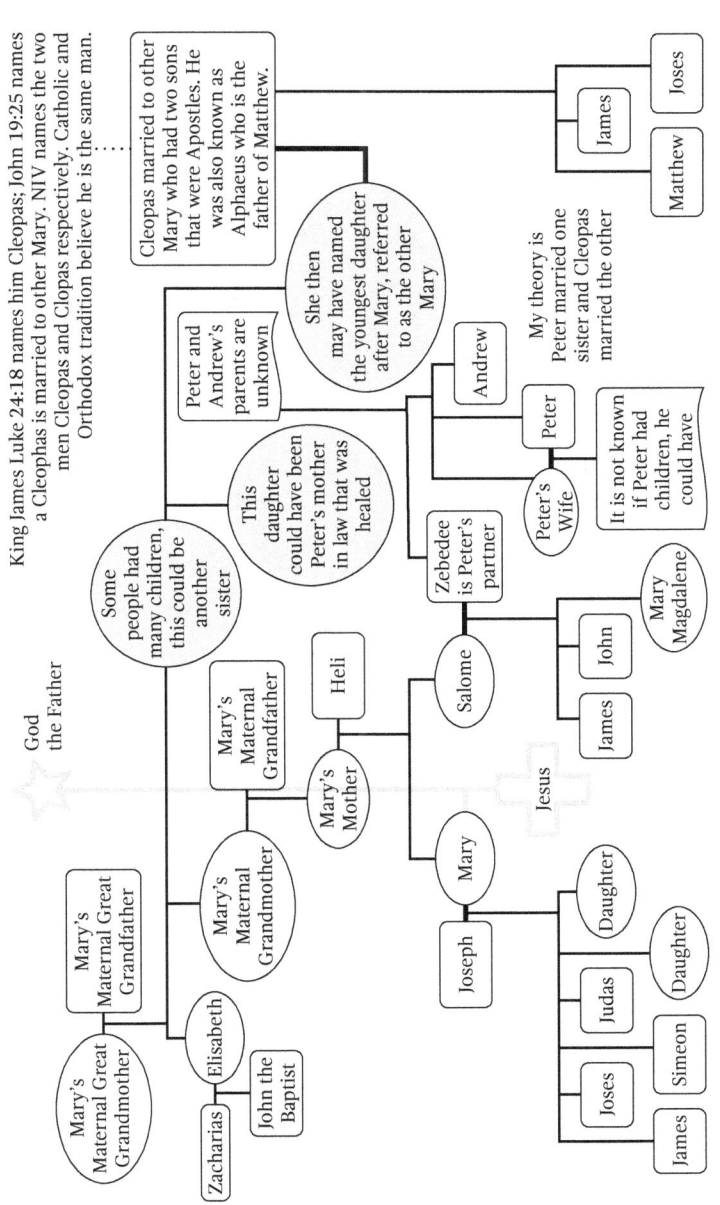

Notes

Preface

1) "THE MIRACLES OF JESUS CHRIST." *THE MIRACLES OF JESUS CHRIST*. N.p., n.d. Web. 02 Jan. 2017. Used in this chapter and throughout.

Chapter 1: Homage to the King in Nazareth

1) The Holy Bible: Containing the Old and New Testaments: Translated out of the Original Tongues and with the Former Translations Diligently Compared and Revised Conformable to the Edition of 1611, Commonly Known as the Authorized or King James Version. Uhrichsville, OH: Barbour, 2002. Print. Used in this chapter and throughout

Chapter 2: Interpreting the Gospels

1) Jeffcoat III, John L., and Craig H. Lampe, Dr. "English Bible History: Timeline of How We Got the English Bible." *English Bible History: Timeline of How We Got the English Bible.* WWW.GREATSITE.COM, n.d. Web. 18 Jan. 2017.

2) McGee, J. Vernon. Thru the Bible with J. Vernon Mcgee. Nashville, TN: T. Nelson, 1983. Print.

3) "How Many Christian Denominations Worldwide?" *HOW MANY CHRISTIAN DENOMINATIONS WORLDWIDE?* The Way, 09 Dec. 2016. Web. 21 Dec. 2016.

4) "Inspiration, Preservation, and New Testament Textual Criticism." *Bible. org.* N.p., n.d. Web. 16 Jan. 2017.

5) Jwallace. "How the Ante-Nicene Church Fathers Preserved the Eyewitness Gospel Accounts." *Cold Case Christianity.* N.p., 18 May 2014. Web. 16 Jan. 2017.

6) "King James Version." *Wikipedia.* Wikimedia Foundation, n.d. Web. 21 Dec. 2016.

7) "Language of Jesus." *Wikipedia*. Wikimedia Foundation, n.d. Web. 16 Jan. 2017.

8) "Why Paul Calls Peter as Cephas in His Books?" *Christianity Stack Exchange*. N.p., n.d. Web. 22 Dec. 2016.

9) "Chapters and Verses of the Bible." *Wikipedia*. Wikimedia Foundation, n.d. Web. 17 Jan. 2017.

10) "John the Baptist." *62 Bible Verses about John The Baptist*. The Lockman Foundation, n.d. Web. 13 Feb. 2017.

Chapter 3: Mary

1) "La Vista Church of Christ." *Where Does It Say That Salome Was James and John's Mother?*N.p., n.d. Web. 17 Jan. 2017.

2) "Ein Karem." *Wikipedia*. Wikimedia Foundation, n.d. Web. 21 Dec. 2016.

3) "Map of Ancient Israel - Hill Country of Judea." *Map of Ancient Israel - Hill Country of Judea*. Bible. History Online, n.d. Web. 21 Dec. 2016.

4) "Book of Isai" Map of Jesus' Ministry (Large Clickable Map)." *New Testament Cities Distances in Ancient Israel - Map of the Ministry of Jesus (Bible History Online)*. N.p., n.d. Web. 17 Jan. 2017.ah." *Wikipedia*. Wikimedia Foundation, n.d. Web. 22 Dec. 2016.

5) McGee, J. Vernon. *Thru the Bible with J. Vernon McGee*. Nashville: T. Nelson, 1981. Print. Genesis thru Deuteronomy

6) "Google Maps." *Google Maps*. N.p., n.d. Web. 23 Jan. 2017.

Chapter 5: Before the Wise Men Visit

1) "As The Crow Flies" Distance Calculator." *"As The Crow Flies" Distance Calculator*. N.p., n.d. Web. 17 Jan. 2017.

Chapter 6: When was Jesus Born?

1) "Dionysius Exiguus." *Wikipedia*. Wikimedia Foundation, n.d. Web. 21 Dec. 2016.

2) "Magi." KELEMEN, Lawrence. "Origin of Christmas | The History of Christmas and How It Began."*Origin of Christmas | The History of Christmas and How It Began*. N.p., n.d. Web. 17 Jan. 2017. *Wikipedia*. Wikimedia Foundation, n.d. Web. 22 Dec. 2016.

Chapter 7: Fleeing into Egypt

1) "From Bethlehem to Egypt to Nazareth, Jesus' Family Accepted Changes around Them." *The Jerusalem Post | JPost.com.* N.p., n.d. Web. 17 Jan. 2017.

Chapter 8: John the Baptist

1) "John 1:31 I Myself Did Not Know Him, but the Reason I Came Baptizing with Water Was That He Might Be Revealed to Israel.'" *John 1:31 I Myself Did Not Know Him, but the Reason I Came Baptizing with Water Was That He Might Be Revealed to Israel.* N.p., n.d. Web. 17 Jan. 2017.

Chapter 11: Jesus Moves Out

1) Finley, Guy. *The Secret of Letting Go.* St. Paul, MN: Llewellyn, 1990. Print

Chapter 13: A Divided Family

1) Guyfinleynow.org. "Guyfinleynow.org." *Guyfinleynow.org.* N.p., n.d. Web. 23 Jan. 2017. Heard Guy Finley speak on division and that Holiness is Wholeness

Chapter 15: Blessing of Simon Peter

1) Oakes, John. "What Is the Evidence That Peter Was Crucified Upside Down in Rome?"*Evidence for Christianity.* N.p., 20 Mar. 2010. Web. 17 Jan. 2017.

2) *Matthew 26:58 Commentaries: But Peter Was following Him at a Distance as Far as the Courtyard of the High Priest, and Entered In, and Sat down with the Officers to See the Outcome.* N.p., n.d. Web. 17 Jan. 2017.

Chapter 16: There is Something about Mary

1) McGee, J. Vernon. Thru the Bible with J. Vernon Mcgee. Nashville, TN: T. Nelson, 1983. Print. Matthew commentary Chapter two

Chapter 17: The Resurrection

1) McGee, J. Vernon. Thru the Bible with J. Vernon Mcgee. Nashville, TN: T. Nelson, 1983. Print. Used in this chapter and throughout.

2) "Mary Magdalene." Wikipedia. Wikimedia Foundation, n.d. Web. 20 Jan. 2017.

Chapter 18: Jesus Appears to Simon

1) Mark16:12 Commentaries: After That, He Appeared in a Different Form to Two of Them While They Were Walking along on Their Way to the Country. N.p., n.d. Web. 17 Jan. 2017.

2) Gill, John. "Mark 16:12 Commentary - John Gill's Exposition of the Bible." *Bible Study Tools.* N.p., n.d. Web. 17 Jan. 2017.

3) "GodVine." N.p., n.d. Web. 17 Jan. 2017.

Epilogue: This World of Zeros

1) Inspired by event in past. In 1993, while watching TBN Christian Television I heard an unknown guest make a comment: "If you put a One in front of a zero and Jesus is the One."

www.ingramcontent.com/pod-product-compliance
Lightning Source LLC
Chambersburg PA
CBHW071908290426
44110CB00013B/1319